■ACHIEVING SUSTAINABLE COMMUNITIES IN A GLOBAL ECONOMY ■

■ACHIEVING SUSTAINABLE COMMUNITIES IN A GLOBAL ECONOMY ■

Alternative Private Strategies and Public Policies

edited by

Ralph D. Christy

Department of Applied Economics and Management
Cornell University

World Scientific

NEW JERSEY · LONDON · SINGAPORE · BEIJING · SHANGHAI · HONG KONG · TAIPEI · CHENNAI

Published by

World Scientific Publishing Co. Pte. Ltd.

5 Toh Tuck Link, Singapore 596224

USA office: 27 Warren Street, Suite 401–402, Hackensack, NJ 07601

UK office: 57 Shelton Street, Covent Garden, London WC2H 9HE

British Library Cataloguing-in-Publication Data

A catalogue record for this book is available from the British Library.

ACHIEVING SUSTAINABLE COMMUNITIES IN A GLOBAL ECONOMY

ISBN 981-238-809-5

Typeset by Stallion Press

Email: sales@stallionpress.com

Printed in Singapore by World Scientific Printers (S) Pte Ltd

$\mathscr{C}$ontents

$\mathcal{P}$reface

Purpose of This Book

In the fall of 2002 Cornell University hosted the symposium "Achieving Sustainable Communities in a Global Economy." These proceedings report the major papers emanating from this symposium. This volume of readings explores alternative strategies in agricultural and rural development to address the impacts of globalization processes on smallholder agriculturalists and marginalized rural people. The book's goal is twofold: 1) to identify and assess the key processes by which globalization is affecting the smallholder agricultural and rural sectors; and 2) to identify and propose both micro- and macro-level policies and other strategies to deal with the problems that arise. This volume presents writings of leading scholars and practitioners working in the private and public sectors. Their work focuses on both major cross-cutting issues across the developing world and country-specific case studies.

Why Study Globalization

The world's economy has become more integrated in recent decades as a result of declining barriers to trade, market-determined exchange rates, and the growth of global capital markets among other factors. The 1.2 billion poor people in developed and emerging nations have experienced both positive and negative social and economic impacts in the new "globalizing" world economy. Although many have benefited from higher national economic growth, greater employment opportunities and higher purchasing power, concerns about the impacts on the poor are widespread. The rural poor depend on agricultural production both for sustenance and for income generation. This relationship makes the equitable distribution of the impacts of globalization particularly challenging in rural regions. These challenges include:

- Gaining access to competitive markets for inputs and products;
- Increasing instability in prices and incomes;
- Understanding the economic and institutional policy framework under which market, trade and investment rules and regulations are implemented and monitored;
- Maintaining national sovereignty associated with conditionality requirements, particularly when these affect social services and safety nets; and
- Privatizing economic functions formerly administered by the state.

Many of the processes of "globalization," in particular, the international integration of commodity and financial markets, are inexorable and will continue. A central question, though, is to what extent will the fate of the poor rise or fall with globalization, and what will the state sector do about it? Even in a world increasingly characterized by privatization and marketization, the state sector still has considerable resources to affect economic and social outcomes, including through such mechanisms as investments in education, health and infrastructure. In addition, the state is often challenged to deal with what are commonly perceived to be the negative consequences of globalization: financial market crisis; rural-urban migration; and social unrest.

In the agricultural and rural sectors, typically highly dependent on tradable goods, the impacts of globalization are often clear and direct. Common policy prescriptions of the past two decades have included 1) the dismantling of trade barriers, 2) the privatization of marketing functions formerly accomplished by parastatals, and 3) the removal of domestic income and price supports for farmers. Despite major gains in increased efficiency and productivity that have been made in many countries, the impacts are often unresolved. Physical and market infrastructure is often limited. Public sector roles (in extension, for example) have been dismantled but not replaced. Market failure is commonplace. Given these facts, what are the implications in terms of distributional consequences for the poor? With privatization and marketization, who is responsible for managing the consequences of market failure? What are the environmental consequences of incomplete markets and market failure? What is the appropriate role for state institutions in dealing with these and other consequences, particularly when the results are social dislocation, the marginalization of the poor, and environmental deterioration?

Increasingly, the international organizations that have the mandate to address the development and implementation issues associated with globalization — the World Bank, the International Monetary Fund, and the World Trade Organization — are being called to account for the alleged negative impacts of globalization processes on the poor. Yet, with privatization and marketization, public and international organizations often have lesser roles to begin with, and their appropriate responses are typically not apparent. Moreover, as it becomes increasingly evident that the poor do not necessary benefit proportionately from national-level economic growth, these organizations are increasingly being challenged to address the specific problems of the poor. Civil society and NGO-oriented solutions are usually focused at the micro level, leaving a gaping institutional void in national-level consequences of globalization and growth.

This edited volume is organized around three interrelated institutions: Firms, Markets, and Communities. Structuring the debate around those institutions will hopefully make it easier to identify the impacts of and suggest strategies to combat poverty.

Intended Audience

Achieving Sustainable Communities in a Global Economy will appeal to a broad cross-section of development scholars and practitioners in economics and finance, agricultural policy, international trade, community and rural development. It will be of special interest to managers of international organizations and foundations. Students studying economic development will find this book a valuable supplement to their readings in globalization.

Acknowledgements

Publication of these conference proceedings resulted from the efforts of a large number of individuals and programs at Cornell University. A project of this scope cannot escape such a debt. The Emerging Markets Program (within Applied Economics and Management), Cornell International Institute for Food and Agricultural Development (CIIFAD), and the Poverty, Inequality, and Development Initiative were the major sponsors of this conference, "Achieving Sustainable Communities in a Global Economy." CIIFAD's Governing Board was most encouraging of the idea that Cornell host a conference on globalization and it was through the gentle prodding of Professor Norman Uphoff that the Emerging Markets Program at Cornell University took on the challenge of organizing this global symposium.

This symposium, in large measure, owes a great deal of gratitude to the faculty, staff and graduate students within the Emerging Markets Program. Drs. Kenneth Robinson, David Conner, and Ed Mabaya provided excellent intellectual input into the planning and execution of the symposium. Carol Thomson and Ginny Montopoli did a superb job of organizing the local arrangements that facilitated our off-campus guests. The creative talents of Cally Arthur in handling the public relations, graphic arts, and editorial assistance for both the symposium and this book of readings are greatly appreciated. A number of graduate students, namely, Emelly Mutambatsere, Sonali Roy, and Nomathemba Mhlanga, willingly assisted with various activities, ranging from registering participants to hosting visitors, all of which made the symposium a success.

This symposium benefited immensely by having its major sessions chaired by: Willene Johnson, Alicia Vazquez Seijas, Gayle Lewis, and Natasha Blackshear. To add to this debate on globalization, we invited three "provocateurs": Frank Pedraza, Bob Herdt, and Roland Bunch. To each of these individuals, a great deal of gratitude is owed as their critical comments helped sharpen the discussion and improve the content of the chapters presented herein.

Kim Tan and Yubing Zhai, Project Manager and Administrative Manager/Editor respectively at World Scientific Publishing, ably shepherded the manuscript through the production process. Finally, I am honored to acknowledge Wylin Dassie's "Reflections" on this globalization symposium (and these proceedings). Remaining errors are of course my responsibility.

Ralph D. Christy

$\mathcal{R}$eflections[*]

These proceedings have challenged me to reflect on the various paradigms on poverty amelioration. While attenuating the negative affects of unbridled economic growth stemming from globalization, we discussed various strategies. This discussion was embedded in the necessity of developing paradigms within which sustainable community development may flourish. However, we should not allow our conversation to end here.

We must go beyond theory and strategy. There are more insights to be gained in addition to those received from the theoretical analyses and discussion that take place today. My reflections on this symposium (and proceeding) lead me to look deeper and be challenged by the legacies of great humanitarians and servant-leaders such as Gandhi, Nelson Mandela, and M.L. King, Jr. Their legacies challenge me not to live in compassionless detachment, or arrogant individualism that inhibits our ability to respond radically to the needs of the underprivileged (MLK). The great servants reminded me that radical commitment to valuing human life entails a willingness to surrender some of our own power, resources, and comfort to participate in the suffering of others (Dalai Lama). We can reject ideologies, religion, and received wisdom, but we cannot escape the

---

*Wylin Dassie is a founding member of the Emerging Markets Advisory Board and is currently pursuing a PhD in Theology at Emory University in Atlanta, GA.

universal necessity of love and compassion, or the understanding that our welfare inextricably ties to the welfare of others (Dalai Lama).

So, as we fulfill our daily obligations within our respective careers, let us find hope in the essential human need that binds us all — Compassion — in our desire to share and receive it. This hope is what encourages us to continue working tirelessly in a world wrought with disillusionment and hopelessness. In doing so, we find and give life.

Part One

The New Role of the Private Sector in Economic Development

chapter one

Engaging the Global Enterprise to Promote Economic Development

Everett M. Ehrlich
Elliot Schwartz

Events of the past several years have led to a dramatic increase in the public's scrutiny of the corporate sector in the United States. A variety of financial reporting scandals, from Enron to WorldCom to Global Crossing, have shaken public faith in the honesty of corporate officials and the integrity of the information they provide. The same scandals also have led to federal election campaign finance reform and a broader questioning of the role of corporate money in the political process.

Also, the opening of global markets has sparked protests at the World Trade Organization meetings of 1999 in Seattle and at subsequent international meetings. Corporations stand accused of being agents of immiseration in the developing world; critics tie them to problems such as public health, child labor, environmental preservation, and workplace safety in those developing nations where the firms produce and sell.

All of these concerns of expanding global trade and corporate scandals have come together to raise the issue of "corporate engagement" in

The authors are, respectively, Senior Vice President for Research and Vice-President for Economic Studies at the Committee for Economic Development (CED). The views expressed are those of the authors and do not necessarily reflect those of CED.

developing countries, that is, the activities of corporations outside their standard, market-based relationships.[1] We use this term rather than the more conventional "corporate social responsibility" for two reasons. First, corporate responsibility is now frequently used with regard to financial reporting — corporations have the responsibility to report honestly and obey the law. Frankly, this is thin soup; we all have this responsibility, and corporations, as legal entities, share it.

Second, and more important, the term responsibility implies, even if only tacitly, some degree of blame on the part of corporations for the problems around them.

We reject this notion. While individual companies have sometimes behaved regretfully if not deplorably, we believe the record shows that trade and foreign investment have been important forces for economic progress in developing nations. Our concerns over child labor, environmental preservation, and other issues are second to none. But the degree of openness of the developed economies bears no intuitive relationship to these problems.

We grant that the economic growth triggered by foreign investment frequently poses environmental costs. But the technology corporations bring to developing locales is often state-of-the-art, sometimes better than that deployed in older installations in the developed countries. Moreover, the environmental track record of developing nations that have pursued autarchy, as opposed to exposure to trade — nations such as India, or pre-reform China — is no better and conceivably far worse than their more open counterparts. The causes of environmental degradation in the developing world typically are either growth itself or practices unrelated to markets such as deforestation due to foraging for fuel.

Child labor is an even more sensitive issue. The image of a small child sewing sneakers in oppressive conditions is a powerful and disturbing one. Child labor offers low-wage manufacturing firms to make profits through exploitation. But the child labor force was not created, nor children thrown out of school and into poverty, by trade and investment. The alternative for such children typically is primitive

---

[1]See, for example, Committee for Economic Development, *Reducing Global Poverty: Engaging The Global Enterprise*, Spring 2003.

agriculture and a standard of living and prospect for advancement no greater, and possibly less, than the one they face as manufacturing workers. In fact, young girls thrown out of factories have gone not to schools, as reformers had hoped, but into prostitution. Less openness will not make these children less poor, nor would cutting off opportunities to export the products they make.

But recognizing that corporations are generally a productive force in the development of the world's poorest economies does not mean that they have no relationship to the social conditions around them. Views on the inherent relationship between corporations and the society within which they function differ. Conservative economist Milton Friedman once proclaimed: "There is but one and only one social responsibility of business — to use its resources and engage in activities designed to increase its profits so long as it stays within the rules of the game ..." (Friedman, 1962). In contrast, many forward-looking businesses have argued that corporations are *inherently* social and cannot avoid the context within which they function. As Alfred Neal, an influential economist and first president of the Committee for Economic Development (CED) remarked: "The corporation is essentially a political institution, whatever its economic objectives may be" (Walton, p. 17). CED's long-held view has been that businesses are important societal institutions that shape, and are shaped by, their environments. As economic institutions, they must pursue activities that ultimately add to their bottom lines, but the scope of such activities is much broader than generally conceived. Almost without exception, good corporate engagement is good for the firm, and for the economy, and society overall.

As the corporate scandals of the past few years and the opening of trade have unfolded, global enterprises have migrated toward adopting good corporate engagement.[2] In many cases corporations are leading a rise in social standards, in contrast to the often-repeated accusation that global

---

[2]A global enterprise (sometimes referred to as a multinational or transnational corporation) is an organization that operates in multiple nations through foreign direct investment, or affiliated or non-affiliated suppliers and sub-contractors, that are subject to a substantial degree of central control. Global enterprises capture economies of scale or scope through operational leverage leading to lower unit costs, or through marketing leverage using the value of brand names.

enterprises are promoting a "race to the bottom." Although the historical record is far from perfect, many leading global enterprises now are establishing progressive social programs in countries in which they operate. As they expand from their home base to developing countries, social engagement policies and programs of their home country often expand with them. Such efforts extend the benefits of globalization and help to ensure that those benefits will accrue to local populations.

Leading businesses understand that they have a relationship to the conditions within which they operate, and that they must contribute to the betterment of those conditions. That understanding is not entirely charitable or even morally based, however. Instead, many businesses now see their relationship to social problems or conditions as part of a long-term strategy for profits. The question becomes: what are the terms of that relationship? Or, in other words, how should corporations *engage* the society around them, both generally and, more specifically, in the developing world, to pursue their corporate long-term interest?

This report seeks to answer those questions on several basic levels. It will first discuss how progressive corporate "engagement" fits into the process of economic growth and examine the motivations surrounding it. It will then address a series of operational questions regarding its execution: What are its limits? How should it be managed and evaluated?

Corporate Engagement and the Growth Process

How does economic growth occur? Economists have long considered this question, but their answers are often abstract. In concrete terms, we see the process as centered around three parallel forces — *invention*, *investment*, and *reorganization*.

Invention, investment, and reorganization

Invention is the process of developing new ideas and new technologies. It is this force that has allowed the advanced economies to move beyond a standard of living associated with artisans, mule-drivers, and shopkeepers. Were technological progress ever to cease, the world's standard of living would ultimately be stagnant.

But *investment* is necessary to bring inventions to the real world. That is, investment in either physical capital or human capital is how new technologies introduce themselves into the economy. One simple way to consider this reality is to consider the dramatically rising share of total investment occupied by computers in the U.S. At one level, this investment represents the accrual of wealth. But more fundamentally, it is a record of how new technology has swept across the economy. Without investment, both in physical capital and human skill, invention cannot drive the economy.

The third and often unmentioned leg of this triangle is *social organization*. We generally understand that technology changes the way we do things. But we fail to draw the logical inference that, in order to realize the benefits of technology, a variety of economic and social activities must be reorganized. Manufacturing, in almost every geographic and historical setting, has been accompanied by urbanization, for obvious reasons. But this shift compels a variety of changes in public health, education, and infrastructure. In addition, technology may change the way a firm is organized, and therefore its relationship to its workers. More generally, economic growth creates a series of changes and tensions.

Most businesses see the first two phenomena — invention and investment — as their responsibility, but see questions of social organization as outside their province. But our view, bolstered by the actions of leading multinational corporations, suggests that this third leg is as central to a firm's prospects as are the first two. And the type of change that is generally of the greatest concern to them concerns the labor force, the relationship between the worker and the workplace. As technology evolves, workers not only need to learn new skills, but new organizational behaviors and new values. Henry Ford understood this early in the previous century when he recognized the magnitude of the changes implied by assembly line work and responded with a variety of ideas, among them raising the pay rate to $5 per day. Heads of modern corporations also must change the way they think about their firms' relationship to the broader society in order to ensure access to a productive workforce.

The same pressures exist outside the workplace. Corporations need to track and address changes in the locales in which they produce and sell, the preferences of their customers, and environmental concerns. But business is only now beginning to learn how to pursue these ends.

Corporate engagement in social change

This chapter uses the term "corporate social engagement" to describe the range of business interactions with groups or communities to achieve development goals. These interactions go beyond the positive externalities that economists generally associate with foreign direct investment (FDI) or trade. Corporate engagement includes both operational policies that establish new (higher) norms within a market framework and programs that tackle social problems directly, often through charitable channels outside of standard market arrangements.[3] Higher norm setting occurs, for example, through the introduction of labor practices such as the provision of education, childcare, or health services, designed to improve the quality and productivity of the work force.

The activities of global enterprises have drawn interest because of the great potential they have to contribute to goals of economic development and the integration of developing countries with more advanced economies. Importantly, transfers within global enterprises account for the bulk of FDI flows to developing countries. Net FDI flows to developing countries have increased considerably in the past decade, rising each year from 1991 to 1999 (followed by a small drop in 2000 and 2001). The average net FDI inflow over the period of 1991–1995 was $69.3 billion, increasing to $168.9 billion for the period of 1996–2000.

In many cases the development-promoting activities of global corporations are linked with foreign direct investment although, as discussed below, joint ventures, subcontracting, and other linkages also create opportunities for businesses to contribute to development. Other than domestic saving, FDI is perhaps the most important and effective source of economic growth for those developing countries that can attract it. The central reasons are well established (CED, 2002). In short, FDI

---

[3]We would exclude from this definition some activities linked to the idea of "corporate responsibility," even though they help achieve social goals, among them private philanthropy (such as the activities of private foundations created by business leaders), business activities that comply with existing laws and regulations (for example, regarding worker health and safety or financial reporting), or the pursuit of a profitable line of business that fulfills a social need (for example, companies that provide education, health, or housing as a line of business), although these are all important avenues of business support for development.

transfers resources and technology from the economically advanced countries and has significant spillover benefits in the form of improved trade balances, increased levels of employment, improved productivity, and higher domestic government tax revenues. Even when it takes the form of a purchase of a local firm, FDI typically enlarges the firm and improves its efficiency by implementing new management techniques and other modernizations. Both directly and indirectly, FDI can help to raise income, lower poverty, and improve other indices of human development. It is especially effective where forward-looking companies make significant contributions to economic and social development through good corporate practices.

In contrast to other forms of capital inflows, FDI tends to be more stable because it is committed for a longer duration. That long-term commitment often carries with it an overlooked benefit, namely, the involvement and dedication of the foreign firm to the improvement of the host country. In most cases, the success of a foreign firm's investment relies on the success of the local economy, society, and policy. That is why FDI is attracted to developing countries that strive toward good governance and market friendly economic policies, and why some countries are able to attract a greater level of FDI relative to the size of their economy or overall capital investment. Once invested for the long term, most foreign firms cannot easily pull out of the country. The commitment tends to align the firm's self-interest with the country's own development goals. Although firms may not be equally motivated by altruistic reasons, most global enterprises based in OECD countries and operating in developing countries establish policies and programs that support and improve the economic, environmental, political, and social performance of the countries in which they operate.[4] While their motivation of long term profits is, in part, no different than domestic firms, which also may establish such programs, the foreign firm is typically larger and more vulnerable than domestic firms to regulatory or political bias. It is also subject to public opinion in its home country, which may create pressure for the firm to maintain a good

---

[4]As noted below, not all such programs are based on FDI. Corporate social programs derive from various sources and motivations. All, however, require some company presence in the affected nation, even if only through contractual relations with subcontractors.

reputation by engaging in social programs in host countries. Thus, it may have added incentive to create goodwill within the host country by adopting high-profile policies and programs that show its commitment to the domestic economy and society.

Three critical points about FDI need to be emphasized:

- First, the role of foreign-owned businesses in promoting social development can only support local efforts; the primary impetus for social and economic change must come from local social, political, and economic leaders. Foreign-owned businesses typically account for a very small percentage of a country's total economic activity. Local conditions, institutions, and policies are the main determinants of economic development.

- Second, global firms characteristically generate positive economic effects through the normal conduct of business when they establish a business presence in a developing country. Such firms transfer financial, managerial, scientific, and technical resources from the more economically developed countries. FDI increases competition in local product and labor markets, which puts pressure on domestic firms to improve efficiency. In many cases, foreign firms provide basic goods and services such as housing, health care, education, water, and electricity.

- Third, although many observers have described corporate social engagement in terms of a conflict between profit and moral or humanitarian motives, the overriding rationale for any corporation must be based on its understanding of its own self-interest.[5] Although social engagement initiatives may not translate directly into profits in the short term, they generally produce benefits for the firm and ultimately add to the bottom line. Our expectation is that upon full evaluation many businesses will find that the net benefits more than justify their engagement in social initiatives.

---

[5]As put by Adam Smith, "It is not from the benevolence of the butcher, the brewer, or the baker that we expect our dinner, but from their regard to their self-love, and never talk to them of our own necessities but of their advantages."

Why Global Enterprises Undertake Social Initiatives

The motivation and commitment of corporations to the goals of poverty reduction and economic and social advancement have been the subject of much debate and analysis. Some of today's leading practitioners of corporate social engagement, especially among firms in the extractive industries, have historically been closer to the lagging rather than leading edge of enlightened behavior. Several firms in the apparel industry and retail trade have been hit with harsh publicity about labor practices of subcontractors. Thus, in many cases, the concerns exhibited by global businesses to improve social conditions results from the need to restore a tarnished image or make amends for previous behaviors. The depth of business commitment to social progress also has been questioned. Many social activists question whether corporations are interested only in the public relations benefits of their social programs. Based on the evidence gathered, we conclude that the range of activities, motivations, and commitments on the part of global business is very broad. The most forward-looking companies have established policies and made commitments that permeate the corporation from the Board and CEO levels on down to the very lowest stratum of the company. Others have yet to understand fully the business case for corporate social engagement and have not embraced such policies. Further, even those companies that strive most to achieve the highest standards of corporate engagement can fall short on occasion.

Although social activities are voluntary on the part of business, governments of the advanced economies have taken steps to encourage and promote such activities. For example, most governments allow a tax deduction or credit for charitable donations. Governments also use various forms of public advocacy and moral suasion to promote good corporate engagement. The broadest effort to influence the conduct of global enterprises is encompassed in the OECD *Guidelines for Multinational Enterprises*. These guidelines are recommendations of appropriate business conduct by global enterprises. As part of the OECD Declaration on International Investment and Multinational Enterprises, they provide a framework intended both to improve the international investment climate and to encourage the positive contributions of global enterprises to economic, social and environmental goals. The general policies of the guidelines are reproduced in the following box.

OECD Guidelines for Multinational Enterprises — General Policies

Enterprises should take fully into account established policies in the countries in which they operate, and consider the views of other stakeholders. In this regard, enterprises should:

1. Contribute to economic, social and environmental progress with a view to achieving sustainable development.

2. Respect the human rights of those affected by their activities consistent with the host government's international obligations and commitments.

3. Encourage local capacity building through close cooperation with the local community, including business interests, as well as developing the enterprise's activities in domestic and foreign markets, consistent with the need for sound commercial practice.

4. Encourage human capital formation, in particular by creating employment opportunities and facilitating training opportunities for employees.

5. Refrain from seeking or accepting exemptions not contemplated in the statutory or regulatory framework related to environmental, health, safety, labor, taxation, financial incentives, or other issues.

6. Support and uphold good corporate governance principles and develop and apply good corporate governance practices.

7. Develop and apply effective self-regulatory practices and management systems that foster a relationship of confidence and mutual trust between enterprises and the societies in which they operate.

8. Promote employee awareness of, and compliance with, company policies through appropriate dissemination of these policies, including through training programs.

9. Refrain from discriminatory or disciplinary action against employees who make *bona fide* reports to management or, as appropriate, to the competent public authorities, on practices that contravene the law, the *Guidelines* or the enterprise's policies.

10. Encourage, where practicable, business partners, including suppliers and subcontractors, to apply principles of corporate conduct compatible with the *Guidelines*.

11. Abstain from any improper involvement in local political activities.

Source: *Guidelines for Multinational Enterprises: Ministerial Booklet*, OECD, 2000.

The OECD *Guidelines* are far from the only effort to influence corporate behavior in developing countries. Another important multilateral, and tripartite (government/business/labor), effort is the International Labor Organization's *Tripartite Declaration of Principles Concerning Multinational Enterprises and Social Policy*, known as the MNE Declaration. The MNE Declaration is a set of voluntary guidelines and commitments by each of the three participating groups in such areas as development policy, rights at work, and industrial relations. In addition, various business associations and individual businesses have developed codes, guidelines, and principles to encourage and support corporate social engagement. Among other prominent international organizations promoting such activities are the U.N. Global Compact, the World Economic Forum's Global Health Initiative, the Corporate Social Responsibility Forum, and Business for Social Responsibility. Increasingly, firms within well-defined sectors such as apparel manufacturing and mining are joining specific initiatives to establish standards of conduct within their industry. (Examples are the Fair Labor Association, successor to the White House's Apparel Industry Partnership, which addresses workplace standards, and the Voluntary Principles on Security and Human Rights, established by the mining and extractive industry.) In many respects these efforts, taken together, create a form of "soft rules" that, although voluntary, nonetheless govern (normalize) corporate social behavior (Haufler, 2001).

The question of whether a private, commercial enterprise should engage in socially beneficial programs must be answered by each business itself. But the large number of businesses that answer that question affirmatively verifies that sufficient business reasons exist. Motivations run the gamut from proactive brand identification with social causes to strictly defensive measures to ensure against negative publicity and consequent lost sales. In some instances, especially when they find themselves in conflict situations, businesses may feel they have no choice but to play a positive role in supporting social stability and better governance. Not all global businesses, of course, are inspired to implement policies or programs that respond to local conditions. Circumstances differ among developing countries and various lines of business. Some firms have a more narrow and, in our view, shortsighted perspective based strictly on the exploitation of local resources. In addition, smaller firms may be less able than larger firms to afford social programs, or, at least, their programs will be smaller. Below, we set out a few of the reasons that have motivated global businesses to become more socially engaged.

Enlightened self-interest. Perhaps the simplest and strongest explanation for why firms go beyond narrow-gauged market activities is because it is right and serves the longer-term interests of the society, which in turn benefits the longer-term interests of the business by creating a more stable environment, good will, and brand identity.

Many business leaders cite humanitarian motives for social activities, and these are clearly important. But businesses are unlikely to be motivated solely or consistently by altruistic appeals. They are neither charitable nor government institutions, and they should not be expected to act as if they were. Nevertheless, businesses prefer to operate in more stable political and economic environments. A business's success is often tied to the success of the country in which it operates, either directly or through supplier relationships. A stable, non-corrupt government and society provide a less risky climate for investment and trade. A more educated and healthier population is more likely to supply a productive and reliable labor force. Populations with higher incomes generate more consumer demand for the products and services businesses sell. Thus, many businesses see their engagement as enriching these environments in order to improve them as markets, investment locales, or sources for labor or materials. At a practical level, as firms gain experience and deepen their relationships in developing countries they often find that upgrading their social policies and programs becomes more important.

Positive brand identification/goodwill. Some firms undertake social initiatives to enhance their brand image; some act to defend their brand against negative publicity; some have built their brand based on identification with social causes. To varying degrees these motivations are all based on the value that consumers place on a company's image and reputation. The value of its brand can be a significant asset to a firm since strong brands have the power to lift sales and earnings. *Interbrand*, a business-consulting group, estimates that in 2002 the world's 10 most valuable brands had a combined asset value of $388 billion (*BusinessWeek*, 2002). Various studies suggest that among other product traits, consumers value products and companies that adhere to social standards such as child-labor-free clothing and environmentally sound production processes (BSR, 2002). Whether the company acts positively to burnish its reputation or defensively to overcome or prevent negative publicity, brand value can be an important motivation for social involvement. Such efforts may be aimed either towards host or home markets. Consumers in developing countries represent a fast growing segment of many markets. Positive brand recognition based on identifications with social engagement can be important in building consumer loyalty in those markets. In addition, as discussed below, goodwill can have a direct payback as local governments may examine the totality of their relationships with a company when making regulatory or licensing decisions.

Labor markets-at home and abroad. Tight labor markets for skilled workers in developing economies lead firms to improve local labor conditions. Firms might, for example, simply provide higher compensation either in the form of higher wages or improved fringe benefits such as the provision of health services to attract and retain a workforce. Although labor markets characterized by excess supply provide less of an incentive for such benefits, they do not necessarily inhibit business activities in this area. In many cases businesses are investing in the education and training of their workforce to improve its quality and productivity or to improve other aspects of the work environment. The AIDS programs of Volkswagen do Brasil and Daimler-Chrysler of South Africa provide good examples of how a firm can help itself by addressing a social problem. These programs focus on prevention of HIV/AIDS and care of those stricken by the virus. Both companies have found that it is far more profitable to educate and treat their employees than to recruit and train new ones. Mining companies in South Africa have recently implemented similar programs.

Similar considerations in a global enterprise's home market, based on the need to retain and attract talented individuals, have led firms to support social programs that benefit developing countries. Firms that identify their brand with a social cause, such as "no sweat" labor conditions and "green" environmental practices, are often more attractive to prospective employees, especially recent college graduates, than are firms with negative reputations. In addition, many U.S. firms provide employees with paid time off from work to engage in volunteer activities that among other causes have benefited developing countries.

Profitability. Numerous studies have linked corporate social activities to better business performance as measured by profitability or return on equity, and evidence of a narrowly defined "business case" for social engagement, although weak in some dimensions, is clearly positive[6], (Margolis and Walsh, 2001). In addition to various studies that link corporate social commitments to improved financial performance, three simple observations are relevant. First, mutual funds that invest in socially screened firms do no worse and often much better than more broadly based funds.[7] Second, the simple fact that many firms choose to engage in social initiatives even if they cannot measure their specific contribution to financial performance, suggests that they can justify such activities on other financial grounds. Some contributions, such as donations of depreciated equipment or excess inventories, are easily justified because they are eligible for a tax deduction.[8] Finally, anecdotal evidence links political and social goodwill generated by corporate engagement to short-term payoffs in the forms of faster licensing and regulatory approvals, greater flexibility on the part of government authorities, and contracts granted on the basis of selection criteria that favored firms committed to social improvement (IFC, 2002).

Some social activists have promoted a broader definition of the business case through the concept of a "triple bottom line of sustainable development" which focuses on society, economy, and environment.[9] Others such as Transparency International, Human Rights Watch, and Greenpeace have emphasized the importance of shareholder activism in support of social causes and the need for public corporations to respond to shareholder interests.[10] Shareholder activism is supported by such

---

[6]The weaknesses stem mainly from methodological shortcomings of the various academic studies, including the issue of whether social engagement is responsible for higher profits or the other way around.

[7]Social Investment Forum and Wiesenberger/Thomson Financial Services, *Socially Screened Mutual Fund Statistical Summary* (December 1998), available at http://www.socialinvest.org/areas/research/other/FundStats_12-31-98.htm. Accessed July 31, 2002.

[8]See, for example, Gifts in Kind International.

[9]SustainAbility, *Introduction to the Triple Bottom Line*, available at http://www.sustainability.com/philosophy/triple-bottom/tbl-intro.asp. Accessed July 31, 2002.

[10]Americas E-Forum on Corporate Social Responsibility, June 10–July 5, 2002, www.worldbank.org/wbi/csr/eforum.html

organizations as the Investor Responsibility Research Center, a source of independent research on corporate governance, proxy voting, and corporate responsibility issues.[11] Strong shareholder interest, when broadly demonstrated, provides a significant business motivation to include social leadership indicators in measures of business success. The success of the original Sullivan Principles at enlisting corporate support for social change in South Africa is a prime example of the force of shareholder activism.

Some Lessons and Examples of Corporate Engagement

Experience and research have raised some important issues with regard to corporate social activities, both for firms that engage in them and countries that receive them, including where and how to spend, how much to spend, how to manage, and how to evaluate (Margolis and Walsh, 2001; Haufler, 2001). Below, we examine these questions and provide some illustrative examples of corporate programs.

Where and how to spend? No rules dictate to firms where or how they should spend in social programs, but as discussed above, substantial guidance exists through the Global Compact, OECD Code of Conduct, and other efforts to help inform their decisions. Such decisions depend on the country context, the nature of the business enterprise, its size, visibility, and motivations for acting, the costs and benefits to be derived, and the nature of the relationship between the business and the social initiative. For example, the social initiatives conducted by most firms take place where the firm has invested and set up local facilities. However, many retail-based firms, such as Levi Strauss, Nike, Target, and Wal-Mart, are primarily concerned about the behaviors of subcontractors in countries where, although they have no physical presence of their own, consumers have linked negative practices to their brands. These firms have instituted company policies, such as contractor codes, and specific remedial programs aimed at improving conditions or moderating subcontractor practices in those countries.

Some firms have established programs that are closely related to their principal business activity and thus build on their specific core competence.

---

[11]"About IRRC," www.irrc.org/subnav/about.html

For example, pharmaceutical companies such as Merck and Pfizer have promoted health related programs in Africa and other developing countries, through donations of medicines, price concessions, subsidization of clinical training, funding of health infrastructure and other mechanisms whose principal aim is to enhance access to quality health care. Both companies have taken the lead in health programs that seek to improve health outcomes for patients in the host countries.

The nature of the company's operations, rather than its product, can also play a significant role in determining the types of social activities undertaken, regardless of location. FedEx and UPS, which operate large air fleets, have found that they can reduce environmental impacts (high fuel consumption and noise pollution) and save money by using quieter and more fuel-efficient engines. Both companies have worked with the Alliance for Environmental Innovation on initiatives aimed at decreasing waste, noise, and other forms of pollution that result from their operations. In addition, FedEx and UPS are companies with high fixed-cost distribution channels and are able to use those channels at low marginal costs to distribute highly valued social goods. Similarly, Coca-Cola has agreed to use its extensive distribution network in Africa to support local AIDS prevention, education, and treatment programs.[12]

How much to spend? Returns on social spending are often either poorly measured or very long-term in nature. Thus, no easy answer exists to the question of how much of its resources a firm should devote to such spending. The limit on social spending by businesses is a question for each business to answer based on its judgment of the benefits. But there is little doubt that many businesses can spend more, especially considering that some start from zero.

Although it is relatively easier to identify social activities that take the form of discrete, charitable programs, the leading edge social practices directly related to labor, environment, and other production-based standards are probably more significant in terms of impact. For example, global enterprises operating in developing countries frequently pay more and have higher working standards than the national norm. Wages paid

---

[12]UNAIDS, UNAIDS Signs Up Coca-Cola in Battle against AIDS, press release, June 20, 2001, Geneva, www.unaids.org/whatsnew/press/eng/pressarc01/Coca-Cola 200601.html.

by global enterprises to workers in the manufacturing sector in low-income countries are on average double that of their counterparts working for domestic firms (Graham, 2001). Royal Dutch/Shell reports that the lowest wage it paid to any of its employees worldwide in 2001 was $50 per month plus $18 transport allowance and medical and life insurance benefits in an African country, compared to the local minimum wage of $28 per month (Royal Dutch/Shell, 2001). Such workplace practices, which set higher domestic norms, can have significant, lasting, and beneficial impacts on the local economy. The impact of such programs comes from their direct integration into a firm's operations and the demonstration effect they can have in pulling other firms upwards towards their standards. However, such integration makes it virtually impossible for them to be quantified.

Corporate philanthropy lends itself toward better quantification, although reporting is poor and disaggregation between domestic and international programs is limited. Within the United States, corporate and personal philanthropy is focused overwhelmingly on domestic causes. In 1990, international causes received 1.3 percent of all private giving. However, a shift toward international causes is discernable as total charitable giving between 1998 and 2001 rose by 12 percent and giving to international causes rose by 32 percent.[13]

How to manage? Social engagement must be managed by the corporation in a manner that simultaneously provides benefits for recipients and for the corporation. Clearly, activities that are integral to company operations are managed within the company. Some charitable programs are also managed directly by the corporation; others are formed as joint partnerships with NGOs, governments, and multinational institutions such as the World Bank.

To assist in managing social programs, several of the organizations concerned with charitable programs have established management handbooks, guidelines, and codes of conduct. Most maintain websites, which contain useful information and case studies of successful efforts. For example, the U.N. Global Compact maintains a "learning bank" and other information databases to help businesses that want to achieve social goals.

---

[13]Data from AAFRC Trust for Philanthropy www.aafrc.org, as cited by Sebastian Mallaby, "Fresh Prince of Philanthropy," *The Washington Post*, November 18, 2002, p. A21.

Similarly, the Good Practice Manual has been prepared by the International Finance Corporation (IFC) to provide guidance to private sector entities operating under IFC programs.[14] The handbook emphasizes public disclosure of information, consultation with the public, and operating in a manner that is sensitive to local environmental and social goals. Companies receiving IFC support are required to comply with stringent labor and environmental standards. The handbook, however, could also be a useful guide for companies not operating under IFC auspices.

Other organizations, mostly in the private sector, have established codes and certifications that can help firms integrate social considerations into their operational policies. Many individual firms establish their own codes or statements of principles. Other codes are the product of international agencies. Still others are created by NGOs. A recent survey by the OECD identified 246 codes, which set forth standards and principles for business conduct.[15] (See box.) All are intended to help the firm to improve its management of labor, environment, and other social issues and give the firm recognition for its compliance with such standards. For example, ISO 14000 is a set of voluntary standards under the auspices of the International Standards Organization that address technical issues in environmental management systems, auditing, labeling, performance evaluation, and life cycle assessment. AccountAbility has established its "AA1000 Framework: *Standard, Guidelines and Professional Qualification*," a systematic approach used to frame corporate responsibility policies, stakeholder dialogue, social, ethical and environmental accounting auditing and reporting, professional training, and research and related standards work. Social Accountability International has developed its SA8000 workplace standard that covers key labor rights and certifies compliance through independent, accredited auditors. The Global Reporting Initiative promotes international harmonization in the reporting of relevant and credible corporate environmental, social and economic performance information to enhance responsible decision-making.

---

[14]The IFC is the private sector arm of the World Bank Group. Its focus is to promote economic development by encouraging the growth of productive enterprise and efficient capital markets in its member countries.
[15]*Corporate Responsibility: Private Initiatives and Public Goals*, Organization for Economic Cooperation and Development (Paris: 2001).

OECD Evaluation of Codes of Corporate Responsibility

The Organization for Economic Co-operation and Development examined an inventory of 246 codes of corporate conduct issued by individual companies, business associations, and stakeholder partnerships. According to the OECD, all of the codes are voluntary expressions of commitments that surpass legal requirements. They address governmental and public concern over the economic, social, and environmental impact of global enterprises.

The examination focused on whether, and how, nine key issue areas were addressed. These areas are: environmental stewardship; labor standards; science and technology; competition; information disclosure; taxation; bribery and corruption; and consumer protection.

The results indicate most major firms issue codes of business conduct that emphasize a commitment to the three major components of sustainable development (economic, social, and environmental stewardship). Despite some uniformity of coverage, the codes vary in many ways. Most notable are differences in commitment and implementation.

For example, virtually all individual firm's codes address the problems of bribery and corruption as well as environmental standards. Many also address labor relations. Some codes treat these issues broadly while others include more detailed topics, such as union association privileges. Documents addressing corruption are much more likely to discuss implementation procedures and disciplinary action than those dealing with environmental oversights. Within specific issue areas, guidelines show significant distinctions between actions expected of company employees and suppliers and business partners. In some, the language promotes internal assessment of company performance while in others it may focus more on punitive action if codes are not upheld.

Source: *Corporate Responsibility: Private Initiatives and Public Goals*, OECD.

Many firms initiate charitable programs in developing countries that build on programs they have started in the United States or other advanced economies. Such programs may have established reputations for recognized achievements. Often these programs need modification to fit within the developing country context, but they have the advantage of starting from a base of experience. As in most business enterprises, managers often learn by doing. Trial and experimentation lead to program improvements.

Program management also raises the question of how a firm's individual social programs intersect with other national, bilateral, and multinational development programs. Corporate policies that help establish higher workplace norms are probably less subject to coordination problems than defined social programs. As noted elsewhere, corporate programs are highly diverse and company specific. To achieve the highest effectiveness, company sponsors may need to work closely with local development authorities or engage in coalition efforts such as the Merck and Pfizer programs described above.

How to evaluate? Corporate social programs are as vulnerable to waste and abuse as national and international development programs. Funds can be misdirected or fail to achieve optimal results. Decision makers need some means to evaluate program effectiveness and make decisions about the program's future course. In addition, NGOs and other independent organizations seek the means to verify that businesses are living up to commitments they make in signing on to a code. Various solutions have emerged in response to the need for evaluations. Private accounting and auditing firms such as KPMG and PricewaterhouseCoopers carry out verification and evaluation services. In addition, NGOs and specialized private firms monitor compliance with codes, as does the ISO with respect to its standards.[16]

An increasingly central element in evaluation is published self evaluation. Increasingly, companies are publishing annual "triple bottom line" and GRI reports, or other detailed reports that credibly evaluate their performance in developing countries against set standards, published business codes and sets of principles. The best of these reports involve corporations undertaking internal reviews, discussing their performance in detail with NGOs and other stakeholder groups, and involving audit firms in aspects of the review. The annual Shell report, *People, Planet and Profits*, sets a high standard of this review process.[17] By staking its reputation

---

[16]OECD, *Corporate Responsibility*, pp. 78–79.

[17]Royal Dutch/Shell Group of Companies, *People, Planet and Profits: The Shell Report 2001*, available at http://www2.shell.com/home/royal-en/downloads/shell_report_2001.pdf

on this kind of public monitoring Shell has had to develop effective incentives for its managers. Starting at the top, every country chairman in the Shell Group must provide a comprehensive annual report on performance against the Shell business principles. Bonus payments take into account their performance in this social area. Thus, public accountability forces firms to seek excellent performance, which demands establishing meaningful management practices for the growing range of social policies and programs that global enterprises need to pursue as they build their global operations and demonstrate global corporate engagement.

Evaluation is also important from a social perspective. How can society ensure that its priorities, beyond those of the firm, are being met? How can private programs be integrated with national and multinational development programs? How can society guard against unintended consequences that might result from corporate social programs? For example, corporate programs may inadvertently empower one social group at the expense of another, thereby creating or exacerbating social frictions. Alternatively, a program may create new problems, even as it tries to solve an old one. And state intervention to correct the problem may make things even worse. The experience of Nestlé is instructive.[18] In 1981, UNICEF and WHO prohibited Nestlé from distributing free infant formula in developing countries, because dependency on unclean sources of water to mix with powdered formula led to infant deaths. Twenty years later, infants are dying from AIDS that they contracted from their mother's infected breast milk, and activists are calling on Nestlé and other formula makers to contribute free infant formula to reduce dependency on mother's milk.[19] But restarting that program would only make sense if clean water can be guaranteed, a function more appropriate to governments.

One concern that has been articulated with regard to social activities is that corporate social spending not lead to the substitution of business spending for programs more properly sponsored (run and paid for) by government. No clear boundary separates corporate social engagement programs from government programs. Nevertheless, business-based programs are likely to derive from different motivations, be operated with

---

[18]Margolis and Walsh, *Misery Loves Companies*, p. 41.
[19]The ban, however, is still being upheld.

different objectives, and be responsible to different constituencies than government-run programs. Recognition must also be paid to the potential role that NGOs can play in the delivery of social programs and the promotion of social goals. Care must be taken to preserve the appropriate roles of government, business, and civil society, even when their relative competencies may make it expedient to rely on business to accomplish social goals in the short term. The ultimate goal must be to build the capacity of domestic government and not to become overly dependent on business largess for critical social programs.

Conclusion

Global companies make practical business decisions to invest in, buy from, and sell to developing countries. Those activities promote economic growth and poverty reduction. Decisions to invest in corporate social policies and programs are no less practical or business-based. They are valuable both to the business and to the recipient nation. Global businesses however can do more to improve conditions in the developing countries. On close examination, many firms will find that when they invest in initiatives that help the host country, they, in turn, benefit because their commercial success is directly affected by local economic and social conditions. Although businesses should neither be expected to perform the functions of government nor mandated to perform non-commercial social activities, significant room remains for global businesses to voluntarily engage in the types of initiatives described in this chapter.

References

"The Best Global Brands." *BusinessWeek*, August 5, 2002, pp. 92–99.

Business for Social Responsibility, *Introduction to Corporate Social Responsibility White Paper*, available at http://www.bsr.org/BSRResources/WhitePaperDetail.cfm?DocumentID=138. Accessed June 11, 2002.

Committee for Economic Development, *A Shared Future: Reducing Global Poverty*. New York, NY: CED, 2002.

Friedman, Milton (1962). *Capitalism and Freedom*. Chicago: University of Chicago Press, p. 133.

Fundamental Issues in Business Structure and Performance. In Clarence C. Walton, ed., *Business and Social Progress: Views of Two Generations of Executives*. New York: Praeger, p. 17.

Graham, Edward M. (2001). *Fighting the Wrong Enemy: Antiglobal Activists and Multinational Enterprises*. Washington, D.C.: Institute for International Economics, pp. 81–104.

Haufler, Virginia (2001). A Public Role for the Private Sector: Industry Self-Regulation. In *A Global Economy*. Washington, D.C.: Carnegie Endowment for International Peace, p. 15.

International Finance Corporation, SustainAbility and the Ethos Institute, *Developing Value Business Case Matrix*, available at http://www.sustainability.com/developing-value/matrix.asp. Accessed July 30, 2002.

Margolis, Joshua D. and Walsh, James P. (2001). *Misery Loves Companies: Whither Social Initiatives by Business?*. Working Paper No. 01-058, Cambridge, MA: Harvard Business School; and Business for Social Responsibility, *Introduction to Corporate Social Responsibility White Paper.*

Royal Dutch/Shell , People, planet and profits — The Shell Report 2001, p. 35.

chapter two

$\mathcal{L}$inking Globalization, Economic Growth and Poverty: Impacts of Agribusiness Strategies on Sub-Saharan Africa

Dave Weatherspoon
Joyce Cacho
Ralph Christy

> *Most of the people in the world are poor, so if we knew the economics of being poor, we would know much of the economics that really matters. Most of the world's poor people earn their living from agriculture, so if we knew the economics of agriculture, we would know much of the economics of the poor. People who are rich find it hard to understand the behavior of poor people. Economists are no exception ...*
> — T. W. Schultz, Nobel Lecture, 1979

For most of the last decade, economic prescriptions for many emerging nations have focused predominantly on "getting prices right" by adjusting macroeconomic policy, privatizing state-owned or sponsored enterprises, or opening domestic markets to international trade in agricultural commodities and currencies. The implicit assumption is that structural adjustments will attract foreign capital through the domestic and international private sectors.

Dave Weatherspoon is an Assistant Professor of Agricultural Economics at Michigan State University; Joyce Cacho is a Vice President of Food & Agribusiness Research at Rabobank International, New York; and Ralph Christy is the J. Thomas Clarke Professor of Emerging Markets, Department of Applied Economics and Management, Cornell University.

This chapter was published in the *American Journal of Agricultural Economics*, Vol. 83, No. 3, August 2001, pp. 722–729.

This new capital would then enable both general market-based solutions and specific firm strategies that contribute to the economic growth and development goals of the nation (Williamson).

More recently, evaluation of the interrelationships among macroeconomic policies, firm strategies, and societal issues has been the source of great debate. There is little evidence to show that increased private sector investment improves economic development. Analysis of a firm's performance is based on a different analytical construct that pivots on specific profits and long-term growth goals, criteria that are internal to the firm.

A key characteristic of developing economies is the importance of agriculture to their national economies. The Green Revolution fueled rapid growth of agricultural productivity in Asia. Advances in economic development in Latin America, however, occurred in a tiered policy structure that favored installing value-added, agricultural-based industries and niche products for export markets with convertible foreign currencies. While Asia and Latin America identified mechanisms to stimulate economic development, sub-Saharan Africa placed greater emphasis on the political economy at the expense of economic growth and development (Collier and Gunning). Poverty rates in sub-Saharan Africa suggest that the focus on political structure left few resources to invest in key rural economic development areas such as persistent poverty, shortage of preventive healthcare, and fragmented infrastructure. In sub-Saharan Africa countries, the gap between the national economic landscape and that of developed countries has widened, while a similar gap has narrowed for the emerging — and competing — regions of Latin America and Southeast Asia.

This chapter analyzes the increased role of the domestic and multinational private sectors in economic development within sub-Saharan Africa. The globalization process demands that private sector strategies must now be assessed by their contributions to emerging economies, as well as by company goals.

Agribusiness Strategies in Emerging Economies: Forces and Outcomes

The globalization process is fueled by such forces as the simultaneous opening of financial capital markets and the dismantling of closed trade in agricultural commodities, which raises questions about the links between private sector strategies and the economic welfare of a country. If the globalization process is to be a catalyst for economic growth and development in emerging and developed markets, then understanding these links is crucial. Rapid developments in communication and biological technologies that reduce costs are expanding the range of strategies that agribusiness firms can use to integrate distant rural markets into national economies, and national markets into global economies.

Globalization inevitably increases competition between industries for financial capital, productive resources, and consumer markets. The unpredictability of agricultural production cycles, however, makes it extremely difficult for food and agribusiness firms to compete against other industries for financing in public markets that demand returns on a quarterly basis. Competitive agribusinesses financed primarily with private capital may invest across borders to mitigate supply risk, expand consumer markets, and diversify products.

In developed markets, agribusinesses may be motivated to internationalize through globalization when there are opportunities to exploit technologies that improve productivity and processing, while at the same time moving to new, growing consumer markets and escaping rising regulatory costs. Expanding industrial agriculture production, in developed markets, may be constrained by government policies about waste management. Growth in developed countries' consumer markets is shaped by price, plus consumer concerns about animal welfare, the seed development process, labor welfare, and the level of chemical inputs.

Interest in overseas investments is also fueled by a need to establish a country or regional presence in order to expand the consumer markets necessary to achieve firms' long-term growth targets. Proximity to emerging market consumers is also important to better understand local tastes and preferences and other factors that influence purchasing decisions and food marketing. Although the risk of doing business in the developing world is substantial, the potential for high returns and access to new markets may make it worthwhile to take the risk.

Firms' investment decision not only focuses on short-term profits, but also relies on ensuring that its profitability growth goals are achieved. As firms move offshore to invest in emerging economies, investment decisions not only focus on short-term profits, but also depend on the potential to reach profit growth goals. One approach may be to play a greater role in the development of the overall economy. From the perspective of the developing country, the increased role of the international private sector focuses on the broader potential to improve social welfare.

Foreign investment, social distributional benefits from introducing new technologies, quality assurance systems and standards, and human capital development are important to the developing country, especially when the country is resource poor. In exchange, developing countries' incomplete or imperfect markets offer investors a higher risk/return ratio, and in the long term, offer consumer markets that support their goals of profitability growth.

Corporate strategies on entering foreign markets vary widely, ranging from indirect exporting to direct investment,[1] and correspond to increasing levels of commitment, risk, control, and profit potential. In addition, expectations by the firm and the developing country about contributions to economic development also differ. Expectations for either indirect or direct exporting strategies are low, principally because these strategies indicate a limited commitment or a short-term view of the developing country market. These low expectations help reconcile the different goals of the firm and the developing country.

Three of the strategies for entry into foreign markets — contracts, joint ventures, and direct foreign investments — present greater challenges when faced with different goals: social welfare for the developing country and profits for the firm. These market entry strategies may affect multiple market participants and provide the opportunity for a differing risk/reward ratio. The profit potential of each entry mode depends on characteristics of the market to which the strategy is applied.

We now consider some distributional effects within sub-Saharan Africa economies associated with each entry strategy.

Distributional effects of contracts in emerging economies: Lessons from Africa

The use of formal contract arrangements among input suppliers, farmers, and food processing firms began in the 1930s in America and

---

[1]Indirect or direct exporting strategies are based on a relationship with a single agent whose role is principally distribution. For indirect exporting, the agent is within the exporters home country, and direct exporting involves an agent in the developing country.

gained prominence in industrialized nations by the 1960s, at which time the concept of agribusiness was emerging. Contract farming was introduced in Africa, Latin America, and Asia in the form of "out-grower schemes" during the 1980s, when farmers were contracted to grow a crop that was marketed through a multinational company (Grosch). In many emerging nations, especially in sub-Saharan Africa, contracts are usually unwritten agreements between export or processing firms and smallholder farms, cooperatives, or producer organizations. The use of contracts, more than other strategies available to the firm, is more closely related to the industrialization of the agricultural sector.

What is the rationale for contract farming in developing economies? Contract coordination in Africa, for example, is believed to be a type of institutional innovation that helps farmers by providing new technology, ready markets, secured inputs and prices, and increased cash incomes. Further, contract coordination offers a mechanism that ensures "self-sustained" development. Governments can benefit through foreign exchange earnings and food security improves if the contracted commodity is a food crop. Private firms are assured in advance of delivery of specific products at predictable times, thus reducing reliance on unpredictable spot markets.

Critics of contract coordination believe that it increases local socioeconomic differences because private firms prefer to work with "progressive" farmers and dependency of the agricultural community on imported inputs. Contracting introduces new export crops that often shifts land away from food crops and allocates resources to production of urban or export-oriented crops, thereby disrupting local domestic production patterns. Farmers lose autonomy because contracting firms control most production decisions and may skew risk and profit sharing in their favor. The contracting firm benefits by achieving greater control over a crop than would have been possible under spot markets, yet they avoid costs and risks associated with investments in production. Farmers then face a monopsonist who is able to dictate prices and exploit quality standards to suit his objectives. Specialization and use of inputs provided by the contracting firm traps farmers in a dependent relationship where they ultimately lose their ability to participate in highly competitive and unstable markets (Glover).

Some form of contract farming (out-grower schemes) is used in all countries in sub-Saharan Africa. The most notable efforts in a growing body of literature on contract farming in Africa are from the Institute for Development Anthropology (IDA) for the Africa Bureau of the United States Agency for International Development. In the mid 1980s, IDA published a number of comparative studies based on surveys carried out in Kenya, Gambia, and Senegal (De Treville, Rassas, Jaffee). Although contract farming schemes are typically unique, several general conclusions can be drawn from these empirical studies.

Jaffee and Jaffee and Morton found that contracts were associated with higher cash incomes for the participating households, created employment, and introduced new technologies that were transferable to crops that were not grown under contracts. In addition, income increased over the years and women farmers had more control over handling and allocation of household finances. Jaffee concluded that the success of a scheme depends on the ability of the firm to improve farmer productivity and the ability to control leakage of money, inputs, and products. Because enforcement of contracts is not feasible, firms must rely more on trust, hence a good relationship with farmers and local leaders became important. The research of Kimenye supports the positive income effect of contract farming with smallholders. He found that on average contract farmers received 37 percent higher yields and 80 percent higher net margins than non-contract growers, and that farmers who used contracts had more access to technical advice and market information.

Despite the overwhelming positive results from these empirical studies, reports of contract farming failures are numerous due to "breach of contract" and/or "bad faith dealing" on the part of farmers and agribusiness firms. Because institutional factors associated with farming play an important part in determining economic outcome, theoretically misallocation of resources can occur on farms where owners employ contracts to vertically integrate with input or processing firms. For example, the changing pattern of fully independent farm owners to a vertically integrated system (via contracts) alters property rights in ways that both positively and negatively affect the economic performance of the agricultural sector.

Beckford argues that major distortions in resource use arise from the inherent conflict between the interests of the principal and those of the agent. This conflict arises because each party uses inputs that are owned by the other. In reality, the outcomes vary depending on the terms of trade between small-scale farmers and contracting firms. With the recent increase in contract farming, little qualitative or quantitative information is known about the relative bargaining power between contracting parties and the resulting distributional effects. There is insufficient information on the long-term effects of contract agriculture on productivity, food prices, food security, and the environment in emerging nations. Institutional issues must be reexamined to restructure agreements between small-scale farmers and agribusiness firms, strengthen contract law, and improve ways to enforce contracts.

Distributional effects of joint ventures

Joint ventures are an alternative approach to enter emerging markets. Joint ventures are investments between two or more firms, based on exchange of financial capital and/or stock equity in horizontal or vertical markets. Approximately 20 years ago, firms throughout industry chose mergers and acquisitions over employing financial capital to build new facilities to expand business. The opportunity to capture additional value from synergies found in complementary assets, beyond economies of size and strengthening the balance sheet, is a strong motivation for joint ventures. Achieving synergies between joint venture firms can be a formidable challenge. The cost of missing the joint venture synergy mark is magnified by the expense of disentangling a failed joint venture attempt.

Joint ventures have occurred predominantly between firms in developed countries. In the strictest definition, preference for joint ventures has ebbed in developed countries because strategic alliances are employed more frequently. Benefits can be derived by acting as a single firm, while at the same time mitigating risk by establishing a formal understanding rather than exchanging financial instruments.

Examples of food or agribusiness joint ventures with firms in sub-Saharan Africa are almost absent. In the literature, this topic is dominated by examples from China and a few examples from Eastern Europe. In sub-Saharan Africa, countries with diverse vestiges of political systems, institutional frameworks, labor force readiness, and economic instability all raise the transaction costs of joint venture investing relative to competing emerging markets. Nonetheless, joint ventures have great potential to catalyze key domestic markets, which in turn could improve socioeconomic conditions.

The joint venture strategy may be the most desirable option for domestic and foreign firms entering emerging markets. In forming a joint venture, local and foreign partners define their commitment to a joint profit objective. The capital and knowledge of the host environment that the local partner brings to the joint venture, including the social welfare challenges, are factors in the investment decisions made by the foreign firm.

Host environment "knowledge" may include the local distribution network, consumer tastes and preferences, as well as cultural factors that influence labor force productivity and food purchasing decisions. Beyond the foreign firm's financial capital, their management and technology systems make investing with an international joint venture partner attractive to local emerging-market investors. Management and technology systems introduce production processes that increase the probability of improved productivity, product quality, and flow consistency. Success of a new joint venture — defined as achieving a profit within the shortest time possible while expanding the foreign firm's consumer market — hinges on a business development strategy that views non-financial contributions from the local and foreign firms as assets.

Joint venture investments have historically been a notable opportunity to exploit sub-Saharan Africa and the overall environment of emerging markets. The role of joint venture local partners was limited to reducing the transaction costs to extract resources, without interest in fostering a longer-term relationship with the local market. This "feigned" commitment provided limited probability for financial capital, or knowledge multiplier effects.

Expanding consumer markets from national to international requires a corporate strategy that considers information about host country market forces — demography, social and cultural characteristics, economic factors, technology base, legal and regulatory framework, and competing local products. This information is usually not readily available to the public, and varies in quality on a national or regional basis.

The increased importance of local consumer markets that has accompanied globalization also raises the bargaining power of local parties that may own underperforming assets. Injecting financial capital and management and technology systems that improve productivity may be the catalysts for these assets to reach their full potential. In a joint venture, a well-defined legal framework is important to use knowledge assets from the local and foreign investors to produce profits and social welfare benefits.

When joint ventures are chosen as the mechanism to enter emerging markets, implications for risk management are heightened. For sub-Saharan Africa firms and international investors, joint ventures offer the opportunity to reduce the cost of financial capital by expanding the choices and improving the bargaining power of the joint venture with financial institutions. Further, joint ventures offer the benefit of diversifying the product portfolio, which is especially valuable when there is intra-company trade between emerging and developed market products. Conceptually, these benefits of risk management establish that the joint venture has notable profit potential.

An alternative view of the joint venture mechanism focuses on the challenges of melding two different business and social cultures, and in many instances, differing value structures. Significant differences in capacity and economic integration between rural areas in emerging and developed markets can make it difficult to harmonize expectations of productivity. Investing the time to understand these differences is important if the joint venture is to capture benefits from risk management and synergies, as well as establish a solid foundation to improve productivity. The joint venture improves its asset performance through its socially responsible approach as a component of the business decision to pursue higher risk/reward ratios offered by investing in sub-Saharan Africa.

Distributional impacts of foreign direct investment

Rather than exporting, some food and agribusiness firms are choosing to serve their international clientele by establishing foreign production subsidiaries that they own completely. Simultaneously, most nations are actively recruiting firms by offering incentives to locate in their country. The combination of opening economies, incentives, and firms seeking international markets have contributed to the dramatic increase in foreign direct investment (FDI) in emerging markets. FDI in emerging markets increased from approximately US$10 billion to more than US$180 billion from 1980 to 1998 (United Nations Conference on Trade and Development [(UNCTAD)/2000]). Part of this increase can be explained by the higher average returns in emerging markets than industrialized countries, e.g., 15.3 percent for emerging markets versus 12.5 percent for all countries (UNCTAD/1998).

Regional rates of return differ greatly (Africa, 36.9 percent; Asia-Pacific, 19.3 percent; Latin America and Caribbean, 12.8 percent), but in their FDI decisions, firms bypassed the highest rate of return — Africa (UNCTAD/1998). Although total foreign investment in Africa rose from US$1 billion to US$8 billion from 1980 to 1998, FDI in the Asia-Pacific and Latin America and Caribbean regions was far greater. Revolutionary advances in communications and biotechnology have strong implications for the ability of sub-Saharan Africa to curb increases in poverty and malnutrition rates. Making effective use of those technologies will require governments to invest in infrastructure and other public goods to leverage FDI. Public policy is a key factor in effectively reducing poverty through investments.

Modernization and dependency theories suggest that initially FDI increases income inequality within emerging countries (Tsai). The modernization theory stresses that sufficient output must be first produced before it can be redistributed, hence the presence of investment is more important than its origin. The path of the income effect of capital investment, regardless of the source, can be characterized by Kuznet's inverted-U curve. Dependency theorists state that FDI is utilized by the local labor elites in emerging markets to create an inter-country coalition to maximize their own interests. In this scenario, persistent income inequality is possible through this alliance of the state, labor elite, and foreign capitalists. These observations emphasize the need for a national strategy to leverage FDI to ensure positive results.

The spectrum of entry strategies into a country's market can yield both positive and negative distributional effects. A major positive distributional effect of FDI is that consumers usually have greater access to consistent quality and capital-intensive products, at a lower price. The country also benefits from the infusion of permanent physical capital, which is not always the case for joint ventures or contracts. On the other hand, firms that acquire or directly invest in SSA may negatively influence domestic competition and smallholders. This crowding-out effect occurs in many ways, but the most common is that foreign firms usually introduce grades and standards to the market. These new standards systematically reduce the market size for domestic firms and smallholders. Global firms source little domestic talent for their foreign operations, hence, the multiplier effect is somewhat reduced (Tsai). Few rural firms and smallholders are able to participate in the new markets, which leads to this question: How can rural firms and producers be engaged and enhanced as a result of an increase in foreign capital?

The benefits of FDI can be marginalized and costs minimized depending on government policy and the overall investment environment. Positive results are possible if the government has a strategic plan to leverage foreign investment and domestic resources, including human resources, to maximize economic growth and reduce income inequality. A country without a strategic plan is in essence relying on foreign capital to create an enabling environment for everyone in the country. This approach to policymaking is insufficient and misguided. The next section will examine various strategies for governments and private firms to consider when promoting economic growth and development through foreign investment.

Negotiating an enabling environment: The role of the public sector

In the past, many sub-Saharan Africa governments have made poor economic decisions that have exploded into dire poverty and poor health conditions throughout the region. FDI targeted at emerging nations has not been directed at sub-Saharan Africa. Additionally, international aid to sub-Saharan Africa has diminished within the last decade — net official development assistance and official aid declined from US$17.5 billion to US$14.2 billion from 1993 to 1998 (World Bank). The lack of FDI, diminished overseas development assistance, and the uncertainty associated with globalization combine to place sub-Saharan Africa economies in a challenging situation. Globalization may provide the on-ramp for these economies or further widen the gap between North and South.

Creating an enabling environment for a healthy private sector is possible if a nation is committed to achieving a *competitive* advantage (Porter). Specifically, it is vital for sub-Saharan Africa nations to evaluate regional competitive advantages and target those industries along with some of the high technology industries. In selecting industries, governments should factor in the market difficulties experienced by smallholders and small firms in the various growth strategies especially since 70 to 80 percent of the population falls in this category. Success depends on sufficient domestic consumption of these goods followed by a strong export market.

Assuming that value-added agriculture is a targeted industry, governments can improve the competitive nature of the sector through several actions. Education is primary when upgrading production factors, along with transparent and seamless market information and infrastructure investments. Strategic partnerships with industry on these factors, along with creating domestic consumption, are vital.

Sub-Saharan African governments realize that agricultural research and development firms will not locate in the region. To reach the next level of value-added products, scarce resources will need to be committed to publicly-sponsored research and development activity. In agriculture, this investment means that partnerships with multinational firms must be negotiated such that the innovations can be re-engineered or adapted legally to regional crops, animals, or machines. This strategy is a slow process, but over time, innovative activities attract additional innovative firms, and eventually a sizeable talented pool of researchers will generate new markets within and outside the region.

Agricultural, trade, and development assistance policies contribute to the investment behavior of agribusiness firms. In today's globalization era, however, agribusiness firms compete for financial capital against firms in industries that have historically looked beyond industry-specific policies for opportunities. The expanded public policy set includes corporate tax policies. Tax expenses — the amount and payment timing — can be instrumental in determining the value of any investment. Desai and Hines shows that tax policy, targeting foreign tax credits, for example, can determine the investment value and entry mode of cross-border investments. The lower a country's tax rates, the more likely that U.S. multinational investors will use a financial capital structure that is higher in debt and pay more royalties to their U.S. parent firm. This capital structure focuses on short-term, extractive opportunities in high GDP growth, high research and development intensity countries — characteristics not present in sub-Saharan Africa emerging market countries.

A fine line separates fostering growth and creating white elephants. The current economic predicament of sub-Saharan Africa countries is unprecedented and hardly fits any modern models of development. In the past, sub-Saharan Africa public policy was heavily involved in private industry and has fostered insulated, dependent, and non-competitive firms. This time around, governments can encourage domestic rivalry to influence sophisticated supply and demand.

In addition to national policy, worldwide leadership is crucial for these governments to negotiate future trade terms. Worldwide reduction of tariff barriers has dramatically increased world trade in fresh and processed agricultural commodities. Today, producers and processors around the world are in direct competition with one another. The globalization of food and agribusiness has begun to shift the standard setting and enforcement processes to international agencies such as the World Trade Organization (WTO), the International Organisation for Standardization and the Organization of Economic Cooperation and Development. Harmonizing standards to transcend national borders will be a central feature of the food and agriculture system for the foreseeable future. Sub-Saharan Africa should focus on efforts to determine the details of these agreements and how they can help the region to improve conditions for all producers — regardless of their size — and increase exports.

Private sector initiatives in emerging markets

Profits depend principally on using assets efficiently and reducing costs. Increasing profitability growth depends on strategic investments — not only for raw material supplies, but also for consumer markets. In the earlier era of closed markets, profitability growth strategies focused on price in the firm's domestic market, and developing export markets in emerging markets using government economic development assistance programs.

Along with a profitability strategy, linked to the opening of financial and commodity markets (the globalization process), firms must embrace a long-term view of emerging markets. By investing in underperforming assets in emerging markets, firms need to acknowledge that in the shorter-term, the investment contributes to the profitability growth goal by improving the social welfare and purchasing power of future consumers. In the longer term, the investment assets will contribute to measurable future profits. By leveraging the investing firm's technology and knowhow, that qualitative value and contribution, can catalyze realizing measurable profits in sub-Saharan Africa markets, as well as reduce rural urban migration and persistent hunger, and increase the availability of preventative medical care.

Firms based in developed markets have the skills and technology that can reduce the cumbersome administrative processes in emerging markets. For example, in many sub-Saharan Africa countries, information management for efficient, low-cost credit administration is in great demand. This is a notable difference from developed markets where computer-based data and process management is commonplace. With limited training for local staff and adaptation of hardware and software systems, the basics of agribusiness management can be established.

Financing insured by a group has proven to be an effective substitute for the collateral of physical assets used in developed markets. The mutual trust and accountability characteristics of group financing are associated with 98 percent loan repayment at acceptable market interest rates. The Grameen Bank in Bangladesh, where small loans (US$20) are managed and insured, typically by groups of five women, is the most notable example. This type of "micro-credit" financing is appropriate for sub-Saharan Africa's rural, agriculture-based environment. A huge obstacle confronting grass roots/rural organizations, especially in debt-ridden sub-Saharan Africa, is the availability of start-up capital. Developed market, private investors can readily provide the needed initial capital as an investment to upgrade the quality of productive resources. The effectiveness of employing this mechanism to ensure improvements in quality and quantity of agricultural products and the social welfare in the host country pivots on understanding the relationship between gender and crop production.

Focusing on private/public partnerships is key to capturing value that multinational agribusinesses need to sustain profitability growth. As sub-Saharan Africa governments work to meet the challenge of public debt that increases as their exchange rates decline, private partners can offer technical and management training — a principal catalyst to improving the rate of economic growth and development.

Sustainable profitability depends on increasing the number of middle class consumers. The benefits from private firms that partner with state or federal governments to establish schools, roads, or wireless telephone communication are linked to the longer-term goal of increasing consumer purchasing power — which is considered a "positive" by investors and governments.

Conclusions

The globalization process has the potential to benefit the economic development of sub-Saharan Africa. It has fused the theoretical stages of economic development, and raised the premium on the traditional, sequential approach. Sub-Saharan Africa governments are investing in the necessary components to foster economic stability and increase the middle-class, including infrastructure, opening telecommunication markets, and internet-based distance learning programs. Competition for capital, driven by globalization, is pushing private sector agribusiness to seek opportunities to capture higher returns in the longrun.

This approach encourages a shift in strategies for internationalizing. Rather than trade in final consumer goods, multinationals are leveraging — either by production contracts, joint ventures, or wholly-owned companies — their technical expertise to introduce production efficiencies while, at the same time, learning about the tastes and preferences of the soon-to-be middle class in sub-Saharan Africa. It is agricultural trade and macroeconomic public policies, along with corporate tax policy and firms' new interest in translating soft assets or qualitative factors into profits — all working simultaneously — that defines the opportunity to include sub-Saharan Africa as beneficiaries of the globalization process.

References

Beckford, G. L. (1983). *Persistent Poverty*. Morant Bay, Jamaica: Maroon Publishing House.

Collier, P., and J. W. Gunning (1999). Why Has Africa Grown Slowly? *Journal of Economic Perspectives*, 13, pp. 3–22.

Desai, Mihir A., and J. R. Hines, Jr. (1999). Basket Cases: Tax Incentives and International Joint Venture Participation by American Multinational Firms. *Journal of Public Economics*, 71, pp. 379–402.

De Treville, D. (1986). *Contract Farming, The Private Sector, and the State: An Annotated and Comprehensive Bibliography with Particular Reference to Africa.* Binghamton, NY: Institute of Development Anthropology.

Glover, D. J., and K. Kusterer (1990). *Small Farmers, Big Business, Contract Farming and Rural Development*. New York, NY: St. Martin Press.

Grosch, B. (1994). Contract Farming in Africa: An Application of the New Institutional Economics. *Journal of African Economies*, 3, pp. 231–61.

Jaffee, S. (1987). Case Studies of Contract Farming in the Horticultural Sector of Kenya. Working Paper No. 83, Institute of Development Anthropology, Binghamton, NY.

Jaffee, S., and J. Morton (1995). *Marketing Africa's High Value Foods: Comparative Experiences of an Emergent Private Sector*. Dubuque, IA: Kendall/Hunt Publishing Co.

Kimenye, L. N. (1994). Contract Farming in Kenya: A Case Study of Smallholder French Bean Production. Dept. Ag. Econ. Staff Paper No. 94–22, Michigan State University, East Lansing, MI.

Porter, M. E. (1990). *The Competitive Advantage of Nations*. New York, NY: Free Press.

Rassas, B. (1988). Contract Farming in the Horticultural Sector in Senegal. Working Paper No. 85, Institute of Development Anthropology, Binghamton, NY.

Tsai, Pan-Long (1995). Foreign Direct Investment and Income Inequality: Further Evidence. *World Development*, 23, pp. 469–83.

United Nations Conference on Trade and Development. Foreign Direct Investment. TNC Database, 2000.

———. Rates of Return on United States Foreign Direct Investment. Data based on United States, Department of Commerce, 1998.

Williamson, J. (1993). Democracy and the 'Washington Consensus'. *World Development*, 21, pp. 1329–36.

World Bank. World Development Indicators 2000, www.worldbank.org/data/wdi2000/pdfs/table6_11.pdf.

Part Two

Can Markets Matter for the Poor?

chapter three

ᴄℳaking Markets Work for the Poor

Eleni Gabre-Madhin
Nithya Nagarajan

Even as the forces of market liberalization and globalization sweep across the world, it seems the jury is still out on whether market reforms have benefited the poor. While we know that markets can be good for the poor by creating productive economic opportunities, little consensus exists on the actual impacts of past reforms on the poor. For example, in the case of the agriculture sector, the emerging consensus suggests that while reforms did improve market efficiency and price transmission, the supply response has been mixed. Interestingly, studies that directly examine the poverty impacts in terms of changes in producers' terms of trade and changes in price volatility, results point to negative or at best mixed outcomes associated with reform (Christiansen and Pontara, 2002; Dercon, 2001; Sahn, Dorosh and Younger, 1997; Peters, 1996; Kheralllah et al., 200; Bocar et al., 1999; Meerman, 1997).

The mixed success of reforms has fueled extensive debates in the past decade. It has underpinned a shift beyond the "getting the prices right"

The authors are, respectively, Research Fellow, Markets and Structural Studies Division, International Food Policy Research Institute and Consultant, World Bank.

paradigm to an agenda that focuses on the institutional features required for a well-functioning market. In this chapter, we hope to take this discussion a step further and examine specifically the relationships between markets and the poor. The impetus for this chapter comes from a renewed interest in poverty reduction as the organizing mandate for country development strategies and a specific interest in examining how markets can be made more "pro-poor" (World Bank, 2000; DFID, 2000). We argue that improving the poor's outcomes associated with market participation requires going beyond "getting markets to work," but to understanding how dimensions of poverty can impact access to and returns from market participation. Drawing from the transactions costs literature, we explore what are the implications of being poor for dealing with the market.

At the outset, it is important to clarify what we mean by making markets work for the poor. A recent literature has emerged around the notion of "pro-poor markets" (Christensen and Pontara, 2002; DFID, 2000). Embedded in the idea of pro-poor markets is the concept that market outcomes should disproportionately benefit the poor. This concept is problematic, however, since it is not clear how market processes, in and of themselves, would accrue gains in a disproportionate manner to a relatively less-endowed segment of the population. Well-functioning markets and market structures do not imply equitable outcomes. This view has theoretical underpinnings in the fundamental theorems of welfare economics, which show that competitive and complete markets yield efficient outcomes (Arrow, 1951; Debreu, 1959), but say nothing about distributional outcomes.

The concept of making markets work for the poor is not simply about improving the functioning and efficiency of the market, as has been the focus for much of reform efforts in past decades. Rather, the basic thesis posited in this chapter is that if we are concerned about markets and the poor, we have to consider how dimensions of poverty impact access to markets and returns accruing from market activity. In this chapter, we seek to shed light on this issue by employing an analytical framework that integrates poverty dimensions into the analysis of market performance. The framework links the New Institutional Economics paradigm and the literatures on social capital in markets and market power with the literature on poverty and the Sustainable Livelihoods framework.

In this discussion, we first discuss the opportunities that markets can create for the poor, and briefly identify some lessons learned from past reform experiences with respect to outcomes for the poor. Second, we build on the New Institutional Economics paradigm and the Sustainable Livelihoods Framework to develop an integrated analytical framework that maps dimensions of poverty and factors that impact market functioning. Specifically, we argue that markets and market outcomes must be understood in terms of underlying transaction costs of coordination, information, and enforcement (Williamson, 1985); in terms of the social capital embedded in market exchange (Granovetter, 1985; Putnam, 1985); and finally in terms of the power relationship among market actors (Bates, 1981). We then map how the dimensions of poverty, with respect to assets, vulnerability, social exclusion, and powerlessness impact the three concepts of transaction costs, social capital, and power with respect to market outcomes. In the final section, we discuss some policy implications for making markets work for the poor.

Markets and the Poor: Opportunities and Experiences

While well-functioning markets in and of themselves do not imply equitable distributional outcomes, the development of markets is nevertheless important for the poor. In all developing economies, the poor rely on formal and informal markets to sell their labor and products, finance investment, and insure against risk. Well-functioning markets can provide productive opportunities for the poor, and impact households through multiple channels. These include:

- **Facilitating access to assets**: Human, financial, social, physical, and natural assets (e.g. land, wells, cattle, tools, houses, skills, health, roads, etc.) are crucial to the welfare of the poor. Markets can facilitate the poor's access to assets and enable them to use those assets to generate livelihoods and to reduce their vulnerability.
- **Improving the productivity and returns on assets**: Markets also provide a mechanism to generate monetary returns to assets as well as increase the productivity of assets already owned by the poor. Markets assign value and prices to assets owned by the poor, including their labor and land, and to the goods and services they produce. Markets

thus permit the generation of income and livelihoods for the poor.
Depending on the sources or nature of growth that takes place, markets
can increase the demand for and return on the assets of the poor.

- **Meeting basic consumption needs**: Poor households usually rely on
markets to secure their basic subsistence consumption basket (DFID,
2000; Arulpragasam and Pontara, 2001).

The role that markets can play in generating allocative efficiency, as
well as incentives for productivity enhancements, has guided much of
reform efforts in the past decades. Reforms have aimed to liberalize and
deregulate markets and to promote private entrepreneurship. The rationale
is that economic opportunities created through reform can be critical in
enabling the poor to escape from poverty.

Lessons from the poor

The actual experience of reforms, particularly their impacts on the
poor, however have had mixed successes. While we do not aim to provide
here an exhaustive review of the literature, we identify some lessons learned
based on past experience.

First, the impact of market reforms on the poor varies and is impacted
by a number of factors, including pre-reform initial conditions. A major
feature of the pre-reform environment is the extent to which the poor
and smallholder producers were taxed or subsidized. For example, in pre-
reform West Africa smallholders were taxed heavily. Reform led to an
initially positive, although limited, impact on production. In contrast, in
eastern and southern Africa, market reforms have removed input and credit
subsidies. The effects of which have not been offset by the gains from lower
cost, private distribution systems.

Second, characteristics of the poor, such as their location (rural vs.
urban) and market position relative to the sectors undergoing reform (net
buyer vs. net seller), will affect the outcomes from reform. In the case of
Malawi, for example, Chilowa (1998) found that the losers from market
reforms were the net food buyers among smallholder farmers, low-income
urban consumers, and remote smallholders, while the winners from reform
were net food sellers among smallholders, and traders. Similarly, Peters
(1996) concluded that structural adjustment reforms in Malawi did not

benefit the rural poor disproportionately. Although liberalization provided new income opportunities for relatively better-off households in terms of expanded tobacco and maize sales, the poorest 25 percent of rural households studied experienced a relative worsening of income and food security.

Third, outcomes and supply responses have varied depending on whether the crops produced are export or cash crops. Supply response has been stronger for export crops than for food crops, mainly because liberalization has moved relative prices in favor of tradables, and the use of imported inputs such as fertilizer has become more profitable for export crops than for food crops. Evidence indicates that the most responsive sectors have been the cash crop sectors such as cotton in Benin and Mali, cashew nuts in Mozambique, and coffee in Uganda. In some instances, because of resource constraints such as land scarcity and seasonal labor shortages, a relative price shift in favor of one crop may result in a shift of resources into that crop at the expense of another resulting in no increase in overall agricultural production. In countries such as Benin and Burkina Faso, where cotton inputs are available on credit through the government, input use has increased and has had positive spill-over effects on food production. Because of the complementary nature of food and export crop production in many areas, the returns generated from export production can be used to buy inputs for food production.

Fourth, the impact of reform is also contingent on the level of market development. Among the issues are the development of market supporting institutions for contract enforcement and property rights, reducing the legal and bureaucratic barriers that confront entrepreneurs, and developing strong public administration and judicial systems to promote governance. In recent years, practitioners have been paying extensive attention to the prerequisite institutional and policy environment necessary for well-functioning markets (see Box 1) (World Bank, 2001; Klein, 2001).

The lessons learned point to the fact that the impact of market reforms on the poor is contingent on a set of factors, which includes the pre-reform environment, position of the poor relative to sectors undergoing reform, and levels of market development. While getting markets to function well can have important beneficial effects for all segments of the population, an interest in the poor warrants a specific examination of how dimensions

Box 1: Promoting an Enabling Environment for Markets
Well-functioning markets require an enabling environment, which encompasses:

- Framework of commercial, environmental, health, and social regulations that limit what owners can and cannot do with their property;
- Reasonable level of certainty about government policy;
- Sound financial system, with prudential frameworks;
- Good physical infrastructure;
- Macroeconomic stability
- Well-defined property rights
- Sound legal, judicial, and contracting systems
- Freedom of entry and exit.

Source: Mahmood, 2002

of poverty impact access to, and outcomes associated with, market participation.

Dimensions of Poverty and the Institutional Foundations of the Market: An Integrating Framework

An analytical framework examines how the concepts of transactions costs, social capital, and power influence the functioning of the market, and how multiple dimensions of poverty interact with these factors to impact livelihood strategies and outcomes of the poor. In examining these issues, we draw on the conceptual literature from the new institutional economics approach, including concepts of social capital and market power, and integrate it with dimensions of poverty as elaborated in the sustainable livelihoods framework.

Transactions cost economics, social capital, and power

Transactions cost economics

Following the work of Ronald Coase (1937), who explicitly introduced transaction costs into economic analysis, two distinct strands of thought have emerged in what has come to be known as the new institutional economics. One approach is concerned with the evolution of institutions as economizing transaction-costs and views those institutions as the key to the performance of economies (Coase, 1937, 1960; Alchisn and Demsetz, 1972; North, 1981; Williamson, 1985). The second strand has grown out of the theory of imperfect information and has adopted a more rigorous framework for analyzing institutions as substitutes for missing markets in an environment of pervasive risks, incomplete markets, information asymmetry, and moral hazard (Akalof, 1980; Stiglitz, 1985).

Williamson (1985) takes the view that the main (not sole) purpose of institutions is to economize transaction costs. Arrow (1969) defined transaction costs as the "costs of running the economic system." Transaction costs are distinguished as *ex ante* and *ex post* — the first include those of drafting, negotiating and monitoring an agreement, while the latter include the cost of maladaption, haggling, setup and running associated with governance, and bonding costs to securing commitment (Williamson, 1985).

Practitioners of the transaction cost approach view transaction costs as the broad set of costs related to information, negotiation, monitoring, coordination, and enforcement of contracts. When transaction costs are absent, the initial assignment of property rights do not matter from the viewpoint of efficiency, because rights can be readily adjusted. But when costs are substantial, the allocation of property rights is crucial and the separability of efficiency and equity break down (Bardham, 1989). Standard Walrasian economics postulates that equilibrium prices apply equally to every participant. With transaction costs, each agent faces specific effective prices. Thus, optimum resource allocation will differ for each agent, with fundamental implications. In neoclassical theory with perfect markets, every commodity has a single opportunity cost and ownership does not matter for resource allocation. Thus, incomes and equity are determined *ex post*. With transaction costs, efficiency in resource use depends on the distribution of assets and property rights. Thus, if the poor have lower transaction costs on labor and production is labor-intensive, then higher efficiency and equity can be achieved through transferring assets to them (Sadoulet and de Janvry, 1995).

Embeddedness, trust, and social capital

While not formally a part of new institutional economics, a related body of research has emerged in recent years, originating in sociology, that addresses the importance of social capital in economic development (Putnam, 1985; Coleman, 1990; Kranton, 1996; Knack and Keefer, 1997). Following Polanyi (1957), it is widely recognized that market transactions, particularly in developing countries, are often embedded in long-term, personalized, relationships (Geertz, 1968; Meillassoux, 1971; Granovetter, 1985; Plattner, 1989; Harriss-White, 1993). Personalized exchange emerges in response to high commitment failure, in which the risk of breach of contract or opportunism is high, resulting from the lack of market information, inadequate regulation, and the absence of legal enforcement mechanisms.

A key notion in the literature on social capital is that social networks and other social links may form for economic reasons and may guard against market failures caused by asymmetric information (Arrow, 2000). There are two possible meanings of social capital. The first definition sees social capital as a "stock" of trust and an emotional attachment to a group or society that facilitates the provision of public goods (Fukuyama, 1995; Grief, 1993; Coleman, 1988; Putnam, Leoardi and Nanetti, 1993). The second views social capital as an individual asset that provides private benefits to a single individual or firm (Granovetter, 1995).

Within the literature that identifies social capital with the existence of trust, the role of networks and coalitions have been examined. In particular, it is found that trade associations, solidarity networks, ethnic or religious ties arise to build trust and promote reputation (Greif, 1993; Fafchamps, 1996; Platteau, 1994). Fafchamps and Minten (1999) demonstrate that these trust-based relationships, which are established primarily by repeated interaction, are used as contract enforcement mechanisms and also impact access to assets.

Market power

Having emerged out of neoclassical economics, a large part of the new institutional economics theory has focused on allocative-efficiency improving institutions and is thus devoid of considerations of power (Bardhan, 1989). Yet, those are equally important in determining market outcomes and market relations. A seminal contribution to understanding how political power was used to manipulate markets is the work of Bates (1981) who demonstrates how pre-reform price policies were generally harmful to the interests of farmers. Bates notes that, in Africa, agriculture was both taxed and subsidized, with output taxed and inputs subsidized. This paradoxical situation is explained in the power relations between urban elites, who needed plentiful supplies of cheap food, and the rural poor producers, who had no voice and participation in the policy process.

More recently, another literature has emerged that explicitly focuses on the issues of power, but in a liberalized market setting. This is the work of Gereffi (1994) and others, who have developed the global commodity chain approach, building on the paradigm of world systems theory. This literature views the emergence of global value chains in which production and consumption are linked in tightly coordinated chains, for example for fresh produce and textiles among others. In this chain, the analysis focuses on the concept of power, particularly the power of the large retail chains in the industrialized countries, which dictates market conditions and prices to the powerless producers at the origin of the chain. With globalization, the rise and consolidation of international markets creates major concerns for smallholders, who are increasingly marginalized from these supply chains.

The Sustainable Livelihoods Framework and the Many Dimensions of Poverty

The sustainable livelihoods framework has emerged recently as a highly relevant and dynamic tool to explain how, over time, asset endowments and risk profiles specific to the poor shape their livelihood strategies. This framework is useful because it embodies two key notions: one is that starting conditions matter; and the second is that strategies, rather than just outcomes, matter. The concept of strategies is very powerful in that it embeds the idea that actors have choices and that decisions are based on considerations of starting conditions as well as potential outcomes. This framework is dynamic in that strategies lead to outcomes, which in turn influence the accumulation of assets and risk profiles.

Among the key strengths of this framework is that it contains the multiple and broad dimensions of poverty. The understanding of poverty goes beyond traditional notions encompassing material deprivation, but also includes attainments in health and education, as well as vulnerability and social exclusion. In order to better understand these dimensions of poverty, it is useful to think about the assets owned by people, and the returns they obtain from these assets (DFID, 2002). Those assets include:

- Financial capital, which includes savings (cash as well as liquid assets), credit (from formal and informal sources), as well as inflows (state transfers and remittances). A major cause of material deprivation is limited access to finance. Credit constraints stemming from problems of information asymmetry and moral hazard, combined with inadequate access to collateral, particularly restrict access to finance for the poor. In Kenya, for example, only 4 percent of the poor have access to credit through banks and another 3 percent through cooperatives (Narayan et al., 2001).

- Physical capital, which includes transportation, roads, buildings, shelter, water supply and sanitation, energy, technology, and communications.

- Human capital, which includes education, skills, knowledge, health, nutrition, and labor power. The relationships observed between human capital — health and education — and income poverty are stark. In many countries, indicators such as child mortality rates, malnutrition, incidence of illness, access to schooling and educational achievement are significantly worse for the income-poor than the non-poor. For example, in a sample of Asian and African countries, the proportion of children born in the past five years but no longer living is between three and six times larger for the poorest decile than for the richest. Steady improvement in this variable is observed as wealth increases. Similarly, with respect to education, a study of five Latin American countries shows that low income households attain fewer years of education than richer households (Kanbur and Squire, 1999).

- Social capital, which includes networks that increase trust, ability to work together, access to opportunities, reciprocity, and informal safety nets, as well as more formal membership in organizations. Poverty as defined in economic terms is often accompanied by social marginalization, and thereby results in exclusion from social networks. Exclusion can take the form of discrimination based on ethnicity, caste, or gender, and also has implications for asset ownership. For example, evidence from India shows that scheduled castes and tribes face a higher risk of poverty. Among rural scheduled caste women in India, the literacy rate was 19 percent in 1991 compared with 46 percent for men and 64 percent for the entire country (World Bank, 2000).

- Natural capital, which includes land, water, forests, marine resources, air quality, erosion protection, and biodiversity.

In addition to these five kinds of capital, lack of power — in the economic sphere and with respect to state institutions — can also be a key dimension of poverty. While empirical evidence between income poverty and powerlessness are scarce, participatory poverty assessments reveal the nature of concerns felt by the poor. For example, in the economic sphere, people in poverty consistently express concerns about exploitation by middlemen and traders. With respect to state institutions, the poor report being harassed, ignored and unable to make their voices heard (Narayan et al., 2001).

Finally, and importantly, the framework captures a key dimension of poverty, which is vulnerability and exposure to risk. Vulnerability stems from seasonality in prices, production, and employment opportunities, shocks such as changes in human or animal health, natural disasters, and conflicts, and trends in prices and technology. While all individuals face risk from a variety of sources, the importance of the agricultural sector to the poor and vulnerability in labor markets[1] exacerbate the risks faced by the poor. Given their limited ability to cope with risk due to resource constraints and absence of formal risk insurance markets, the poor are left vulnerable. With limited options to manage risk through formal market mechanisms, they experience significant fluctuations in income, which makes consumption smoothing difficult (World Bank, 2000; Jalan and Ravallion, 1997).

The sustainable livelihood framework is intended to be dynamic, recognizing changes due to both external fluctuations and the results of people's own actions. Assets interact with policies, institutions and processes in shaping the choice of livelihood strategies. These in turn shape the livelihood outcomes, which are the types of impact that we are interested in.

---

[1]Studies show the first workers to be laid off during public sector cutbacks are typically those with low skills, who then join the ranks of the urban poor — a phenomenon observed in both Africa and Latin America during the structural adjustment reforms of the 1980s and 1990s (World Bank, 2000).

Mapping Poverty and Market Outcomes

Asset ownership, including access to information

Asset ownership or access to private endowments are among the most important dimensions of poverty and affects the extent to which households benefit from reforms. This has been found consistently in a number of micro-level studies. For example, studies from sub-Saharan Africa show the importance of initial private endowments in education and land as key conditioning factors that influence the extent to which households benefit from reforms (Christiaensen, Demery and Paternostro, 2002). Similarly in India, Datt and Ravallion (2002) find that initial literacy affects the extent of the poor to benefit from growth, or the capacity of the poor to participate in opportunities created. Asset ownership impacts the gains from market reform both because it affects transactions costs and productivity.

Access to information such as market information systems and grades and standards is a key asset that impacts transactions costs. In many countries, market information systems perform poorly or are non-existent due to inadequate financing and the inability of government agencies to collect reliable market information. Following liberalization, new information systems to replace those previously administered by the state marketing channels are very underdeveloped, particularly since the private sector has not been able to assume the institutional role previously fulfilled by the state (Chaudhury and Banerji, 2001). Poor producers and consumers who lack the scale to collect their own information are particularly adversely affected. Transactions costs, such as costs of acquiring information or search for marketing and trading partners, increase. In a study of grain markets in Ethiopia, Gabre-Madhin (2001) finds that search costs for small traders are higher than for traders of higher volume, resulting in their higher dependence on market intermediaries. Ultimately, these high search costs restrict the scope and scale of markets and smaller traders' ability to respond to the needs of the poor. Similarly, inadequate access to standardized system of grades and standards, which can provide a greater level of certainty about the quality of produce, also increases search and screening costs. It implies that traders must visually inspect each product. More generally, inadequate access to market information implies that the poor are unable to plan their production, harvesting and sales according to market demand, or to sell their products in the most lucrative markets.

Limited access to physical assets such as infrastructure (roads, electricity) or storage and transport facilities, combined with the spatial dimension of poverty, also impact transactions costs for the rural poor. Empirical studies from food market reforms show that access to roads and land were among the most important factors for groups who benefited from reform (Dercon, 1998). Inadequate infrastructure and distance from markets implies that transactions costs rise not only due to higher transport costs, but also due to the increased costs of screening, bargaining with, and monitoring distant trading partners (Staal et al., 1997). A case study of dairy transactions in East Africa illustrates some of these issues (see Box 2). It represents a case where liberalization of the sector provided producers more options with respect to marketing outlets they could use, but the ability to use these alternative outlets — some of which offered higher prices and more stable payments — was determined by their level of transactions costs. Communities further from markets restrict the parties with whom they make transactions.

Limited access to assets has several implications for the livelihoods strategy of the poor. First, reliance on intermediaries and limited access to reliable market information implies that smallholders often end up selling their products at harvest, when prices are their lowest, rather than storing output until prices increase. Second, access to information, particularly for communities far from markets, impacts their decision to commercialize. For example, studies by SEWA show how poor women in a region called

---

Box 2: Dairy Transactions in East Africa

A study of transactions in the East African dairy market shows how access to infrastructure, storage and transport systems, and spatial factors impact transactions costs, and thereby marketing behavior of small scale producers.

Until the liberalization of the dairy industry in 1992, the Kenya Cooperative Creameries (KCC) had a monopoly on fluid milk sales in urban areas. Dairy cooperatives sold their milk to private buyers or collection centers belonging to KCC, which was effectively a parastatal.

Prices that KCC paid to the cooperatives was set by the government, and the pricing policies adopted were pan-seasonal and pan-territorial. But, these pricing schemes severely compromised KCC's financial position over time. The squeeze on its balance sheets meant that KCC was not able to increase milk prices to keep pace with increases in input prices, and furthermore delayed their payments to the cooperatives. As a result, producers began to shift sales to the informal raw milk market, and supplies to KCC fell substantially.

In 1992, the Kenyan government liberalized the dairy industry and revoked KCC's monopoly on urban milk sales. There was a rapid development in milk market innovations, including "self-help" groups which collected and marketed raw milk. In addition, cooperatives began themselves to market a greater portion of the milk to urban markets. But in order for cooperatives to sell to other marketing outlets, where they typically received higher prices and more stable payments, they had to be willing to incur the costs of searching for alternative market outlets, screening trading partners and bargaining with them, and monitoring contractual agreements with new trading partners. In addition, the cooperatives, many of whom did not have adequate transportation or cooling equipment, incurred losses due to spoilage.

A survey of dairy cooperatives in three districts provides evidence of the impact of these transactions costs on dairy marketing. It shows that all three districts enjoyed growth in alternative marketing outlets, but the district closest to Nairobi had a dramatic decline in the share of output going to KCC. In contrast, the districts further away showed only a marginal decline in milk sales to KCC, despite the fact that producers received lower prices and unstable payments than they would have through alternate channels in Nairobi. For districts further away, which are likely to have higher transactions costs due to the transport costs, spoilage, and screening/monitoring, the transactions costs outweighed the losses imposed by the uncertainty of payments by KCC and the lower prices. Hence, while liberalization permitted the growth of new marketing channels and outlets, the level of transactions costs determined the extent to which different producers could actually utilize different marketing channels.

Source: Staal et al., 1997

Banaskantha, in northern part of Gujarat, India, did not commercialize their traditional craft work because they had no understanding of the market value or demand for their products. As a result, they simply bartered their craftwork with traders for plastic buckets, which were significantly below the value of their own handicrafts. Only following SEWA's intervention, educating the poor women about market prices and commercial value for their products, did they begin to commercialize and generate a livelihood from this source (Aurther field visit, 2002). Similarly, a study in Zambia shows that smallholders with cash liquidity constraints were vulnerable to private agents which led them to barter transactions at disadvantageous terms (Kalinda et al., 1998). Finally, information asymmetry between poor producers and traders lowers the bargaining power of the poor producers.

It is important to bear in mind that asset ownership affects gains from reforms, not only by increasing transactions costs, but also has important implications for productivity. Asset ownership, in particular access to credit, notably makes a difference in the productivity of existing assets, which affects the ability to expand the scale of present activities, or enter into value added activities. For example, the importance of financial capital is particularly evident for the underlying competitiveness of the poor in land markets. Imperfect credit markets, subject to information and moral hazard problems, lead to credit rationing for small and near-landless farms. Hence, the rural poor may not be able to compete for land, and moreover, face a severe disadvantage in improving the productivity of their land and labor without access to working capital. In a theoretical model, Carter and Zegarra (2000) show how constraints in access to credit (and multiple market imperfections) can interact to reduce the underlying competitiveness of producers in the land market and result in different land market outcomes. In addition, weak credit supply for smallholder agriculturers constrains adoption of more productive agricultural technology, despite extensive liberalization. Analysis of the sub-Saharan experience liberalization succeeded in boosting trader entry only in segments of the marketing chain. Inadequate information and access to working capital were among the key barriers preventing market entry into more value-added segments. The food market liberalization in Madagascar illustrates the inability of traders to enter certain value-added niches of the food marketing chain due to these mobility barriers (Barrett, 1997; Fafchamps, 1999).

Box 3: Liberalization and Trader Entry in Madagascar

Following liberalization, there was limited trader entry into value-added niches of food marketing in Madagascar due to "mobility" barriers. As a result, the producers that remained in these niches continued to face limited competition, and retained considerable market power.

Madagascar operated a single-channel, parastatal food marketing system prior to the comprehensive liberalization of its food marketing. The Malagasy government had a legal monopsony in the purchase of rice, maize, manioc, and dried beans, and a monopoly in the processing, distribution, and commercial storage of those crops. Heavy state controls were supported through a state enforcement agency and were blamed for stagnating food production, subsistence farming, and the nation's high food import bill. Starting in 1983, Madagascar announced liberalization reform plans, which were implemented over the following decade.

However, there was limited trader entry into value-added niches, alongside increased entry into others. Some major barriers to inter-group movement within food marketing channel included access to working capital, market information, bulk storage and transport, and a reliable network of customers and suppliers, and policy unreliability that made the private sector reluctant to invest for fear of expropriation. Significant entry into marketing chains only took place in certain niches, which were not protected by capital, information, or relationship barriers.

Source: Barrett, 1997

Vulnerability and risk

In addition to asset ownership, vulnerability and risk also have important implications for transactions costs faced by the poor, and the livelihood strategies they adopt. Marketing strategies to minimize risk can exacerbate transactions costs. In developing countries, and especially for lower income producers, formal institutional strategies for consumption smoothing — crop insurance, formal credit markets, or commodity futures markets — are unavailable or have high associated transactions costs. In addition, the informal methods of coping with risk available to low income farmers are often costly and inefficient. For example a study of Malagasy grain traders show that as traders do not rely on formal legal institutions for contract enforcement, exchange is made in a flea market style. Traders personally inspect quality on each delivery and guard stocks in person. Furthermore, in the presence of risk and inability to withstand shocks, combined with screening and enforcement costs, traders restrict parties with whom they have commercial interactions. Traders prefer to trade based on trust and reputation, and with people they already know (Gabre-Madhin, 2001).

Vulnerability and risk also have implications for livelihood strategies. Liquidity constrained households may choose risk management strategies to lower the variability of household income such as choosing crops with a lower yield or price variability, and diversifying crops. These strategies can have costly negative effects on productive efficiency. For example, in India, World Bank (2000) reports "poor farmers devote a larger share of land to traditional varieties of rice and castor than to high return varieties. Similarly, Tanzanian farmers without livestock grow more sweet potatoes, a low-risk, low-return crop, than do farmers who own livestock. As a result, returns to farming per adult household member are 25 percent higher for the wealthiest group than for the poorest." In a study of cattle-rearing in western Tanzania, Dercon analyzes the link between wealth, risk, and activity choice. In the presence of credit constraints, risk, and the fixed set up costs to obtain cattle, poor households are less likely to invest in cattle-rearing activities, though it is a more profitable activity (Dercon, 1998).

Finally, vulnerability and risk also impact accumulation and depletion of productive assets, which as discussed earlier, impacts benefits from market participation. Households facing high borrowing costs or are constrained in their ability to borrow may attempt to smooth consumption through accumulation and depletion of productive assets, which can increase costs, and detrimentally affect productive efficiency (Rosenzweig and Wolpin, 1993).

Social marginalization and lack of power

Aside from asset ownership and vulnerability, social marginalization and lack of power in the economic sphere also affect outcomes from market participation. As explained earlier, a growing literature on social capital explains the role of personalized relationships, trust, and social norms in facilitating market interactions in a world characterized by imperfect information and enforcement. When markets are not functioning well, social capital can reduce transactions costs associated with information asymmetry. While social relations can accelerate the transmission of market information and the creation of knowledge and systems of mutual assistance, the reverse applies for those who are excluded from society. Having few social relations may limit access to information, ideas, and capital. And since social marginalization is also associated with poverty, it has a number of implications for market outcomes.

Having inadequate access to social networks with some economic power, the poor may be excluded from transactions and access to assets. Personalized relationships can facilitate circulation of information about prices and market conditions, the provision of trade credit, the prevention and handling of contractual difficulties, the regularity of trade flows, and the mitigation of risk. In the presence of information asymmetries and the high cost of monitoring and enforcement, transactions may only take place between groups for whom people have information or know to be reputable. The inability of the poor to engage in reciprocity may imply that they are effectively excluded from transactions (World Bank, 2000). Examples of this are seen in the context of trade credit and commodity markets. In a study of the determinants of trade credit in Zimbabwe, Fafchamps (1997) finds that network effects and statistical discrimination affect screening of trade credit applicants. African firms have more superficial relationships with suppliers, and are therefore, less likely than other firms to obtain trade credit, controlling for factors like firm size, age, and sector of activity. Black entrepreneurs are disadvantaged by their lack of business contacts, and ethnic barriers may be limiting African firms from obtaining credit. Similarly, in a study of agricultural traders in Madagscar, the role of relationships was a crucial factor to the success of businesses (Fafchamps and Minten, 1999).

The effects of social exclusion can be particularly onerous in the context of labor markets. Discrimination may be overt or hidden as well as officially sanctioned against certain groups based on gender, race, or caste. The economics of discrimination in the labor markets can be understood in two ways. First, to avoid the cost of acquiring information about individual workers, employers might rank and screen employees based on easily observable group characteristics. This type of profiling can reinforce prejudices. Second, as a way of reducing monitoring costs or having leverage over workers, employers might prefer to hire workers with some level of social collateral. A World Bank study in Pakistan shows a close correlation between employment opportunities and caste kinship or social grouping. Personal recommendations and guarantees were found to be a significant factor in job clustering, and caste and kinship networks were an important determinant of economic opportunity and mobility (World Bank, 2002).

Traditionally an agriculture-based community, villagers in Faisalabad, Pakistan, have diversified to other livelihoods. It is evident, though, that caste relationships played an important role in the diversification options available to them. A number of families belonging to the Dogar, a local cultivating caste, entered into the transport business. The first truck worker was a Dogar man, who over time developed a fleet of trucks that runs from Faisalabad to Karachi. Most of the truck drivers and cleaners also are from the Dogar community. In contrast, the predominant portion of the low caste Christian families in the village are involved in brick-kiln work in a neighboring village. Following the first member of the community, practically one person of every Christian family in the village is now working at a kiln, mostly as indebted piece rate workers.

Policy Implications

Improving access to markets and returns from market participation for the poor requires that policies of liberalization are complemented with interventions that directly address their specific constraints.

Specific areas that would need to be addressed are:

- Improving access to market information and infrastructure;
- Supporting collective action;
- Supporting alternative institutional schemes;
- Addressing risk and vulnerability;
- Addressing discrimination and social barriers;
- Building the asset base of the poor.

Improving access to market information systems and infrastructure

Improving access to market information systems and infrastructure is critical to reducing transactions costs and improving the bargaining power of the poor. Providing the public with market information systems is particularly important in developing countries, where the cost of collecting and disseminating information is high due to lack of records and inadequate communications infrastructure. This is particularly important in countries where reforms left an institutional vacuum, where producers would have had access to the required needs from parastatals or other institutions. While the record of success in public provision of market information systems has been poor, due to inadequate financing among other reasons, some cheaper options are available (Chaudhery and Banerji, 2001). For example, in Andhra Pradesh, India, prices of products are published daily on the Internet (Christiaensen and Pontara, 2002).

In some countries, governments have actively ensured that market reforms are accompanied with programs to improve infrastructure, market information systems, and productivity for poor and smallholders. The case of the Malian rice sector illustrates how government and donor support contributed to the success of the rice sector reforms, and in particular to improving the participation of smallholders (see Box 4).

Supporting collective action

In the context of poorly functioning markets due to information asymmetries and limited asset ownership of the poor, collective action can play an important role in reducing transactions costs. Collective action schemes such as cooperatives and associations can allow for risk pooling and sharing of "lumpy" capital, and thereby, facilitate access to inputs, credit, and technical assistance that might otherwise be costly to obtain. It can also improve the bargaining position of its members, particularly in contexts where product or input markets are uncompetitive.

Collective action schemes can take various forms. For example, in Honduras, UNIDO has piloted the idea of "network brokers" who work with small businesses that have similar characteristics and growth constraints. Brokers provide these small firms with analysis and information about common problems and encourage collective action. Action might include pooling resources to purchase raw materials in bulk, applying for joint loans, and sharing equipment. A subsidy is currently provided for the services of the network broker, though over time, the aim is to

Box 4: Success of Smallholders in Mali

Mali's transformation of its rice sub-sector is a great success story in West African, and it illustrates the importance of aligning sectoral market reforms with programs to improve infrastructure, market information systems, and technology. Following the reforms of the rice sector in the 1980s, domestic production in Mali grew at an annual rate of 12 percent between 1991 and 2000. Smallholders incomes grew as land and labor productivity increased, with yield per hectare rising from 2.5 tons per hectare to 4 to 5 tons per hectare, leading to a tripling of rice production between 1985 and 1998. Returns to family labor in rice production was three to five times higher than the local daily wage rate.

A defining characteristic of the market reforms in Mali was that reforms were coordinated by a multi-donor financed program known as PRMC (Programme de Restructuration du Marche Cerealier). Alongside the World Bank and IMF programs, which were aimed at reducing state involvement in market activities, the PRMC "accompanied" the state in its transition, through various support measures. Notably, the measures supported the management of a grain board, the establishment of a national emergency grain reserve, provision of market information, and subsidization of trade credit for traders and village associations. Specifically, the following measures were taken.

1. Market information systems were established in 1989 as part of the broader cereals markets reform. This system provided important information via the radio and news media to producers, traders, and other market participants.
2. Grading and standardization systems, which were informally introduced by traders in the 1990s, were then formalized through donor support. The grades and standards established a market premium for long grain and clean rice, and increased the incomes of smallholder producers producing quality rice.
3. Massive investments were made in infrastructure, including irrigation rehabilitation, all-weather roads, and canals. Donor support was crucial in these schemes.

In addition to the above schemes, mechanized threshing was introduced to smallholders, which reduced threshing time and labor requirements, as well as equipment for small-scale rice mills, which led to higher efficiency of small mills and their rapid growth and the resulting decline in oligopoly power of the main rice importers. Participation of smallholders in village associations and their empowerment via access to credit are also factors that contributed to success of the Mali rice sector.

Source: Gabre-Madhin et al., 2002.

transition to a fee-for-service model (Narayan, 2002). Other examples include the Anand Diary Cooperative in India and the Andhra Pradesh District Initiatives Project, which illustrate how collective action successfully facilitated access to needed market information and supporting infrastructure for the poor (see Box 5).

The role of the government in promoting collective action is two-fold. First, governments must ensure that there exists an enabling environment of regulations and infrastructure for cooperatives. This requires reducing bureaucratic obstacles to effective formation and management of cooperatives. Second, governments can help build capacity within cooperatives by supporting flow of information, providing resources for training and decision making, and supporting access to credit for priority capital expenditures (Staal et al., 1997).

Box 5: The Role of Collective Action in India
Gujarat: The Anand Dairy Cooperative in the western Indian state of Gujarat is often cited as one of the most successful cooperatives in the developing world. It helps organize small producers in dairy cooperatives, provides them with the necessary inputs and services, and markets their outputs. Especially the poorest households — i.e. those with one or two milk animals - have benefited. Particularly women have been employed, whose social status subsequently improved and whose incomes from crop production increased because agricultural inputs were now available, as well as cash from milk sales to buy them. Other features of the Anand model include: (1) its benefits are accessible to everybody, including the poorest of the community; (2) there is a strong externally audited managerial system, which limits the scope for internal financial

malpractice; (3) the model is based on learning-by-doing and on experimenting with new technologies (e.g. cross-bred cows).

Source: Excerpt from Christiaensen and Pontara (2002)

Andhra Pradesh: Among the most economically marginalized communities in the villages of Andhra Pradesh, India, the poor earned a livelihood collecting neem seeds from the nearby forests. For 1 rupee per kilogram, they sold their seeds to a traveling middleman, unaware of the prices and markets to which he was selling their output. The Andhra Pradhesh District Initiatives Project (APDPIP), which is overlooking a series of projects in these communities, decided to investigate and inquire about the end markets to which these seeds were being sold. They discovered that these neem seeds contained medicinal properties and were being bought by pharmaceuticals companies. APDPIP consulted with the major local pharmaceutical buyers to identify what would be required to sell to them directly. They learned that appropriate storage of the seeds was critical to the seeds retaining their medicinal value. Having obtained the information on the necessary storage procedures, APDPIP forwarded the information to the community.

The community council, with the assistance of APDPIP, established a village cooperative that purchased the seeds from the individual pickers in the village and invested in transportation and storage equipment. With the seeds in the appropriate condition and in possession of bulk quantities, the village cooperative was in a position to bargain directly with the pharmaceutical company. They sold the seeds at 3 rupees per kilo.

Following this initial agreement, one of the village cooperative members contacted other companies to inquire about the prices for neems seeds and found a company in Bombay willing to pay 6 rupees per kilo. This provided the impetus for the cooperative to renegotiate with the existing client and a new price of 6 rupees was agreed upon. Minus the costs of transportation and storage, the new prices were passed directly to the pickers, who effectively saw a nearly six-fold revenue gain from this activity.

Source: Author interview with K. Raju, APDPIP Executive Director, 2002.

Supporting alternative institutional schemes

Laws and policies should be designed to support alternative institutional arrangements and innovative contract design schemes, which minimize information asymmetries and reduce monitoring and enforcement costs. Among the most well-known examples of such innovations are inter-linked contracts such as contract farming for access to credit and inputs, as well as microfinance or group lending schemes in credit markets. In the context of credit markets, policies to enhance the role of informal mechanisms include a supportive legal and regulatory framework that accommodates the needs of less formal institutions. Box 6 illustrates how three Asian countries provided such flexibility to rural financial institutions so that they could utilize innovative institutional arrangements to sustain themselves and successfully serve the poor.

In general, restrictions and regulations should apply with gradually increasing stringency as institutions rise in size and formality. For example, in credit markets, informal institutions such as membership groups and savings collector should not be overly regulated. Self-regulation and some registration requirements may be suitable for small semi-formal activities, such as savings and credit associations (Steel et al., 1997).

Box 6: Success of Alternative Financial Institutions in Asia
In contrast to a number state or donor sponsored rural finance operations, which have fallen short of expectations and have become a costly drain on government budgets, four schemes in Asia are preeminent examples of rural financial institutions that have succeeded. Their success is due in large part to flexible policies and innovative institutional arrangements. The schemes include the Bank for Agriculture and Agricultural Cooperatives (BAAC) in Thailand, the Badan Kredit Kecamatan (BKK) and Bank Rakyat Indonesia Unit Desa (BDU) in Indonesia, and the Grameen Bank (GB) in Bangladesh. Some key features of these program include:

1. Mechanisms to address strict collateral requirements, which are incompatible with small-scale loans. Three of the four institutions

departed significantly from the traditional requirements established by credit institutions and have devised successful methods of securing their loans. For example, BAAC had joint liability for short-term loans by using a small homogenous group, in which peer pressure could be brought to bear. Similarly, the Grameen Bank also used joint liability mechanisms, while BKK used character references.

2. Flexible repayment patterns, which were based on needs of specific clientele. Some institutions have weekly payments plans, while others have monthly ones. Such flexibility has allowed finance for a wide variety of activities.

3. Use of existing social structures and peer groups, which ensure that borrowers are selected appropriately and that repayments are made on time. The two Indonesian financial institutions have used official village leadership to help screen loan applicants and secure prompt loan collection. The Grameen Bank and BAAC have leaned heavily on self-help groups to promote and deliver loans, and therefore generated substantial savings in transactions costs.

4. Use of a variety of incentives, which helped maintain financial discipline and build positive relationships between lender and borrowers. For example, BKK and Grameen Bank, which have targeted the lowest income clientele, have required obligatory savings. This has introduced and enhanced financial discipline among first time, small scale borrowers, and reduced risk of the rural financial institutions.

Hence, the use of alternative and flexible arrangements have allowed these institutions to overcome the traditional problems faced by RFIs and to recover loan payments and effectively serve their clients.

Source: Yaron 1994.

Addressing risk and vulnerability

Mechanisms to manage and cope with risk are important complements to market reforms. Promoting multi-pronged risk management schemes entail enhancing market integration, supporting innovations of nontraditional financial institutions, and developing public sector provision of risk management, particularly for co-variate risk.

Encouraging policies that support market integration over a geographical area help to spread the effects of supply shocks and mitigate price fluctuation, as well as to broaden the opportunities for income diversification. In this context, promoting cross border trade can be important in order to equalize supply and demand and therefore to stabilize prices. For example, in southern Mozambique, the effective operation of cross-border trade with South Africa, together with the existence of good roads, have resulted in greater maize price stabilization than in other parts of the country (Christiaensen and Pontara, 2002; Dorosh, 2001). In addition to trade, improvements in infrastructure, and investment in market information systems are also important to promote market integration. In the context of the labor markets, policy barriers that contribute to segmentation of the market need to be reduced.

Other market-based insurance schemes can also be explored. Examples of these include price risk management tools such as forward and future/options markets for commodities, guarantee schemes, and contracts that package insurance with agriculture/small business credit. In the context of agriculture, systems of warehouse receipts, which allows for seasonal spacing of sales, and weather risk insurance can be particularly useful (Christiaensen and Pontara, 2002; Jaffee et al., 2001).

Promoting innovations using nontraditional financial institutions also can help the poor cope with risk. Examples included offering poor households partial insurance through limited liability loan contracts in the context of land markets as a way to mitigate the effects of risk (Carter and Zegarra, 2000). In addition, microfinance programs can be very successful in reducing vulnerability of the poor by allowing for income diversification and asset accumulation. Especially effective at reducing vulnerability are microcredit programs, which when coupled with savings and insurance products allow clients to avoid taking out loans when faced with illness or death.

The Self-Employed Women's Association (SEWA) in India is an example of a program that provides a savings and insurance scheme to its members. SEWA is a registered trade union for women in India's informal sector, provides conventional labor union functions and worker security, but also operates a bank and a social security scheme. The bank offers savings accounts and loans to members, while the social security scheme, which insures about 14 percent of SEWA members, covers health, life, and asset insurance. Slightly more than half the cost of the insurance program is covered by premiums, whereas the other half is financed by SEWA and a public subsidy. The combination of banking, insurance, and union services has helped raise SEWA's membership and the incomes of its members.

Finally, devising public sector programs for risk management and insurance are important particularly because markets for risk and insurance are often underdeveloped and because informal institutions do not guard against co-variate risk. A key rationale for government involvement is that it can undertake national risk pooling. State support of risk insurance can include health insurance, old age assistance and pensions, unemployment insurance and assistance, workfare programs, social funds, and cash transfers (World Bank, 2000). The suitability and success of these options depends on the resources and administrative capacity of the public sector and the extent to which the poor can actually benefit from these schemes. For example, irregular and unpredictable earnings, which is typical of the informal sector, can make it hard for workers to participate in contributory insurance programs. In such cases, it is necessary to promote alternative schemes to support poor, informal sector workers (see Box 7).

Addressing discrimination and social barriers

Developing anti-discriminatory legal, institutional and policy reforms are critical to reducing social inequities, which can hinder access to assets and market opportunities. Reforms can address a range of issues, including gender biases in access to land, using subsidies to close gender gaps in education women's rights, and mobilizing collective action (World Bank, 2000).

Addressing gender bias in land titling, which are typically rife with inequities, can be important to improve women's access to land. For example, in a number of countries in Latin America, statutory law required that beneficiaries of earlier land reform programs be heads of households. Since custom dictated that men were the head of the household, it was difficult for women to benefit from such programs. But during the 1990s, reform measures gave special attention to gender issues, and more progressive reform measures were introduced. For example, in 1994, the

Box 7: Insurance for the Informal Sector

Simple expansion of statutory coverage of formal sector social insurance programs (pensions, unemployment insurance, disability insurance) to small enterprises will not meet the risk management needs of the informal sector. Schemes need to accommodate the lower contributory capacity and greater earnings volatility of self-employed and informal workers.

Schemes need to be more innovative by allowing for partnerships between various providers (state, private insurance, communities, organizations representing informal sector workers, and NGOs), and having a mix of contributory self-financed insurance schemes and assistance paid out of general tax resources.

An example of a recent innovation is in Andhra Pradesh, India. Under the Employees' Provident Fund Act, pension coverage has been extended to about 425,000 home-based workers in the beedi (leaf-rolled cigarettes) industry. A simple procedural mechanism, through the issuance of identity cards, was crucial to the success of the program. In addition, a welfare fund for beedi workers was set up by the central government, funded through an earmarked tax collected from employers and manufacturers in the beedi industry. This delinks collection of contributions and the delivery of welfare services from individual employee-employer relationships, and thereby, removing a major bottleneck to including informal sector workers in contributory schemes.

Source: Excerpted from World Bank, 2000

Colombian Agrarian Law gave top priority to redistributing land to households headed by women and to women who lacked protection or had been displaced by war. Other countries in Latin America have implemented similar programs. A study tracking the gender effect of these reforms shows that women made up a larger share of the beneficiaries under current land titling programs than under previous ones.

In addition, mobilizing collective action among groups that are socially oppressed and improving social capital is also important.[2] In particular, encouraging the development of social networks and associations can be

---

[2]For further details on action areas, refer to Empowerment and Poverty Reduction: A Sourcebook, 2002 and World Development Report 2000.

used to curb market power of dominant players, or facilitate entry of the poor into new markets. In Madagascar, governments and donors were actually involved in the emergence of new subgroups into the cereals market. A cereal bank network was created that competed locally with commercial interseasonal grain stockers (Barrett, 1997).

In several countries in Latin America, explicit measures are being undertaken to address gender and social inequities as part of a broader strategy for reform. As part of its national strategy for reform, Bolivia has identified gender equity as one of its main cross-cutting themes. Policies have been developed to support women's role in productive market activities by enhancing women's access to market information resources and technology, education, and health care, and providing support for female entrepreneurs.

Honduras, a comprehensive treatment of women's issues is part of the country's national development strategy. Programs have been developed to improve development of women's labor market skills, access to land title, adult education programs for women in rural and marginal urban areas, and information centers for women's rights have been established.

Nicaragua has identified programs to address its indigenous population through interventions to improve nutrition, demarcation of indigenous land, transport and communications in the areas in which they live, and having specific health and education strategies for the population.[3]

Building the asset base of the poor

Improving the asset base of the poor, which is a recurrent theme in the context of poverty reduction strategies, requires careful attention in the context of market reforms. The ability of poor households to benefit from economic opportunities created through market reforms are limited if the poor do not have the ability to acquire assets or capabilities to enhance the productivity of their activities. The importance of facilitating access to technology and inputs, as well as training to poor communities is well illustrated in the case of the tribal communities in India. Interventions, with support from the state, were critical to enhancing returns from market activities (see Box 8).

---

[3] Poverty Reduction Strategy Papers for Boliva, Honduras, and Nicaragua PRSP; Mukherjee and Arulpragasam, 2002.

Box 8: Building Capacity in Human Capital and Technology in India
The livelihood of more than 10,000 poor, landless, tribal families of
Andhra Pradesh depends on the harvest and sale of gum karaya, a tree
fiber. Due to lack of information on commercial uses for the gum or
knowledge about how to upgrade the quality of their gum, the tribals
received a low price for the gums as well as having to bear the full brunt
of commodity price swings for the low quality product. However,
intervention supported by government of Andhra Pradesh and through
the Girijans Corporation Council (GCC), significantly helped upgrade
the quality of their gum, which resulted in a tripling of incomes for the
tribal population.

In 1991, following significant price decreases for gum, the head of
the GCC undertook research to understand the market demand for gum
of differing quality and to identify how the gum produced by the tribal
population in Andhra Pradesh could be upgraded. Following interviews
with buyers and traders, GCC learned that gum karaya was primarily
exported, and the export price received was a function of quality, reflected
in viscosity, swelling ability and color. Gum karaya is a commercial gum,
which has multiple uses in the manufacturing, food, and medical
industries. GCC subsequently began to hire scientists to understand
whether the current methods adopted for gum retrieval, transportation,
drying, and storage could be upgraded to allow the tribals to produce
higher quality gum.

Following extensive field visits, it was understood that the prevailing
handling practices and lack of appropriate equipment resulted in
deterioration of the gum, spoilage, and discoloration. GCC launched
training programs to disseminate information about the appropriate
methods of gum collection, grading, and storage. In addition, equipment
such as improved sickles, surgical grade stainless steel forceps, and electric
dryers were provided to upgrade the tapping, collection, and handling
procedures by the tribals.

The interventions made by GCC translated into quality
improvements within a year. Information regarding the improvements
was supplied to foreign buyers and domestic traders and as a result, prices
that the tribals received began to increase. Two years later, the value of
their gum was tripled to what it was before the intervention. Nearly 8,500
tribal families shared the benefits from the quality improvements.

Source: Mehta, undated.

Conclusions

In examining the implications of a pro-poor focus on market reforms, we adopt the position that the notion of a "pro-poor" market, i.e. market structures and processes that disproportionately benefit the poor, is not a legitimate concept to address poverty alleviation. While market development in and of itself can be important to reduce transactions cost and productivity for all market participants, a focus on the poor warrants a closer examination of how dimensions of poverty impact access to, and returns from, market participation.

The main constraints faced by the poor can be grouped as follows:

(1) Limited asset ownership, in particular access to information and physical capital, which exacerbate transactions costs;
(2) Exposure to risk and vulnerability, which can exacerbate transactions costs and provide incentive for poor to invest in low-risk, low-return activities;
(3) Social exclusion due to information asymmetries and imperfect markets, which restricts access to assets such as credit, as well as restricts labor market opportunities;
(4) Lack of power stemming from economic and social marginalization that reduces bargaining power and returns from trade.

Our key message is that policies of liberalization need to be augmented with a broader package of reforms that support policy and institutional reforms required to address the constraints faced by the poor. We have not provided an exhaustive discussion of all reforms required for a well-functioning market (e.g., macroeconomic stability, governance, investment climate), but rather employ the "lens of the poor" to examine policy priorities required to address constraints to market participation and institutional mechanisms to support participation.

While we have identified the overarching constraints and policy ramifications, several questions remain. In particular, the importance of asset ownership for participation in markets raises questions about the design and sequencing of reforms with regards to policies to improve asset ownership. For example, should public expenditure policies be targeted towards those assets needed to exploit opportunities in a particular market, concurrent to market reform? Furthermore, given the importance of social capital as a mechanism to minimize transactions costs and provide access to markets, how can policies encourage the inclusion of the poor in associations and relevant networks? These issues warrant further study.

References

Akiyama, T. et al. (2001). Commodity Market Reforms: Lessons of Two Decades. Washington D.C.: World Bank.

Alchian, A. A. (1961). Some Economics of Property. Rand Paper P-2316, Santa Monica, CA: The Rand Corporation.

Alchian, A. and H. Demsetz (1972). Production, Information Costs, and Economic Organization. *American Economic Review*, December.

Alderman, Harold (2001). The Implications of Private Safety Nets for Public Policy: Case Studies of Mozambique and Zimbabwe. Africa Region Human Development Working Paper Series, World Bank.

Arrow, K. J. (1951). An Extension of the Basic Theorem of Classical Welfare Economics. In Neyman, J., ed., *Proceedings of the Second Berkeley Symposium on Mathematical Studies and Probability*, Berkeley, CA: University of California Press.

Arrow, K. (1969). The Organization of Economic Activity: Issues Pertinent to the Choice of Market versus Non-market Allocation. In *The Analysis and Evaluation of Public Expenditures: The PBB-System*, Joint Economic Committee, 91st Congress, 1st session, Vol.1, Washington, D.C.: Government Printing Office.

Arulpragasam, Jehan and Nicola Pontara (2001). Role of Markets. Mimeos Overarching Framework; Financial Markets; Land Markets. World Bank Poverty Reduction Group.

Bardhan, P. B. (1989). Alternative Approaches to the Theory of Institutions in Economic Development. In *The Economic Theory of Agrarian Institutions*, edited by P. Bardhan. Oxford: Clarendon Press.

Barrett, Christopher (1997). Food Marketing Liberalization and Trader Entry: Evidence from Madagascar. In *World Development*, 25, pp. 763–777.

Bell, C. (1977). Alternative Theories of Sharecropping: Some Tests Using Evidence from North-East India. *Journal of Development Studies*, 13, pp. 317–46.

Besley, Timothy (1994). How Do Market Failures Justify Interventions in Rural Credit Markets?, *The World Bank Research Observer*, 9, pp. 27–47.

Beynon, J., S. Jones and S. Yao (1992). Market Reform and Private Trade in Eastern and Southern Africa. *Food Policy*, 17, pp. 399–408.

Bocar, Diagana, and Francis Akindès, Kimseyinga, Savadogo, Thomas, Reardon and John, Staatz (1999). Effects of the CFA Franc Devaluation on Urban Food Consumption in West Africa: Overview and Cross-Country Comparisons. *Food Policy*, 24, pp. 465–478.

Carter, Michael R and Eduardo Zegarra (2000). Land Markets and the Persistence of Rural Poverty: Post-Liberalization Policy Options. In *Rural poverty in Latin America*, edited by Ramón López and Alberto Valdés. New York: St. Martin's Press.

Chaudhury, N. and A. Banerji (2001). Agricultural Marketing Institutions. Background paper for the World Development Report 2001, Institutions for Markets. Washington, DC: World Bank.

Chilowa, W (1998). The Impact of Agricultural Liberalization on Food Security in Malawi. *Food Policy*, 23, pp. 553–569.

Christiaensen, Luc and Nicola Pontara (2002). Poor Markets or Markets for the Poor?: The Role of Agricultural Marketing Arrangements. Mimeo. World Bank Poverty Reduction Group.

Christiaensen, L., Demery, L. and S. Paternostro (2002). Economic Growth and Poverty Reduction in Africa: Messages from the 1990s, Mimeo. Washington, DC: World Bank.

Coase, R. (1937). The Nature of the Firm. *Economica*, 4, pp. 386–405.

——— (1960). The Problem of Social Cost. *Journal of Law and Economics*, 3, pp. 1–44.

——— (1988). *The Firm, the Market and the Law*. Chicago: University of Chicago Press.

Coleman, J. (1988). Social Capital in the Creation of Human Capital. *American Journal of Sociology*, 94, pp. s95–s120.

Datt, Gaurav and Martin Ravallion (2002). Is India's Economic Growth Leaving the Poor Behind?, World Bank Policy Research Working Paper.

Debreu, G. (1959), *The Theory of Value*. New York: Wiley.

Department for International Development (2000). Making Markets Work Better for the Poor: A Framework Paper. U.K.

Department for International Development UK. (2002). www.livelihoods.org.

Dercon, S. (1995). On Market Integration and Liberalization: Method and Application to Ethiopia. *Journal of Development Studies*, 32, pp. 112–143.

Dercon, Stefan (1998). Wealth, Risk, and Activity Choice: Cattle in Western Tanzania. *Journal of Development Economics*, 55.

Dercon, Stefan (2000). Income Risk, Coping Strategies, and Safety Nets. Center for the Study of African Economies, Working Paper Series, WPS/(2000).

Dercon, Stefan (2001). Economic Reform, Growth and the Poor: Evidence from Rural Ethiopia. Working Paper Series, U.K.; Center for the Study of African Economies. No. WPS/2001-8:1–41.

Dong, Xiao-yuan and Gregory Dow (1993). Monitoring Costs in Chinese Agricultural Teams. *Journal of Political Economy*, 101, pp. 539–53.

Dorosh, P. A. (2001). Trade Liberalization and National Food Security: Rice Trade Between Bangladesh and India. *World Development*, 29, pp. 673–689.

Dorward, A., J. Kydd and C. Poulton (1999). The Baby and the Bathwater: Agricultural Parastatals Revisited. Paper presented at a symposium on the African Rural Crisis Revisited at the Annual Conference of the Agricultural Economics Society, Stranmillis University College, Queen's University of Belfast, 28 March (1999). London, UK: Agrarian Development Unit, Wye College, University of London, 3–28.

Fafchamps, Marcel (1997). Trade Credit in Zimbabwean Manufacturing. *World Development*, 25.

Fafchamps, Marcel (1999). Networks, Communities, and Markets in Sub-Saharan Africa: Implications for Firm Growth and Investment. Center for the Study of African Economies. Working Paper Series, U.K.

Fafchamps, M. (1996). Market Emergence, Trust and Reputation. San Francisco, CA: Stanford University, Mimeo.

Fafchamps, Marcel and Bart Minten (1999). Property Rights in a Flea Market Economy. Center for the Study of African Economies. Working Paper Series, U.K.

Fafchamps, M. and B. Minten (1999). Returns to Social Capital Among Traders. International Food Policy Research Institute MSSD Discussion Paper No. 23, Washington, DC.

Frisvold, George (1994). Does Supervision Matter? Some Hypothesis Tests Using Indian Farm Level Data. *Journal of Development Economics*, 43, pp. 217–38.

Fukuyama, F. (1995). Social Capital and the Global Economy. *Foreign Affairs*, 74, pp. 89–103.

Gabre-Madhin, Eleni (2001). Market Institutions, Transactions Costs, and Social Capital in the Ethiopian Grain Market, Research Report 124. Washington, D.C: International Food Policy Research Institute.

Gabre-Madhin, Eleni et al. (2002). Success in Rice in West Africa: Mali, Senegal, and Guinea. Mimeo. International Food Policy Research Institute.

Geertz, Clifford (1968). The Bazaar Economy: Information and Search in Peasant Marketing. *American Economic Review*, 68, pp. 28–32.

Gereffi, G. (1994). The Organization of Buyer-Driven Global Commodity Chains: How U.S. Retailers Shape Overseas Production Networks. In Gereffi and Korzeniewicz, eds., pp. 95–122.

Granovetter, M. (1985). Economic Action and Social Structure: The Problem of Embeddedness. *American Journal of Sociology*, 91, pp. 481–510.

Greif, A. (1993). Contract Enforceability and Economic Institutions in Early Trade: The Maghribi Traders' Coalition. *American Economic Review*, 83, pp. 525–548.

Greif, A., P. Milgrom and B. Weingast (1994). Coordination, Commitment, and Enforcement: The Case of the Merchant Guild. *Journal of Political Economy*, 102, pp. 745–76.

Harriss-White, B. (ed.) (1999). *Agricultural Markets from Theory to Practice: Field Experience in Developing Countries*. New York: St. Martin's Press.

Hazell, Peter, Carlos Pomerada and Alberto Valdés (eds.) (1986). *Crop Insurance for Agricultural Development: Issues and Experience*. Baltimore: Johns Hopkins University Press.

Holzmann, Robert and Steen Jorgensen (2000). Social Risk Management: A New Conceptual Framework for Social Protection, and Beyond. Social Protection Discussion Paper No. 6, World Bank.

Hoff, Karla and Joseph Stiglitz (1990). Introduction: Imperfect Information and Rural Credit Markets — Puzzles and Policy Perspectives, *The World Bank Economic Review*, 4, pp. 235–250.

Hoff, Karla, Avishay Braverman and Joseph Stiglitz (1993). *The Economics of Rural Organization: Theory, Practice, and Policy*. New York: Oxford University Press.

Jaffee, S., et al. (2001). Modernizing Africa's Agro-Food Systems: Towards an Operational Strategy for the Africa Region, Mimeo. Washington, DC: World Bank.

Jalan, Jyotsna and Martin Ravallion (1997). Are the Poor Less Well-Insured? Evidence on Vulnerability to Income Risk in Rural China. World Bank Policy Research Working Paper.

Jayne, T. S., et al. (2001). False Promise or False Premise? The Experience of Food and Input Market Reform in Eastern and Southern Africa. In Jayne, T. S., Argwings-Kodhek, G. and I., Minde, eds., *Perspectives on Agricultural Transformation: A View from Africa*, New York: Nova Science Publishers.

Jayne, T. S. and S. Jones (1997). Food Marketing and Pricing Policy in Eastern and Southern Africa: A Survey. *World Development*, 25, pp. 1505–1527.

Kalinda, T. H. et al. (1998). Access to Agricultural Extension, Credit, and Markets among Small-Scale Farmers in Southern Zambia. *Development Southern Africa*, 15, pp. 589–608.

Kanbur, Ravi and Lyn Squire (2000). The Evolution of Thinking about Poverty: Exploring the Interactions. In *Frontiers of Development Economics: The Future in Perspective*. Geral Meier and Joseph Stiglitz, eds., New York: Oxford University Press.

Kherallah, M, C. Delgado, E. Gabre-Madhin, N.Minot, M. Johnson (2002). *Reforming Agricultural Markets in Africa*. Baltimore: The Johns Hopkins University Press. Published for International Food Policy Research Institute (IFPRI).

Kherallah, Mylene and Kumaresan Govindan (1997). The Sequencing of Agricultural Market Reforms in Malawi. International Food Policy Research Institute, Discussion Paper No. 13.

Klein, Michael (2001). *Private Sector Development Strategy*. The World Bank.

Knack, S. and P. Keefer (1997). Does Social Capital Have an Economic Payoff? A Cross-country Investigation. *Quarterly Journal of Economics*, 112, pp. 1251–88.

Kranton, R. (1996). Reciprocal Exchange: A Self-Sustaining System. *American Economic Review*, 86, pp. 830–851.

Mahmood, Syed (2002). *Private Sector Development and Poverty Reduction*. Mimeo. World Bank.

Mehta, Aasha. Undated. Administrative Responsiveness and Competitiveness: The Case of Gum Karaya in Andhra. Mimeo. Indian Institute of Public Administration.

Meillassoux, C. (1971). *The Development of Indigenous Trade and Markets in West Africa*. Oxford: Oxford University Press.

Meerman, J. (1997). Reforming Agriculture: The World Bank Goes to Market. Washington, DC: World Bank Operations Evaluation Study.

Milgrom, P., D. North and B. Weingast (1990). The Role of Institutions in the Revival of Trade: The Law Merchant, Private Judges, and the Champagne Fairs. *Economics and Politics*, 2, pp. 1–23.

Morduch, Jonathan (1995). Income Smoothing and Consumption Smoothing. *Journal of Economic Perspectives*, 9, pp. 103–114.

Morduch, Jonathan (1999a). Between the State and the Market: Can Informal Insurance Patch the Safety Net. *The World Bank Research Observer*, 14, pp. 187–207.

Morduch, Jonathan (1999b). The Microfinance Promise. *Journal of Economic Literature*, 37, pp. 1569–1614.

Mukherjee, Nayantara and Jehan Arulpragasam (2002). Review of Pro-Poor Growth in Full PRSPs. Mimeo. The World Bank.

Narayan, Deepa et al. (2001). *Voices of the Poor Series*. Washington, DC: World Bank.

Narayan, Deepa (2002). Empowerment and Poverty Reduction: A Sourcebook. Washington, DC: World Bank.

North, D. C. (1981). *Structure and Change in Economic History*. New York: W.W. Norton.

——— (1990). *Institutions, Institutional Change and Economic Performance*, Cambridge: Cambridge University Press.

Palaskas, T. B. and B. Harriss-White (1993). Testing Market Integration: New Approaches with Case Material from the West Bengal Food Economy. *Journal of Development Studies*, 20, pp. 1–57.

Peters, P. E. (1996). Failed Magic or Social Context? Market Liberalization and the Rural Poor in Malawi. Development Discussion Paper 562. Harvard Institute of International Development.

Plattner, S. (1989). Economic Behavior in Markets. In *Economic Anthropology*, edited by S. Plattner. Stanford: Stanford University Press.

Platteau, Jean-Philippe (1994a). Behind the Market Stage Where Real Societies Exist: Part I. The Role of Public and Private Order Institutions. *Journal of Development Studies,* 30, pp. 533–577.

Platteau, Jean-Philippe (1994b). Behind the Market Stage Where Real Societies Exist: Part II — The Role of Moral Norms. *Journal of Development Studies*, 30, pp. 753–815.

Polanyi, K. (1957). Trade and Market in the Early Empires. New York: Free Press.

Poverty Reduction Strategy Papers, Bolivia, Honduras, and Nicaragua. www.worldbank.org.

Putnam, R. D., R. Leonard and R. Y. Nanetti (1993). *Making Democracy Work: Civic institutions in modern Italy*. Princeton, N.J.: Princeton University Press.

Putnam, R. (1985). Affirmative Action as Earnings Redistribution: The Targeting of Compliance Reviews. *Journal of Labor Economics*, 3, pp. 363–84.

Raju, K., Executive Director, Andhra Pradesh District Initiative Project, Personal interview in Washington, D.C., June 2002.

Ravallion, Martin (2001). Growth, Inequality and Poverty: Looking Beyond Averages. World Bank Policy Research Working Paper.

Roe, Alan (1990). Financial Systems and Development in Africa. Conference Report on EDI Policy Seminar. Nairobi.

Rodrik, Dani (1999). Institutions for High Quality Growth: What They Are and How to Acquire Them. Mimeo. Harvard University.

Rosenzweig, Mark and Kenneth Wolpin (1982). Governmental Interventions and Household Behavior in a Developing Country: Anticipating the Unanticipated Consequences of Social Programs. *Journal of Development Economics*, 10, pp. 209–25.

Rosenzweig, Mark and Kenneth Wolpin (1993). Credit Market Constraints, Consumption Smoothing and the Accumulation of Durable Production Assets in Low Income Countries: Investmetns in Bullocks in India. *Journal of Political Economy*, 10, pp. 223–244.

Runsten, David and Nigel Key (1996). Contract Farming in Developing Countries: Theoretical Aspects and Analysis of Some Mexican Cases. United Nations Economic Commission for Latin America and the Caribbean, Research Report No. 3.

Sadoulet, Elisabeth and Alain de Janvry (1995). *Quantitative Development Policy Analysis*, Baltimore: Johns Hopkins University Press.

Sahn, D., P., Dorosh and S., Younger (1997). *Structural Adjustment Reconsidered: Economic Policy and Poverty in Africa*, Cambridge, UK: Cambridge University Press.

Seppala, P. (1997). Food marketing reconsidered: An assessment of the liberalization of food marketing in Sub-Saharan Africa. Research for Action No. 34. Helsinki, Finland: United Nations University, World Institute for Development Economics Research UNU/WIDER. .

Soto, Hernando de (2000). *The Mystery of Capital: Why Capitalism Triumphs in the West and Fails Everywhere else*. New York: Basic Books.

Staal, Steven, Christopher Delgado and Charles Nicholson (1997). Smallholder Dairying Under Transactions Costs in East Africa. *World Development*, 25, pp. 779–794.

Steel, William, et al. (1997). Informal Financial Markets under Liberalization in Four African Countries. *World Development U.K.*, 25, pp. 817–30.

Stewart, F. (1995). *Adjustment and Poverty: Options and Choices*, London, UK: Routledge.

Srinivasan, T. N. (1980). Farm Size and Productivity: Implications of Choice under Uncertainty. *Sankhya Indian Journal of Statistics*, Series B 34, pp. 409–20.

Stiglitz, Joseph (1989). Markets, Market Failures, and Development. *The American Economic Review* 79, pp. 197–203.

Stiglitz, Joseph E (1998). More instruments and broader goals: moving toward the post-Washington consensus, Helsinki: United Nations University, World Institute for Development Economics Research.

Stiglitz, J. E. (1974a). Incentives and Risk-sharing in Sharecropping. *Review of Economic Studies*, 41, pp. 219–55.

Stiglitz, J. E. (1974b). Alternative Theories of Wage Determination and Unemployment in LDCs: The Labor Turnover Model. *Quarterly Journal of Economics*, 87, pp. 194–227.

Stiglitz, J. E. (1985a). Information in Economic Analysis: A Perspective. *Economic Journal Supplement*, 95, pp. 21–40.

Stiglitz, J. E. (1985b). Economics of Information and the Theory of Economic Development. NBER Working Paper no. 1566.

Van de Walle, Dominique (1998). Protecting the Poor in Vietnam's Emerging Market Economy. World Bank Policy Research Working Paper.

Udry, Christopher (1990). Credit Markets in Northern Nigeria: Credit as Insurance in Rural Economy. *The World Bank Economic Review*, 4, pp. 251–269.

Williamson, O. (1985). *The Economic Institutions of Capitalism*, New York: The Free Press.

World Bank (1990). *World Development Report 1990*. New York: Oxford University Press.

World Bank (2000). *World Development Report 2000/2001: Attacking Poverty*. New York: Oxford University Press.

World Bank (2002). *World Development Report 2002: Building Institutions for Markets*. New York: Oxford University Press.

World Bank (2002). Pakistan Poverty Assessment.

Yaron, Jacob (1994). What Makes Rural Finance Institutions Successful. *The World Bank Research Observer*, 9.

Zimmerman, F. and M. Carter (1996). Dynamic Portfolio Management Under Risk and Subsistence Constraints. Staff Paper 402. Department of Agricultural and Applied Economics, University of Wisconsin-Madison.

chapter four

$\mathcal{G}$lobal Markets and Rural Poverty: Do the Rural Poor Gain or Lose from Globalization?

Clive Y. Thomas
Carlton G. Davis

Do the rural poor gain or lose from globalization? If global markets "worked" as theory suggests, then the answer would be yes they would gain. But in practice, they do not, and in the first section of this paper we discuss six reasons why, in our opinion, this is the case. The reasons are: (1) the prevalence of trade manipulation; (2) the nature of markets in poor countries; (3) exceptions to neoclassical efficient market theory; (4) theoretical and empirical inconclusiveness regarding the relation between open trade policies and growth; (5) income inequality; and (6) the institutional framework of global trade. The second section uses the example of trade in food and the United Nations Millennium Development Goals (MDG) for food security and poverty reduction to substantiate the arguments advanced in the first section. The third section

Clive Y. Thomas is a Professor in the Economics Department, and Director of the Institute of Development Studies at the University of Guyana, Georgetown, Guyana, South America. Carlton G. Davis is a Distinguished Professor in the Food and Resource Economics Department at the University of Florida, Gainesville, Florida, USA.

This chapter was published in the *American Journal of Agricultural Economics*, Vol. 78, No. 5, December 1996, pp. 145–156.

offers some conclusions and policy recommendations to address the problems and issues considered in this chapter.

Why the Rural Poor Don't Gain from Globalization

Our primary objective is to explore the impacts of globalization on markets, trade and rural communities. From this perspective there is no singular answer to the question: Do the rural poor gain or lose from globalization? The term "globalization" has different meanings to different people as pointed out by Davis, Thomas and Amponsah in a recent article. To avoid a long discourse on the meaning of the term globalization, we adopt the United Nations Development Program (UNDP) 1997 (p. 82) definition that: "globalization is the widening and deepening of international flows of trade, finance, and information in a single global market." Its necessary corollary is, of course, the active pursuit of policies of market liberalization in all areas of the economy. Based on this definition the impact of globalization on the rural poor is captured in the truism: globalization offers opportunities (e.g., access to third markets, enforceable rights and so on) as well as challenges to the livelihoods of the poor (arising out of obligations of poor countries to open their markets, follow WTO-rules and so on).

Markets matter for the poor in the sense that *if* they work — producing incentives, opportunities, and rewards — they should be able to offer: (1) predictable access for the rural poor to sell their products and/or their labor in conditions of growing and stable demand at remunerative prices; and (2) opportunities to acquire finance and obtain their input requirements and consumption needs at competitive non-disadvantageous prices. If these two conditions are fulfilled, then the welfare of the rural poor is likely to be enhanced. Indeed, we might go further and state that the situation described here provides the rationale for the assertion that liberalized markets and global trade together constitute the engine of growth for poor countries. As the World Bank puts it: "Integration into global markets offers the potential for more rapid growth and poverty reduction" (World Bank 2002, p. 4). According to this view, if existing market barriers prevent poor countries from seizing these opportunities then the correct response would be greater efforts to have those barriers removed. For a variety of reasons however, these two conditions are rarely fulfilled in practice and the substantial — let alone full — removal of market barriers remains a very distant prospect. Six of these reasons are important. They are: (1) the prevalence of trade manipulation; (2) the nature of markets in poor countries; (3) exceptions to neo-classical efficient market theory; (4) theoretical and empirical inconclusiveness over the relation between open trade policies and growth; (5) income inequality; and (6) the institutional framework of global trade.

Trade manipulation

First, traditionally, and up to today, politics, ideology, geo-political and geo-strategic concerns play the lead role in shaping global market outcomes. Irrespective of the legal standing of commitments to de-regulate trade, covert and overt control and manipulation of markets by governments and large firms are the rule rather than the exception in all the major global markets that impact on the livelihoods of the rural poor — whether the markets are agricultural commodities, raw materials, energy, transportation, manufactured equipment and tools, chemicals, communications, or services. The emerging literature on "rent-seeking"[1] behavior in trade is an attempt to develop a theoretically plausible explanation for this phenomenon (Kruger; Just, Hueth and Schmitz; de Gorter, Rausser and Schmitz).

Nature of markets

Second, the general nature of markets in poor countries poses special difficulties that are not readily overcome. Intrinsically, all markets are networks for transactions between buyers and sellers and these networks are mediated through a number of institutions, including traders, dealers, financiers, and the courts. These flanking and support institutions mature very slowly. Historically, they have evolved through distinct development stages, with each stage broadly reflecting the overall condition of the economy. In rural areas of poor countries, financial markets have not evolved to a mature level. We find that in poor countries, in

---

[1]The rent seeking literature deals in large part with the waste of resources to society at large to capture (or create) the private benefits and/or to avoid private costs resulting from actual/potential government policy or institutional settings.

contradistinction to rich ones, rural markets typically suffer from incompleteness, asymmetry of information, the prevalence of moral hazard, weak incentives, ill-defined or undeterminable contractual limits, the absence of rules and enforcement mechanisms, weak organizational support, and minimal regulation and oversight. In such circumstances, markets have been aptly labelled as either imperfect, informal, localized or segmented. Very often, particularly in rural areas, crucial markets, such as rural credit, insurance, and futures markets are missing. In this context, if market failure occurs, as it frequently does, contagion is rampant and its negative effects aggravated by the significant inequality of income and assets that prevail in these communities (Abbott; Bonnen, Eicher and Schmid).

Exceptions to neo-classical efficient market theory

Third, neo-classical economics efficient market theory, which provides the rationale for market liberalization, tells us that resources are efficiently allocated if, and only if, each product's price is equal to its marginal cost of production. If the price exceeds that, then the product will be "under-produced;" if it were less, then the opposite would occur. Where this rule is violated, and in particular for reasons that are *intrinsic* to the nature of the product and its production process, market failure occurs and state involvement with its production is deemed consistent with economic rationality.[2] The form of that intervention however, may be quite varied and could include direct action with respect to production of the product in question, fiscal incentives and penalties, tradable permits, or the encouragement of "private remedies" along the lines of Coase. Furthermore, the same theory also tells us that because private markets do not possess a self-regulating mechanism to ensure continuous dynamic macroeconomic balance at the aggregative level, and by force of circumstance, markets are continuously exposed to exogenous and/or endogenous shocks, government macroeconomic stabilization has become a necessary feature of all liberalized market economies. To complicate matters further, recent financial and

---

[2]Market failure exists in neo-classical economics when social costs or benefits diverge from private costs or benefits.

economic crises in Asia, Russia, Brazil and Argentina, allied with the global slump since 2001, have heightened concerns about the relationship between macroeconomic stabilization on the one hand, and the linkage between trade and development on the other (Drabek and Laird). As Weller and Hersh indicate, a number of studies show that: "the probability of financial crises in developing countries rise in direct relation to rises in unregulated short-term capital flows." Lustig also identifies macroeconomic crises as the single most important factor in explaining increases in poverty in Latin America and the Caribbean.

The neo-classical efficient market theorem recognizes the well-known cases of "public goods," which unlike private goods are not depletable (that is, they are non-rival in their use) and can be consumed readily by non-payers, (that is, they are non-excludable). The marginal cost of producing these types of goods is theoretically zero, and here again, a case for government involvement in production can also be established, consistent with neo-classical economics rationality. In like manner, the production of some goods also entails positive externalities (marginal social cost exceeds marginal private cost) and negative externalities (marginal social cost is less than marginal private cost). Here also, governments can enhance market efficiency if they involve themselves in the production of these goods, since high positive externalities will lead to a situation where there is insufficient market incentive for private producers. This type of situation often occurs in key areas of development such as education, training, and research and development.

Governments may involve themselves in economic activity for other related reasons. One set is socioeconomic (for example, to protect employment); another set is based on the desire to contain exploitation by private monopolies. Likewise, the prevalence of imperfect information, high transaction costs, and moral hazard in poor countries cause market failure and make government intervention consistent with market efficiency. Finally, given the manner in which a market rate of interest is arrived at in most economies, it is difficult to reconcile this with an "objective" or optimal discount factor, which avoids market failure and guarantees inter-generational equity.

Two observations appear to be particularly appropriate and relevant at this stage. The first is that many of the conditions of market failure identified in neo-classical economics prevail in the agricultural economies of most countries. This consideration has caused in large measure the widespread practice, prior to formation in 1995 of the World Trade Organization, of governments protecting domestic agriculture from import competition, with richer countries better able to accomplish this effectively than poor ones. The contribution of this reasoning to the existing distortions in global agricultural markets can hardly be exaggerated. Second, lest the case for intervention is overstated, *government or policy failure* is also recognized in neo-classical market theory as a likely occurrence, for a number of reasons. The one that is usually emphasized in the literature, is the role of self-interested behavior by those who control the state along the lines of public choice-theory. To avoid a long discourse on the neo-classical tenets of policy/government failure, it is sufficient for our purposes to point out that these conditions exist when: (1) the public sector fails to redress market failure through legal, regulatory, economic or other means when it is clearly feasible to do so or; (2) when public sector activity magnifies existing market failure (Miranda and Muzondo). Following along these lines of observations, Panayotou argues that the prevailing configuration of market and policy regimes under which poor countries operate results in dissociations between resource scarcity and price, benefits and costs, rights and responsibilities, actions and consequences. But, the tendency for market configuration to generate dissociations and hence market or policy failures, can be compromised by institutional reforms and policy intervention. It is within this context the argument has been advanced that, "A market failure is nothing but a policy failure, one step removed" (Panayotou).

Theoretical and empirical inconclusiveness

The fourth reason why practice tends to diverge from theory is that economic theory and quantitative assessments have failed to provide definitive conclusions on which to base policy, concerning the relationship between the pursuit of an open trade policy and economic development. In the literature, whenever this relationship appears robust, two conditions are usually attached to it. First, it is assumed that the relationship holds true over the long term, and secondly, other complex measures such as macroeconomic stability, governance, institutional support and capacity building exist (Dollar; Dollar and Collier; Dollar and Kraay, 2001a; Dollar and Kraay, 2001b).

Although a trend towards more open trade and market liberalization exists, a number of well recognized difficulties face impact measurement, making the available data difficult to quantify. Thus in practice, for example, there are numerous divergences between "bound" and applied tariff rates across countries; tariff-rate quotas are notoriously difficulty to convert into their *ad valorem* equivalents; tariff administration generates a significant level of difficult-to-measure non-tariff barriers to trade as well as a number of anomalies; existing non-tariff barriers and technical barriers to trade are complex and difficult to quantify; and, the practice of stacking non-tariff barriers alongside tariff-rate quotas further complicates the difficulties.

Some growth models, particularly of the endogenous variety, advance the view that there is a strong positive relationship between the practice of an open trade policy and growth. This is usually attributed to the impact of new products and new ideas in a situation of non-diminishing returns in the rate of growth of output and productivity (Romer). It should be recognized, however, that these models are rooted in conditions of market failure, such as, monopoly market structures, externalities and the prevalence of public goods such as research and development, extension, infra-structural/institutional support, and non-diminishing returns. Because of this, the specific circumstances of each economy, including its initial level of endowment, technology in use, specialization patterns, factor mobility and so forth, are required data before the appropriateness and likely success of policies of freer trade can be determined (Edwards; Mosley; Rodrick and Rodriguez 1999; Rodrick and Rodriguez 2001).

Income inequality

Fifth, abundant evidence suggests that unregulated private markets generate inequalities. That is why governments, as a rule, have a redistributive role to play in market based societies. Markets driven by globalization and liberalization are no exception. Indeed this process has been associated with dramatically widening income inequalities. Thus, after a careful survey of the data Weller and Hersh (p. 1) found that:

"In 1980, median income in the richest 10 percent of countries was 77 times greater than in the poorest 10 percent; by 1999, that gap had grown to a staggering 122 times. Inequality has also increased within a vast majority of countries."

They further contend that the gains in poverty reduction over the previous two decades were relatively small and geographically isolated.

Institutional framework

Our sixth and final point is that the liberalization of capital markets and the consolidation of the institutionalized global trade regime along WTO lines present special challenges for the rural poor. The WTO is premised on the view that trade without discrimination optimizes the welfare of all participants engaged in it. With this in mind its main goals may be summarized as securing a situation in which the following conditions exist:

- All trading partners are treated equally (that is, full reciprocity and the eventual end to all special market access for poor countries);
- Non-discrimination is practised between national and foreign products, services, and nationals;
- The removal of **all** WTO-defined barriers to trade;
- The linkage of freer trade to a growing number of "trade-related" areas;
- Predictability is assured, in that barriers to trade cannot be arbitrarily re-introduced or raised;
- The removal of all unfair trading practices.

Though the long-term goal of freer trade is becoming increasingly the norm, the burdens of implementing WTO commitments and the short-run effects of liberalization on the rural poor have become a major pre-occupation of our times. The biggest concession that the WTO makes to the conditions of the rural poor are contained in its time-bound special and differential treatment of developing and least developed countries, which generally permits greater flexibility and more time in taking on WTO obligations. However, this is designed in a manner to ensure that these remain unquestionably "transitional arrangements," which will cease over the medium term. The issue therefore is that the role of trade in the livelihoods of the poor cannot be separated from the institutional/regulatory framework in which that trade is taking place (Walters, Lowe and Davis).

The data indicate that high and stable rates of growth of the rural/agricultural sector and food supplies have significant impact on the reduction of poverty because of the major role this sector plays in providing livelihoods (Eastwood and Lipton; Lipton and Ravallion). Sometimes, as much as two-thirds of the population in poor countries live in rural communities. Agriculture accounts for 27 percent of GDP and exports of agricultural exporting developing countries, and about 50 percent of their employment. Among the least developed countries, it is even more important and the range of their agricultural products is substantially narrower.

Global Food Trade, Food Security, and Poverty Reduction

In this section we first will discuss U.N.'s millennium development goals (MDG) for food security and its achievements to date. Next, we will assess the impact of globalization and liberalization on food security in the context of the WTO's liberalization agenda. Finally, we will draw certain policy conclusions.

As part of the global initiatives to reduce poverty, 186 countries at the 1996 World Food Summit adopted the Rome Declaration, (FAO, p. 1), which among other things expressed a: "Commitment to achieving food security for all and to an ongoing effort to eradicate hunger in all countries, with an immediate view to reducing the number of undernourished people to half their present level no later than 2015." In 1996 the number of undernourished persons was estimated at 840 million.

During the past 50 years, there have been at least 30 quantitative estimates and projections of future global food security. The most regular producers of these are the Food and Agriculture Organization (FAO) of the United Nations (U.N.) and the U.S. Department of Agriculture (USDA). Other agencies such as the Organization for Economic Cooperation and Development (OECD) and International Food Policy Research Institute (IFPRI) have done so occasionally (McCalla and Revoredo; Pinstrup-Andersen, et. al.). Those studies conclude that since the early 1990s, trends do not give hope that the 2015 target will be met. Recently, the Economic Research Service (ERS) of the USDA reported that only one in three countries has reduced the number of hungry persons in their population. In the case of the 67 low income countries that ERS monitors annually, it found the numbers overall have increased from 2000 to 2001. Its global projections for the next decade indicate an annual decline of 1.6 percent for the total number of hungry people, an amount that falls well short of the target of 3.5 percent needed to meet the commitment in the Rome Declaration. FAO's projections show an even slower rate of annual decline in the number of hungry people worldwide.

At present 800 million people worldwide suffer from severe malnourishment and over 2 billion experience micronutrient deficiencies. About three-quarters of the malnourished and the poor live in poor rural areas, relying on farming for their livelihoods. Diseases due to inadequate, unbalanced, and unsafe food are also prevalent in these areas. Children, female headed households, the homeless, and other vulnerable persons bear the brunt of food insecurity and its related hunger and disease. These terrible trends are expected to persist as global population grows and continues to apply pressures on material resources. It is of course paradoxical that these trends are occurring at a point when the world has never produced so much food, when food has never been cheaper, and when food stocks have never been so high. Since the early 1960s world grain output has doubled and livestock production tripled. The result is, on a worldwide basis, per capita food availability has risen to over 2700 calories per day. These are of course average figures and as such do not take into account the distribution of food at the individual household level, where food security ultimately must be established (Thomas 2000; Thomas 2001, 2002; Thomas and Davis).

The 1996 World Food Summit emphasized availability, affordability, and stability of physical and economic access as the key dimensions of food security. Based on this, the main obstacles preventing progress in achieving food security are: natural disasters; political conflicts; high production variability; population growth in some areas; weakening import capacity/external debt burden; economic shocks; variable global growth; natural resource degradation; distribution/equity concerns; declining official development assistance, weak safety nets; and variability of food aid (FAO).

Poverty is seen as the main cause of food insecurity. The MDG for poverty parallels the goal for nutrition. By 2015 the goal is to reduce by half the number of persons living in extreme poverty as there were in 1990. Extreme poverty is defined as living on less than $1 per day in 1993 PPP US dollars.[3] This target means that there would still be about 900 million people living in extreme poverty in 2015. Between 1990 and 1999, however, the world poverty rate fell from 29 percent to 22.7 percent and the total number of poor persons fell from 1.28 billion to 1.15 billion. If these trends do not improve, the goal to reduce poverty, and therefore the goal to improve food security is unlikely to be met.

Agreement on agriculture and world food security

In the context of globalization and liberalization, food security has to be examined in relation to the institutional framework regulating trade in food. The WTO/Uruguay Round (UR) Agreement of 1995, with its subsidiary Agreement on Agriculture (AOA), provides the umbrella framework under which trade in agriculture is being liberalized. The AOA is not a final undertaking of the signatories to the WTO, rather it is a work-in-progress, subject to on-going revision based on its built-in agenda items and agreed-to work programs. At the Doha 2001 Ministerial meeting, multisectoral trade negotiations were launched as a single undertaking and agriculture was included in these.[4] Significantly, Article 20 of the AOA acknowledges food security concerns as part of the on-going negotiations.

The underlying theoretical rationale that drives the AOA is neo-liberal trade theory, which postulates that a liberal trading regime would ensure that

---

[3]PPP is the Purchasing Power Parity, which is that rate of exchange between the currencies of countries in which the units of national currency expressed in the exchange rate, command equivalent or comparable purchasing power, in terms of specified commodities, in either domestic or international markets.

[4]The WTO held its Fourth Ministerial Conference in Doha, Qatar, November 9–14, 2001. Over 140 countries were represented at the conference. The other three conferences were: Singapore (1996); Geneva (1998); and Seattle (1999).

all countries reap the "efficiency benefits" of competition based on differences in comparative advantage, along with the "transfer benefits" of capital, skills, and technology flowing from resource-rich to resource-scarce countries and regions. In relation to food, these many benefits would permit: (1) the ability to fill gaps as they arise between domestic supplies and demand; (2) minimize the adverse impact on domestic consumption of domestic supply variations; (3) domestic food consumption growing faster than domestic supplies; (4) enlarged opportunities for undertaking domestic production on the basis of access to larger (external) markets than the domestic; (5) wider consumer choice; and (6) overall faster economic growth. This rationale is the direct antithesis of the non-market considerations that presently characterize global food production and trade where state intervention, domestic protection, subsidies, and other forms of regulated production are the norm (Davis, Thomas and Amponsah; Thomas 2000, 2001, 2002; Thomas and Davis).

According to Thomas and Davis, seven mechanisms of the WTO significantly impact trade in food and therefore directly and indirectly food security. These are:

(1) The export subsidies provision of the AOA: This provision states that for developed countries, the *quantity* of subsidized exports should be reduced by 21 percent by 2000, and for developing countries two-thirds of that, or 14 percent by 2004. *Budgetary outlays on subsidized exports* should be reduced by 36 percent by 2000 for developed countries, and for developing countries by two-thirds of that, or 24 percent by 2004. Both objectives are based on product-specific 1986–1990 averages.

(2) The market access provisions of the AOA: Market access entails tariffication or removal of non-tariff barriers and their conversion to tariff equivalents e.g., import quotas, licensing, state trading, etc. The tariff equivalents are based on 1986-88 data. Tariffs are bound and are to be reduced by 36 percent on average for developed economies by 2000, and for developing countries by 24 percent by 2004. The minimum cut per product was set at 15 and 10 percent, respectively. (The practice of "dirty tariffication" should be noted as it entails declaring tariffs at extremely high levels so that after percentage reductions are made, the absolute level of the tariff still remains high).

Tariff-quotas are to replace quotas to maintain current access opportunities through incorporating existing plurilateral/multilateral arrangements based on import levels for the 1986–88 period. They also will afford a general minimum access opportunity for imports up to a minimum percentage of domestic consumption and *minimum access*. In anticipation of dirty tariffication, countries have agreed to maintain current access opportunities and establish quantitative commitments for new access opportunities, if imports in the 1986-88 base period were low or non-existent. The minimum access commitment starts at 3 percent and should rise to 5 percent by the end of the agreement. This provision provides a *safeguard clause*, which allows for the imposition of additional duties if trade is seriously disrupted.

(3) The domestic support provision of the AOA: The insertions are required and represent standard usage in this area. To exclude will distort the sense. The total aggregate measure of support (subsidies) is the sum of commodity specific and sector wide aggregate support given to rural producers. The AOA utilizes the traffic lights metaphor items in the Amber Box. Highly subsidized commodities are the most trade-distorting, and for developed countries these are to be reduced by 20 percent by 2000, based on the base period levels of 1986–88. For developing countries, the ratio is two-thirds of this over a period of 10 years. Support measures that are deemed as non-trade distorting are exempted. These include " Green Box" subsidies; subsidies that have no or minimal trade distorting effects on production and do not provide price support to producers and "Blue Box" subsidies which cover direct payments on product limiting programs. These non-trade distorting subsidies are dominant among the developed countries while support measures prevalent in developing countries e.g., investment and input subsidies are not so exempted. Other provision clauses such as the *De Minimis* allowed for exemptions once a subsidy does not exceed 5 percent of the value of the product or the total value of agricultural production.

(4) The Trade-Related Aspects of International Property Rights Agreement (TRIPS) and patent protection for micro-organisms and biological processes, including genetically-engineered animals and plants, is addressed.

(5) The provisions relating to food aid (international and national).

(6) The provisions governing sanitary and phytosanitary measures and technical barriers.

(7) The general provisions made for the special and differential treatment of developing countries provision covers: (1) least developed countries, which are exempted from reduction commitments; (2) other developing countries, which have smaller commitments (e.g. two-thirds and a longer period to comply, 2004 and not 2000); (3) net food-importing developing countries which are recognized, although no specific commitment to them is made; (4) provisions for food aid and technical assistance to least developed countries; (5) trade in food security stocks at administered prices.

Before offering an assessment of these provisions in relation to food security it is useful to observe seven general characteristics of global trade that are important for our arguments. First, there has been a lowering of the simple average of most favored nations tariffs. However, the less developed a country is, the higher are its average applied tariff rates. Thus the World Bank (2002) reports a simple average tariff rate of 17.9 percent for the least developed countries, 14 percent for other developing countries, and 5.2 percent for industrialized countries. In practice these rates do not capture the full operational range of barriers, which would include technical barriers, sanitary and phytosanitary measures, tariff rate quotas, contingent protection, prohibition, tariff escalation, tariff dispersion (peaks), and administrative hurdles.

Second, global trade is growing faster than global output and with significant shifts in the composition of that growth, generally in a direction away from food. Over the past five decades the total value of world trade has grown at an average annual rate of 10 percent. By the end of the millennium the value of world trade at current prices was 50 times greater than it was in the 1950s.

Third, across all major regions the trade-openness ratio has increased, (exports plus imports divided by GNP). The increase is strongest in East Asia and the Pacific. Sub-Saharan Africa showed a downturn in the 1990s in contrast with its strong performance in the 1960s and 1970s.

Fourth, the developing countries managed as a group to increase their share of world merchandize trade from less than 20 percent in the mid 1980s to 30 percent by the end of the 1990s. East Asia was responsible for much of this achievement while Africa and Latin America and the

Caribbean lost shares. And, the share of merchandize trade as a proportion of total trade among developing countries rose from about 25 percent in 1980 to above 40 percent by the end of the 1990s (World Bank 1999).

Fifth, due to East Asia's activity the share of manufactures in the exports of developing countries has risen from about one-fifth in 1980 to over two-thirds at the end of the 1990s. Over the same period, the share of food products and agricultural raw materials declined from about one-third to one-eight. Notably, the leading subsector within the group manufactures has become food processing especially "newer" products like fish, speciality foods and preserved fruit.

Sixth, commodity prices have been very volatile. During the 1980s and 1990s the prices of many commodities fluctuated from below 50 percent to above 150 percent of their average prices. This price volatility is critically significant. to poor countries. More than 50 poor countries depend on three or fewer commodities for half of their export earnings. In about 20 countries this reliance is over 90 percent. More than 30 developing countries, particularly in Africa, spend more than 20 percent of their import expenditure on food and fuels.

Seventh, since 1950 the price decline in a number of food items including vegetable oils, rice, maize, wheat, soybean, and coffee has been in excess of 2 percent per year. This decline reflects a broader decline in primary commodity prices due to the effects of expanded output, which is a result of improved technology, reduced costs, the more liberal trade environment, subsidies to the sector, and the usual primary commodity price cycles. The World Bank (1999) concluded that "Commodity prices may have taken another step down in the long history of declining prices relative to those of manufactured goods". For poor primary exporting countries, this could be bad news.

The data convey a picture of robust growth in trade that spans the entire period of globalization. Barring major global upheavals and recessions, the trend towards faster trade growth than GNP is likely to persist for some time to come. The World Bank (2002), has claimed in relation to the U.N.'s millennium development goal for poverty that: "More rapid growth associated with a global reduction in protection could reduce the number of people living in poverty by as much as 13 percent in 2015."

It cites estimates of global gains from eliminating barriers to merchandize trade that range from US $250 billion to $620 billion annually, with one-third to one-half of this total accruing to developing countries.

Modeling the future

In recent years, the econometric technique known as computable general equilibrium models have been used to analyze and compute the effects of future agriculture trade policy reforms under the WTO, usually as part of broader projections that cover other trading sectors. These models vary in important areas such as: the extent of projected liberalization; model specification; trade-related effects (e.g. savings, investment, productivity changes); database; number of sectors/regions; elasticities values; exogenous versus endogenous variables; and factor market competition and supply rigidities. The results from these models, which generally share the common assumption of constant returns to scale and limited trade-related dynamic gains, show a broad similarity (UNCTAD). Most of the gains are derived from domestic liberalization, and the gains obtained are roughly equally shared between developed and developing regions. A summary of these results presented in the UNCTAD report is adapted and presented in Table 1 (See also Francois 2000a). Caution is advised, however, as it would be extremely adventurous, to say the least, to place great reliability on the precision of these results, given the complexity of the many issues these simple models sought to address.

UNCTAD also presented the results of its own simulations of agricultural liberalization.

Simulation 1: A worldwide reduction of 50 percent in all agricultural tariffs
General Results: Aggregate welfare gain of US$ 21.5 billion with all regions gaining, but unevenly.
Simulation 2: A worldwide elimination of export subsidies in agriculture without parallel changes in tariffs.
General Results: Modest worldwide welfare losses due to worsened allocation of resources.
Simulation 3: Tariffs reduced by 50 percent on processed agriculture only.

General Results: Aggregate welfare gain roughly one-half that of Simulation 1. The gains are unevenly distributed.

Simulation 4: Non-reciprocal 50 percent cut in tariffs by developed economies only.

General Results: Aggregate gains are limited compared to Simulation 1.

Table 1 Estimates of Global Welfare Effects from Multilateral Trade Liberalization

Studies	Policy experiments	Welfare change estimates (US$ billions per annum)
Nagarajan, 1999	50 percent cut in agricultural protection and implementation of additional trade facilitation measures.	385
Hertel, Anderson, Francois, and Martin, 1999	40 percent cut in agricultural tariff, export and production subsidies	70
Anderson, Francois, Hertel, Hoekman, and Martin, 2000	Full liberalization in agriculture	164
Abare, 2000	50 percent cut in agricultural support	53 (GDP in 2010)
Francois, 2000b	50 percent cut in agricultural protection	27 (monopolistic competition) 21 (oligopoly)
Diao, Somwaru, and Roe, 2001	Full removal of agricultural supports and protection worldwide	31 (static version) 56 (dynamic version)
Scollay and Gilbert, 2001	100 percent cut in agricultural tariffs	69
Brown, Deardoff, and Stern, 2001	100 percent cut in agricultural tariffs	33
Van Meijl and Van Tongeren, 2001	100 percent cut in agricultural tariffs and in domestic agricultural support	44

Source: Adapted from UNCTAD.

From the perspective of food security these results suggest that the evolution of the global trade architecture embodied in the WTO is critical for the determination of the impact of globalization on food security and the rural poor. What can therefore be reasonably anticipated under this institutional regime? The reality is that the WTO has not existed long enough to draw definitive conclusions about its eventual impact on poor developing countries. Certain trends however, appear to be gaining strength. First, opportunities have no doubt expanded and some developing regions (e.g. East Asia) have been able to take advantage of them. This is reflected in their generally robust performances over the past three decades. Second, as the WTO trade regime is being implemented, the scope for national trade policy options is being curtailed. This reduction however, has been uneven across countries and regions and appears to adversely affect poor countries disproportionately. The reason is that within the WTO framework, development-related issues have not been adequately addressed. At the same time, the realization is also growing that the developing countries face unrelenting pressures against such traditional trade practices as non-reciprocity and preferential access, even as they face reduced access to official development assistance as an offset (Madeley; Safadi and Laird; Walters, Lowe and Davis).

Third, agricultural markets remain the most distorted of all global markets because, in practice, the rules of the WTO provide legal space for the developed countries to use their abundant resources, financial and other, to continue practicing market support, subsidies, and protection for their food supplies. For the period 1998–2000, the OECD countries, which are a major market for the agricultural exports of developing countries, gave average support to domestic producers US $331 billion or 2.2 percent of the group's GNP. This is a dramatic increase from the base period 1986-1988 when it gave US $271 billion or 1.3 percent of GNP to domestic producers. In 2002 over two-thirds of agricultural production in the OECD countries receives market price support. Astonishingly, the value of that assistance is twice what is required to meet the global food security target by 2015. It also represents twice the value of all the agricultural exports of the developing countries and five times current official development assistance flows to them. The amount of support also exceeded 40 percent of farmers' income in the OECD countries in 1998–2000.

In terms of *market access*, average agricultural tariff levels in OECD countries are estimated at 60 percent, about six times the level of their industrial tariffs. Generally, tariff peaks are concentrated in agriculture, food products, and footwear in the European Union (EU) and Japan, and textiles and clothing in the U.S.A. and Canada (World Bank 2002). OECD farm prices are estimated at 37 percent above those on world markets (Ford; IMF/World Bank).

Subsidies in the OECD are estimated at over 100 billion U.S. $ annually. The recent (2002) U.S. Farm Bill and the associated raising of subsidies have attracted strong adverse global attention. The situation is that one-third of U.S. cultivated acreage is assigned to food and fibers for export. With domestic markets being described as "saturated," agricultural exports are key to the survival of U.S. agriculture and this links it directly to domestic subsidies. A recent comment by U.S. Trade Representative Robert Zoellick (Becker), is instructive: "The U.S. would be in a better negotiating position at the world trade talks precisely because American farmers are receiving record amounts of subsidies without breaking limits imposed by the WTO."

The EU however, is an even larger user of export subsidies, accounting for as much as 90 percent of the total by some estimates (Ford). The EU system of protection has been in place since its inception four decades ago and expenditure on it accounts for 45 percent of the EU budget, although only 5 percent of its work force is in agriculture. It has also been reported that technical barriers, especially in areas like health, safety, and product standards have been rising rapidly and the inability of the developing countries to cope with this within the WTO structure is limited because of its complexity and cost (Henson et al.; World Bank 2002).

Transfers from consumers and taxpayers have maintained high producer prices in OECD countries. The Diaz-Bonilla, Thomas and Robinson study indicates that as a whole, equivalent domestic prices exceed world prices by 60 percent for the OECD countries with rates as high as 229 percent for Norway and 90 percent for Japan. The net effect is domestic over-production with domestic producers displacing agricultural production from poor countries in their home markets, and in third countries as well when these products are exported at lower prices. Indeed, in some cases (e.g. sugar and the European Union), OECD countries are simultaneously among the world's largest exporters and importers of the agricultural product. As UNCTAD observes: "Another aspect of the linkage between trade and development relates to the effects of policies and practices of other countries and private economic agents. Studies of patterns in the use of trade measures show a systematic bias against the imports of developing countries."

As presently configured, the developing countries have less space and capacity to practise what the developed countries have been doing. In areas of agriculture where they may find opportunities, for example, food security, multi-functionality, and environment, this difference is very notable (Diaz-Bonilla and Tin). As a rule, developing countries have historically favored low agricultural prices in order to keep living costs down, raw materials cheap, and exports competitive, however this approach has been somewhat modified over the past two decades. Except for countries that are preference dependent or net food importers, the evidence is that on the whole, these countries have been undergoing a structural shift away from domestic agricultural production to exports.

Conclusions

An irreversible dynamic favors trade liberalization under the WTO framework. To ensure that in this institutional setting global markets bring gains for the rural poor, *a greater coherence between trade policies and development policies* is required. As we have argued, neo-classical economic theory along with the *modus operandi* of the existing trade architecture assume a robust relation between open trade policies and development, which has not been satisfactorily established either at the theoretical, empirical or policy level. Yet on this basis poor countries have had, mainly as a result of structural adjustment programs, to introduce unilateral liberalization measures, despite the prevalence of distortions in world agricultural markets due to subsidies and other protection by the rich countries that could afford them. It is obvious that for the future, the relationship between the two policy spheres need to be continuously re-evaluated. In particular there is a need for greater flexibility and national control of the *timing and sequencing* of trade policy measures; even with the WTO so well entrenched, much of the national discretion in this area has effectively disappeared from its global agenda and the work program emanating from the 2001 Doha Ministerial Round. Appropriate flanking and support policies to cope with related problems of supply side constraints, capacity building, adjustment costs for poor countries, and so on, have to be put in place if global markets are to bring gains to the rural poor.

This observation is consistent with calls for a greater focus on *development issues in the post-Doha work program of the WTO*, which have emanated from the developing countries. Although the Uruguay Round has had the dramatic effect of bringing agriculture, however loosely, under the commercial and market-oriented disciplines of the WTO, it has had limited impact so far on the effective levels of trade liberalization in agriculture for those products of specific concern to the developing countries. To deal with this impasse, the only credible "good-faith" signal the OECD countries can make at this stage would be a binding commitment to delink their own agricultural production from government financing and other measures in order to reduce their levels of market support, protection, and other trade barriers in the WTO Agreement *first*, without an immediate *quid pro quo* from the developing countries.

Unless this undertaking is given, other important related issues will not be adequately addressed. Those include calls for: (1) a phase-out of all tariff peaks and tariff escalation on agriculture products; (2) restraint on the abuse of TBTs and other trade remedies permitted under the WTO; (3) a more liberalized environment for the treatment of "rules of origin" in developing countries; (4) support by the developed countries for support measures to deal with the distributional and other consequences of the agricultural adjustment challenges in developing countries; (5) a fairer treatment of the phase-out of preferences and special market access; and (6) commodity risk management to cater for the vulnerability of poor countries to commodity price volatility (ComSec). With the high levels of scepticism and distrust over these issues, none of this agenda will advance without an expression of good faith on the part of the developed countries. The contrast between globalization's gainers and losers and deepening inequality over the past two decades have contributed to this outlook.

A major complication is that the poor countries have themselves become a heterogeneous grouping with different preferences in regard to the adjustment of national and global agricultural production. Some poor countries are grouped as major exporters of agricultural products with little reliance on imported food, except in times of crisis; others are major exporters and importers of agricultural products; and, yet others produce little agricultural output and are highly dependent net-food importers. Furthermore, they vary considerably in terms of the extent of their economic differentiation, technological capacity, standard of living, and capacities to deal with shocks and transitional issues. These circumstances preclude a monolithic one-size-fits-all approach to the problems identified in this paper (Walters, Lowe and Davis; WTO).

The question now frequently asked is, where does the responsibility for achieving the global food security target lie? Is it at the international or national jurisdiction? And, if the latter, is it at the governmental, private business, or non-governmental level? There is no *a priori* answer to this question, but we share the view expressed by Thomas (2002) that at this stage of global development, the responsibility falls primarily on national governments. This perspective starts from citizens "rights to food security", and governments' responsibility to ensure their enjoyment of these "rights." The international community, private business, and non-profit agencies are obviously important contributors to this outcome, but as an entitlement of citizenship, the ultimate responsibility for its provision lies with national governments. This perspective, precisely because it is unequivocal, does not easily permit the MDG for food security to fall through the cracks.

Finally, we reiterate the assessment we offered in an earlier study that at present the best approach to food security for a developing country or region is to pursue it as a combined commercial *and* strategic/developmental objective (Thomas and Davis). National interests will always conflict with deregulated trade; strategically therefore, a definite degree of national autonomy and flexibility in basic food supplies should be pursued. Food security is too important to be left entirely to the uncertain outcomes of international trade. This combined objective requires that domestic measures to overcome supply constraints and those designed to ensure that the rural economy plays the desired role in social development are seen as complementary goals. The aim is not autarky or excessive protection; rather it is a call for a nationally self-reliant approach that combines realistic sustained domestic efforts to improve agricultural productivity and judicious trade in food in order to meet the goal of food security. This preference function is underlined by three basic considerations that have informed this study. These are: (1) the persistent structural uncertainties in the present global economy; (2) the historical trend for added value in food production to occur off farm, with the result that the significance of land in relation to other inputs will continue to decline as the agriculture of poor countries becomes radically transformed; and (3) the persistence of asymmetric outcomes and the polarization of winners and losers in the age of globalization and liberalization. Our call for strategic government intervention in global food-trade in pursuit of accelerated poverty reduction and food security is consistent with performance-based economic principles. If there is convincing evidence that market or policy failures are the norm rather than the exception as they relate to food trade, poverty reduction, and food security, then appropriate public sector intervention is justified. After all the elements are considered, we stand firm on our point that market failure is nothing but a policy failure one step removed.

References

ABARE (Australian Bureau of Agricultural and Resource Economics) (2000). *The Impact of Agricultural Trade Liberalization on Developing Countries.* Canberra, Australia: ABARE.

Abbott, J. (1967). The Development of Marketing Institutions. In H. Southworth, and B. Johnston, eds., *Agricultural Development and Economic Growth*, Ithaca, NY: Cornell University Press.

Anderson, K., J. Francois, T. Hertel, B. Hoekman, and W. Martin (2000). Potential Gains from Trade Reform in the New Millennium. Paper presented at the Third Annual Conference on Global Economic Analysis, Monash University, Australia, June 27–30.

Becker, E. (2002). U.S. Defends Its Farm Subsidies Against Rising Foreign Criticism. *New York Times*, Thursday, June 27, p. A5.

Bonnen, J., C. Eicher, and A. Schmid (1964). Marketing in Economic Development, In V. Sorenson, ed., *Agricultural Market Analysis: Development, Performance, Process*, East Lansing, MI: Michigan State University Press.

Brown, D., A. Deardorff, and R. Stern (2001). CGE Modeling and Analysis of Multilateral and Regional Negotiation Options. Paper presented at Research Seminar in International Economics, University of Michigan, Ann Arbor. Discussion Paper No. 468, January 23.

Coase, R. (1960). The Problem of Social Cost. *Journal of Law and Economics*, 3, pp. 1–44.

COMSEC (Commonwealth Secretariat) (2002). Commodity Risk Management in Developing Countries: A Proposed Market Based Approach and Its Relevance for Small States. Paper presented at the Global Conference on Development Agenda for Small States. London.

Davis, C., C. Thomas, and W. Amponsah (2001). Globalization and Poverty: Lessons from the Theory and Practice of Food Security. *American Journal of Agricultural Economics*, 83(3), pp. 714–721.

de Gorter, H., G. Rausser, and A. Schmitz (2001). Rent Seeking and International Trade in Agriculture, In C. Moss, G. Rausser, A. Schmitz, T. Taylor, and D. Zilberman, eds., *Agricultural Globalization, Trade, and the Environment*. Norwell, MA: Kluwer Academic Publishers.

Diao, X., A. Somwaru, and T. Roe (2001). A Global Analysis of Agricultural Reform in WTO Member Countries. In M. Burfisher, ed., *Agricultural Policy Reform: The Road Ahead*, Washington, DC: Economic Research Service, Report No. 802.

Diaz-Bonilla, E., M. Thomas, and S. Robinson (2002). On Boxes, Contents, and Users: Food Security and the WTO Negotiations. International Food Policy Research Institute, Trade and Macroeconomics Discussion Paper No. 82, Washington, DC.

Diaz-Bonilla, E., and J. Tin (2002). That Was Then But This Is Now: Multifunctionality In Industry and Agriculture. International Food Policy Research Institute, Trade and Macroeconomics Discussion Paper No. 94, Washington, DC.

Dollar, D (1992). Outward-Oriented Developing Economies Really Do Grow More Rapidly: Evidence from 95 LDCs, 1976–85. *Economic Development and Cultural Change*, April, pp. 523–544.

Dollar, D., and P. Collier (2001). *Globalization, Growth and Poverty: Building an Inclusive World Economy*, New York, NY: Oxford University Press.

Dollar, D., and A. Kraay (2001a). Growth is Good for the Poor. World Bank Research Department Working Paper No. 2587, Washington, DC.

Dollar, D., and A. Kraay (2001b). Trade, Growth, and Poverty. World Bank Research Department Working Paper No. 2615, Washington, DC.

Drabek, Z., and S. Laird (2001). Can Trade Policy Help Mobilize Financial Resources for Economic Development. World Trade Organization Economic Research and Analysis Division, Staff Working Paper No. ERAD 2001–2, Geneva.

Eastwood, R., and M. Lipton (2001). Pro-poor Growth and Pro-Growth Poverty Reduction: What Do They Mean? What Does the Evidence Mean? What Can Policymakers Do? Paper presented at the Asia Pacific Forum on Poverty-

Reforming Policies and Institutions for Poverty Reduction, Asian Development Bank, Manila, 5–9 February.

Edwards, S (1998). Openness, Productivity and Growth: What Do We Really Know? *Economic Journal*, 108, pp. 383–398.

FAO (Food and Agriculture Organization of the United Nations) (1996). *Rome Declaration on World Food Security and World Food Summit Plan of Action*. Rome, Italy: Food and Agriculture Organization.

Ford, J (2002). Uruguay Round on Agriculture: Retrospect and Prospect for Caribbean Agricultural Development. Paper presented at the 24th West Indies Agricultural Economics Conference, Grenada, West Indies, July 9–12.

Francois, J (2000a). Assessing the Results of General Equilibrium Studies of Multilateral Trade Negotiations. UNCTAD Policy Issues Study Series No. 3 in International Trade, New York and Geneva, United Nations.

————. (2000b) The Economic Impact of New Multilateral Negotiations: Final Report. Report prepared for the European Commission Directorate-General II, Brussels.

Henson, S., R. Loader, A. Swinbank, M. Bredahl, and N. Lux (1999). *Impact of Sanitary and Phytosanitary Measures on Developing Countries*, London, UK: H.M. Government, Department for International Development (DFID).

Hertel, T., K. Anderson, J. Francois, and W. Martin (1999). Agriculture and Non-agricultural Liberalization in the Millennium Round. Paper presented at the 1999 Global Conference on Agriculture and the New Trade Agenda from a Development Perspective: Interest and Option in the WTO 2000 Negotiations, Geneva, October 1–2.

IFAD (International Fund for Agricultural Development) (2001). *The Challenge of Ending Rural Poverty: Rural Poverty Report 2001*, New York, NY: Oxford University Press.

IMF (International Monetary Fund) and World Bank (2002). Market Access for Developing Country Exports: Selected Issues. IMF/World Bank paper. Washington, DC.

Just, R., D. Hueth, and A. Schmitz (1982). *Applied Welfare Economics and Public Policy*. Englewood Cliffs, NJ: Prentice Hall.

Kruger, A (1974). The Political Economy of the Rent Seeking Society. *The American Economic Review*, 64(3), pp. 291–303.

Lipton, M., and M. Ravallion (1995). Poverty and Policy. In J. Behrman and T. Srinivasan, eds., *Handbook of Development Economics*. Amsterdam, Netherlands: North-Holland.

Lustig, N. (2000). Crises and the Poor: Socially Responsible Macroeconomics. Inter-American Development Bank, Sustainable Development Department Technical Paper Series No. POV-108, Washington, DC.

Madeley, J (2000). Trade and Hunger — An Overview of Case Studies on the Impact of Trade Liberalization on Food Security. *Global Studier*, Stockholm, Sweden.

McCalla, A., and L. Revoredo (2000). Prospects for Global Food Security: A Critical Appraisal of Past Projections and Predictions. International Food Policy Research Institute, 2020 Vision Brief No. 71, Washington, DC.

Miranda, K., and T. Muzondo (1991). Public Policy and the Environment. *Finance and Development*, 28(2), pp. 25–27.

Mosley, P. (2000). Globalization, Economic Policy and Convergence. *The World Economy*, 23(5), pp. 613–634.

Nagarajan, N. (1999). The Millennium Round: An Economic Appraisal. Commission of the European Communities, Economic Papers No. ECFIN/ 659/99-Rev.EN.

Panayotou, T. (1992). Is Economic Growth Sustainable. *Proceedings of the World Bank Annual Conference on Development Economics 1991*, Washington, DC: World Bank.

Pinstrup-Andersen, P., R. Pandya-Lorch, and W. Rosegrant (1999). *World Food Prospects: Critical Issues for the Early 21st Century*, Washington, DC: International Food Policy Research Institute.

Rodrik, D., and F. Rodriguez, (1999). "Trade Policy and Economic Growth: A Skeptic's Guide to Cross-national Evidence", in B. Bernanke, and K. Rogoff, eds., *Macroeconomics Annual*, Cambridge, MA: MIT Press for National Bureau of Economic Research (NBER).

Rodrik, D., and F. Rodriguez (2001). The Global Governance of Trade as if Development Really Mattered. Paper prepared for the UNDP (mimeograph).

Romer, P. (1990). Endogenous Technological Growth. *Journal of Political Economy*, 98, pp. S72–S102.

Safadi, R., and S. Laird (1996). The Uruguay Round Agreements: Impact on Developing Countries. *World Development* 24(7), pp. 1223–1242.

Scollary, R., and J. Gilbert (2001). An Integrated Approach to Agricultural Trade and Development Issues: Exploring the Welfare and Distribution Issues. UNCTAD Policy Issues Study Series No. 11 in International Trade, New York and Geneva, United Nations.

Thomas, C. (2002). Food Security: A Neglected Dimension of Caribbean Agricultural Policies. Institute for Development Studies (IDS) Working Paper, University of Guyana (forthcoming).

Thomas, C. (2001). Global Food Security: Advance and Retreat. *Caricom Perspective*, Georgetown, Guyana: Caricom Secretariat.

Thomas, C. (2000). Global Food Security: The Evolution of Recent Thinking and Practice. Paper presented at the Symposium on Poverty and Global Food

Security, American Agricultural Economics Association Annual Meeting, Tampa, FL, July 30–August 2, 2000.

Thomas, C., and C. Davis (2000). Food Security in the Age of Liberalization and Globalization, In R. Zabawa, N. Baharanyi, and W. Hill, eds., *Global Food Security: Exploring the Nexus Between Domestic and International Strategies*, Proceedings of the 57th Professional Agricultural Workers Conference. Tuskegee, Alabama: Tuskegee University.

UNCTAD (United Nations Conference on Trade and Development) (2002). *Back to Basics: Market Access Issues in the Doha Agenda* (UNCTAD/DITC/MISC. 73/Rev.1). Geneva, Switzerland.

UNDP (United Nations Development Program) (1997). *Human Development Report 1997*. New York, NY: Oxford University Press.

USDA (United States Department of Agriculture) (2002). *Food Security Assessment*. Washington, DC: Economic Research Service (ERS) Outlook Report No. GFA13.

Van Meijl, H., and F. Van Tongeren (2001). Multilateral Trade Liberalization and Developing Countries: A North-South Perspective on Agriculture and Processing Sectors. Paper presented at the Fourth Annual Conference on Global Economic Analysis, Purdue University, West Lafayette, Indiana, June 27–29.

Walters, L., G, Lowe, and C. Davis (2002). Economic Asymmetries, Trade Liberalization, and Regional Integrations: Issues and Policy Implications for CARICOM Countries. Paper presented at the 24th West Indies Agricultural Economics Conference, Grenada, West Indies, July 9–12.

Weller, C., and A. Hersh (2002). The Long and Short of It: Global Liberalization, Poverty and Inequality. Economic Policy Institute Research Paper, Washington, DC.

World Bank (1999). *World Commodity Markets, 1999*, Washington, DC: World Bank.
———. (2002). *World Development Report 2002*. Washington, DC: World Bank.

WTO (World Trade Organization) (2000). Agreement on Agriculture: Special and Differential Treatment and a Development Box: Proposal to the June 2000 Special Session of the Committee on Agriculture by Cuba, The Dominican Republic, Honduras, Pakistan, Haiti, Nicaragua, Kenya, Uganda, Zimbabwe, Sri Lanka and El Salvador. (G/AG/NG/W/13). Geneva, Switzerland: WTO.

chapter five

$\mathcal{M}$arkets, Government and Development: Structural Adjustment Programs in a Global Economy

Edward Mabaya
Ralph D. Christy

The Great Debate in Economics on the role of markets and government in economic development was rekindled at the turn of the millennium as empirical results from structural adjustment programs were unveiled and globalization presented uncertainties. While the debate has evolved from the simple dichotomy of state versus markets that occupied early 20th century economists, still, no consensus currently exists on the ideal mix that can maximize the synergy between the two while minimizing the rivalry. The collapse of the former Soviet Union and its allies, mixed results from structural adjustment programs (SAPs), the raise and demise of the East Asian miracle, and the challenges and opportunities of globalization have added more fuel to that debate. Focusing on poverty alleviation in Sub-Saharan Africa, this chapter contributes to the discourse by examining two key questions: (1) What explains the success and failure of the World Bank and International Monetary Fund initiated economic structural

---

Edward Mabaya is a research associate in the department of Applied Economics and Management at Cornell University. Ralph D. Christy is the J. Thomas Clark Professor of Emerging Markets in the same department.

adjustment programs? (2) What has been the impact of globalization on less developed countries?

This chapter is organized as follows: First, we highlight the key elements of the markets versus governments debate and how the debate shaped global political economies (and vice versa). Next we discuss the SAPs of the 1980s and 1990s by assessing the key factors that contributed to their successes and failures. Our discussion of globalization focuses on its economic impacts on less developed countries (LDCs). We then draw some strategic lessons from those two market-led phenomena to guide economic policies in LDCs. Finally, we close by reviewing guidelines for applied economists to understand society's choice between market- or government-based solutions.

The Great Debate Revisited

The polar arguments in the Great Debate are epitomized in two classic works: Adam Smith's seminal *Wealth of Nations* presenting the virtues of perfect markets and Karl Marx's (1867) revolutionary *Das Capital* justifying a command economy. Much of the remaining literature falls between these two polarized views. Before examining the key arguments for each side, a discussion of the measures of success for an economy — efficiency and equity — is in order. It is those two criteria that form the keystone in this debate. While there is no consensus on precise definitions and measures of these terms, we give here the fundamental principles.

Economic efficiency requires that allocations be *pareto optimal*, i.e., it should not be possible to make anyone better off without making someone else worse off. To satisfy this condition requires efficiency in production (equal marginal rates of transformation of resources across producers of the same good), efficiency in consumption (equal marginal rates of substitution across consumers of the same good), and product-mix efficiency (marginal value is equal to marginal cost). Interpersonal welfare comparison, and thus distributional issues, is taboo to strict advocates of economic efficiency.

By contrast, interpersonal welfare comparison is central to any equity considerations. Because of its normative nature, both the definition and measurement of equity are more elusive. However, the consensus among supporters of economic equity is that total welfare can be increased by reallocating resources whenever it makes some or more people better off even at the expense of others or a minority who are judged as worse of to a lesser extent. Income distribution, captured through Lorenz curves and Gini coefficients, is most commonly used to evaluate equity.

The pro-market view is based on an idealized model of a perfectly competitive market that tends toward full employment equilibrium for the macroeconomy and efficient use of resources by the firm and the individual (the microeconomy) (Wolf, 1993). Under certain conditions, a market economy can fulfill consumption, production, and product mix efficiency through use of a price mechanism as an allocation system (Debreu, 1959). In reality however, all the assumed conditions rarely, if ever, hold. Situations under which markets are not the best allocation mechanism — market failures — include: (a) externalities and public goods; (b) jointedness or increasing returns to scale; (c) market imperfections related to accessing information; (d) and the possible social or economic inequity of efficient market outcomes. The applicability of market exchange is further limited by "contractual problems of asymmetrical information, moral hazard and adverse selection" (Lane and Ersson, 2002). The suitability of the market allocation mechanism depends on the prevalence of these market failures and the extent of inequities. With regards to LDCs the direction of causality is subject to debate, but there is some consensus on the prevalence of market imperfections as noted by Stiglitz:

> ... the difference (between less developed and developed countries) can be attributed, perhaps tautologically to differences in economic organization, to how individuals interact, and to the institutions which mediate those interactions. Among the most important of these 'institutions' are markets. (Stiglitz, 1998, p. 103)

The market economy view draws empirical support from the past century's experience of economies in the industrialized West. Arguably, those economies are based on extensive private property institutions and a small public sector. Also used to support the virtues of markets is the experience of the industrialized export-led countries of Southeast Asia (Hong Kong, Malaysia, Singapore, South Korea, Taiwan, and Indonesia) prior to the Asian financial crisis in 1997.

The pro-government stance is based on an idealized model of an informed, efficient, and humane government that is able to identify and remedy failures of the market and to achieve national goals arrived at by democratic means, according to the precepts of formal welfare economics (Musgrave). Theoretically, it is possible for a "ministry of production and consumption" to meet the same efficiency criteria that are required of a market economy (Barone, 1935). However, the practical feasibility of arriving at such an efficient allocation based exclusively on a command system is unlikely given the vast knowledge and information requirements. Beyond the information problem, a command economy would have to address an incentive problem as some participants might still find it strategic to bias information to their advantage (Lane and Errson, 2002). Despite these major limitations, a command economy can resolve some market failures such as the under-provision of public goods and inequity that bedevil the invisible hand of the market. Welfare economics provides rules and guidelines for government intervention to remedy, or at least alleviate, such shortcomings.

The pro-government view draws empirical support from the generally favorable economic performance of the Scandinavian countries and the Netherlands in the post-World War II period, as well as specific instances of efficient government performance such as Europe's national railway system and Japan's macroeconomic policy.

Although the anti-market view is supported by an elaborate theory on market failure, the anti-government view cannot lean for equivalent support on a similarly developed formal theory of government failure because, "That theory does not exist" (Wolf, 1993, p. 4). As a result, an interesting asymmetry emerges in comparing the sources and types of support for the pro-market/anti-government intervention views with that for the pro-government/anti-market position. A more fully developed theory of non-market failure could help provide a better balance in the debate and a better guide to public policy. Important elements in such a comprehensive theory of non-market failure are provided by Buchanan's version of public choice theory and Williamson's transaction cost economics. Public choice theory emphasizes the self-interest of politicians and bureaucrats within the public sector, but it "ignores the role of organizational inertia, tradition, and standard operating routines as contributors to non-market failures" (Wolf, 1997, p. 6). Moreover, public choice theory does not embrace the wider range of activities covered by the non-market sector as a whole — to include, for example, foundations, universities, and nonprofit hospitals (which Kenneth Boulding refers to as "the grant economy"). A comprehensive theory of non-market failure should include the behavior of a wider set of actors beyond government itself.

Understanding Policy Failure

Perhaps a constructive role for social scientists would be determining where policies have failed, thus allowing for the creation of alternative institutions (government-based or market-based) to address such failure, rather than accepting the market as superior in allocating resources in a socially acceptable fashion. Policy failure reflects policies that ignored the problem, were in place but were not effective, or caused unintended — mostly negative — consequences. Those policies created costs that were greater than benefits (Allen and Christy). Addressing the failure calls for a continuous evaluation of the impact of public policies on economic actions and on the economy. An evaluation will recognize that, over time, policies recreate circumstances; that is, government influences the structure, the behavior, and the performance of markets, from which new problems and, thus, new policies eventually arise. This process must be understood by policy analysts. In order to assess the proper role of government, analysts must address both market and government failures (Stiglitz, 1995).

Too much weight has been given to the "polar opposites game," — markets or government. Models that advocate for middle ground have received little attention. Lange, Taylor and Lenner's competitive socialist model which theorizes public enterprise, state-managed, market economies, generated remarkably little discussion in the literature after the collapse of the Soviet Union. So too did the market socialism model in which profit maximizing enterprises are owned by government but independently run by appointed managers. In actuality, all real-life political economic regimes involve some combination of both markets and government that often varies across industries. Instead of the dichotomous "markets or government"

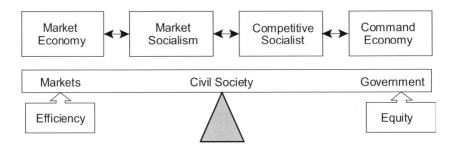

Figure 1 Resource allocation systems

decision facing academics, public policy makers try to maximize the synergy between the two. However, the difference between markets and government is as much ideological as it is empirical: governments stifle efficient markets through regulations, policies and bureaucracy while markets tend to corrupt governments (Streeten, 1992). Figure 1 illustrates the balance between resource allocation mechanisms in pursuit of economic efficiency and equitable distribution.

Post Structural Adjustment Program Assessment

The collapse of state socialist economies in Eastern Europe, coupled with the success of export led growth from the Asian Tigers (Taiwan, Hong Kong, Singapore, and South Korea) in the 1970s scored victory for the pro-markets supporters. In addition, poverty, tyranny, and oppression under the former Soviet Union and its allies came to be associated with the failure of government control. In the last quarter of the 20th century, economists increasingly held the view of markets as the magic pill for both growth and development, essential to providing strong economic incentives, socially efficient allocations, and necessary bulwarks for the preservation of liberty. In the Southern hemisphere, particularly Africa and Latin America, this tidal wave of free market euphoria resulted in massive restructuring of the economies. Throughout the 1980s and early 1990s, Structural Adjustment Programs (SAPs) led by the International Monetary Fund (IMF) and the World Bank reoriented economic policies towards laissez-faire market economies. The debt crisis which peaked in the early 1980s favored acceptance of the SAP packages and limited the negotiating power of governments over the terms and conditions. Furthermore, the United States government leveraged adoption of these policies by conditioning its aid on acceptance of the programs and adherence to the reform process. The SAPs generally entailed reductions in government spending and employment, higher interest rates, currency devaluation, privatization of government parastatals, meeting debt repayment schedules, reduction in tariffs and other trade barriers, and liberalization of foreign investment regulations and labor laws.

The required adjustments were implemented in most Southern countries. The programs were successful in cutting government expenditure, improving debt servicing, eliminating hyperinflation, privatizing state enterprises, and improving economic efficiency in some industries. The currency devaluation, coupled with a reduction in trade barriers, expedited the integration of less developed countries into the global economy. A widely cited success story of the SAP in Sub-Saharan Africa is Uganda, which rose from negative growth rates in the early 1980s to a peak growth rate of 11.6 in 1996.

However, for most countries the anticipated overall growth and development have not materialized to date. Welch and Oringer (1998) argue that "SAPs have bankrupted local industries, increased dependency on food imports, gutted social services, and fostered a widening gap between the rich and the poor." A 2001 study by Easterly shows that, SAP lending lowered the growth elasticity of poverty (the change in poverty rates for a given amount of growth) but found no evidence of a direct effect on growth. The poor people took the brunt of SAPs while a few wealthy entrepreneurs were best placed to take advantage of new economic opportunities. The result was increased inequity. Poverty, unemployment, and food insecurity increased in most countries despite mandated welfare programs and relief measures. Reduced government expenditure squeezed budgets for the soft-sectors (public education, health, housing, and social welfare programs) while military budgets remained untouched. Trade liberalization lead to dumping of cheap manufactured products thereby undermining local infant industries and resulting in massive job losses. Safety nets designed to cushion the most affected either were inadequate, inaccessible, or overwhelmed by the demand. Reflecting the growing inequity, the Gini coefficient for the world increased from 0.63 in 1988 to 0.66 by 1993 (UNDP, 2001). A 1999 World Bank study by Lundberg and Squire of 38 countries between 1965 and 1992 shows that trade liberalization is correlated negatively with income growth among the poorest 40 percent of the population and 'strongly and positively' with income growth among the remaining 60 percent. SAPs have contributed to increasing inequity both globally and at the national level.

SAPs also have been blamed for widespread environmental degradation in LDCs. Currency devaluation and the emphasis on increasing exports promoted extractive enterprises (e.g., timber, mining, and fishing) and chemical intensive export-oriented agribusinesses (Welch and Oringer, 1988). The increasing unemployment and poverty led many urban and rural poor to increase their reliance and pressures on natural resources and environmental services just to survive (Reed, 1996). Most policies were abolished that had been designed to spearhead the integration of smallholder farmers into the mainstream economy and to promote national food security through self-sufficiency. Without price controls and/or consumer subsidies, food prices rocketed. Faced with increasing food prices and low income, smallholder farmers responded by expanding cultivation in marginal areas leading to major environmental degradation.

Why SAPs failed

In the late 1990s, the growing realization of the SAPs failure coupled with a growing civil movement, promoted analytical postmortems of the program. Numerous country specific and regional case studies were written to explain the few success and many failures of the program in each country. Critics of SAPs looked inward at the program design and underlying assumptions, while supporters searched for exogenous causes for the lower than expected performance. The explanations for the failure of SAPs can be summarized in six points:

Poorly designed program with hidden agendas

Activists and stern critics argue that SAPs were doomed for failure from the beginning as they were poorly formulated and designed mainly to improve debt servicing by LDCs. The programs were designed with minimal consultation with local governments, NGOs, and civic organizations. Additionally, the one-size-fits-all approach in the economic policies ignores the unique social, economic and political conditions facing each country. The narrow focus on macroeconomic reform neglected socioeconomic and environmental issues, and no provisions were made to ameliorate the adverse impacts of structural adjustment on the poor.

The limit of markets

Those who have little faith in markets as an allocation mechanism take the failure of SAPs to be an empirical verdict on markets. They argue that markets did not work precisely because markets in general do not work. Indeed the increased inequity under SAPs is consistent with the key limitations of market led development. The trickle down approach to development, implicit in most market led initiatives, failed to deliver. The *laissez faire* approach does not guarantee market efficiency or socially desirable allocations especially in less developed economies where market failures are particularly pervasive (Hayami, 1998; Stiglitz, 1998).

Poor governance

To counter the 'limit of markets' argument, pro-market advocates contend that markets were never given a chance. Failure of SAPs can be blamed on poor governance that failed to create a conducive environment for sufficient competition. For instance, low foreign direct investment into Africa is blamed on conflict and unstable bureaucratic governments. Based on a database of 220 countries, Dollar and Svensson (2000) find political-economy variables to be significant in predicting the success of SAPs.

Heavy foreign debt

Debt servicing to the multilateral institutions is widely blamed for stagnated growth in LDCs. Growing protests and civil pressure led the multi-lateral lending institutions to launch the Heavily Indebted Poor Countries (HIPC) initiative in 1996. HIPC focuses on writing off part of the debts owed by the poorest countries thereby freeing resources for social welfare programs. The initiative has been criticized as doing too little too late; its terms were made more generous in October 1999. It is noteworthy that approval of debt write-off under HIPC is still conditional on satisfactory implementation of SAPs.

Fall in commodity prices

The export led initiative of SAPs was seriously undermined by a plunge in world commodity prices in the 1980s. For example, between 1980 and 1988, sugar prices fell by 64 percent, coffee by 30 percent, cotton by 32 percent, crude oil by 53 percent, and tin by 57 percent (Sparr, 2001). Since commodity export was and still is the major source of foreign currency for Southern Hemisphere nations, the fall in prices slowed industrialization and undermined the ability of these nations to service foreign debt. Though some commodity prices have recovered, heavy agricultural subsidies in North America and Europe continue to depress agricultural commodity prices. Currency devaluation under SAPs also reduced LDCs' income from and increased costs of imports for LDCs.

Natural disasters

For most LDCs it seems as though it either never rains or it pours. In the 1980s and 1990s, droughts ravaged Northern and Southern Africa, while hurricanes destroyed hard infrastructure and livelihoods in South America. The same regions were also, and continue to be, hit hard by the HIV/AIDS pandemic, which has debilitated the labor force. While these natural disasters contributed to the high levels of poverty in the last quarter of the 20th century, the dual causality between the two is undeniable: the economic hardships brought by SAPs have made people in LDCs more vulnerable when natural disasters occur (Adger, 1999). And, because of the natural disasters, the poor economic performance of LDCs over the last two decades cannot be blamed entirely on SAPs.

It would be unfair to judge success and failure of SAPs without looking at the alternative. Has adjustment resulted in more or less poverty, inequity, and environmental degradation than otherwise would have occurred? It can be argued that the heavy government expenditure in LDCs during pre-SAP period was unsustainable and destined for failure; or that, much of the adverse conditions faced by nations in the 1980s and 1990s would have occurred with or without SAPs. However, since no alternative to SAPs was instituted, it is impossible to say if LDCs are better or worse off with SAP.

Globalization

Globalization is a much more complex and multidimensional phenomenon than SAPs. The term is generally used in reference to the compression of the world and the intensification of consciousness of the world as a whole (Robertson, 1992). It also refers to the intensification of economic, political, social and cultural relations across borders (Holm and Sorensen, 1995). While there is no consensus on the causes, nature, spread, measurement, and impact of globalization, its inevitability is widely accepted. We approach globalization from a political economy perspective with a particular focus on economic development in LDCs.

For LDCs, the link and distinction between SAPs and globalization are rather amorphous. Activists and other skeptics of market-led developments insist that globalization is nothing but 'pouring old philosophical wine into new ideological bottles' (Steger).

> In the last two decades, Aglo-American proponents of the nineteenth-century market utopia have found in the concept of "globalization" a new guiding metaphor for their neoliberal message. The central tenets of neoliberalism include the primacy of economic growth, the importance of free trade to simulate growth; the unrestricted free market; individual choice; the reduction of government regulation; and the advocacy of an evolutionary model of social development anchored in the Western experience and applicable to the entire world (Steger, 2002, p. 9).

While acknowledging the close relationship between SAPs and globalization, we contend that the two are different. The distinction is clear in Western economies, Cuba, and North Korea, which have not undergone SAPs, but are dealing with globalization. To shed light on the relationship between the two, we examine the causes of globalization. Note that globalization is a self-propelling phenomenon where cause and consequence are inextricably linked. Globalization leads to more globalization.

Causes of globalization

Major improvements in transport and communications technology are widely held as the primary causes of globalization. In the post World War II period, the cost of transporting goods, traveling, and communicating across the world fell drastically. The cost of a three-minute call between New York and London fell from $60.42 to under 30 cents today; between 1930 and 1990, the cost of air transport dropped by 84 percent, and the price of a computer fell from over a million dollars in 1960 to under $500 dollars today. Cell phones, faxes, email, and the World Wide Web revolutionized communication in the last quarter of the 20th century. The availability of better, faster, cheaper, and more reliable technology catalyzed the integration of international capital markets and trade.

Technological advances were necessary but not sufficient for globalization. A liberalized international trading system was required to allow free movement of capital and labor across national boarders. The adoption of SAPs in LDCs and free trade accords such as the North American Free trade Agreement (NAFTA) and the General Agreement on Tariffs and Trade (GATT) in the industrialized nations reduced the barriers to global trade. Global tariff levels fell from 20 percent of the value of imports in 1946 to about 5 percent in the mid-1990s (Mandel, 2003). The combined effect of technological advances and liberalized trade spurred growth in foreign direct investments. Transnational corporations flourished, becoming more powerful than local, state, and national governments. Of the world's 100 largest economic entities at the turn of the millennium, 51 were corporations and 49 were nations (based on company sales from *Fortune*, July 31, 2000 and country GDPs from World Development Report 2000). Plutocracy — government by the wealthy — is fast becoming the new world order.

Effects of globalization on the poor

Based on the theory of comparative advantage, the increase in global trade should result in higher levels of output or global growth. In addition to the benefits of global specialization, foreign direct investment introduces the latest technology and intellectual capital to LDCs which results in "technology leapfrogging." Free capital flows will ensure the transfer of savings from countries with low marginal product of capital to LDCs where returns to capital investment are high. In theory, both investor and recipient reap the fruits of globalization. Consumers benefit as product range and quality improve while competition drives prices down. As nation-states become increasingly interdependent, political conflict will be reduced, and we shall all live in peace as good neighbors in a global village governed by the invisible hand of the market.

To a limited extent, some of the benefits of globalization have occurred and benefited poor countries. The cell phone boom has allowed many poor countries in Africa, Asia and South America to skip a whole generation of expensive and inefficient cable technology. Women's groups in rural Kenya are selling their unique crafts to the world over the internet. In the southern Indian cities of Bangalore and Hyderabad, the information technology sectors continue to flourish as small indigenous companies take advantage of the time difference and skilled labor to process electronic data and information overnight for American companies. However, along with many benefits, globalization has brought with it a host of undesirable elements and new dangers especially to LDCs. Again, it is hard to distinguish between the effects of SAPs and those of globalization as the two happened concurrently. While acknowledging that globalization transcends economics, our discussion here is limited to the economic impact on the world's poor.

Labor

The market-driven model of globalization assumes many small buyers and sellers. The reality of today's global markets is one of few gigantic transnational companies that have become much more powerful that most governments. Countries and communities compete for the highly mobile capital from these transnationals by minimizing labor, social and environmental costs (Bhagwati, 1994). This process has resulted in the dismal phenomenon known as the "race to the bottom". Countries with the least workplace safety laws, the toughest anti-unionization laws and the lowest taxes attract the most foreign direct investment from transnational seeking the lowest production costs. Nations that attempt to preserve high labor standards are placed at a competitive disadvantage. The comeback of sweatshops around the world in the 1980s testifies to the adverse effects of globalization on working conditions. Poor and unskilled workers are affected the most through the loss of jobs, deteriorating work conditions, lower wages, and cuts in government expenditures.

Environment

The effect of globalization on the environment is multifaceted. First, the race to the bottom phenomenon similarly applies to the environment. Countries with low environmental standards and regulations attract foreign direct investment because of the reduced costs of production. It is a winner's curse. Second, unlike locally owned businesses, transnational cooperations have little or no incentive to plow back their profits into environmental protection. The main stake-holders for transnationals are shareholders, most of who are wealthy and oblivious to the environmental impact of their investment. Third, the boom in international trade has increased the demand for transportation services and fossil fuels. World trade, as measured by value, has increased 15 fold in the last half of the 20th century from $380 billion in 1950 to $5.86 trillion in 1997 (IMF, 1997). Shipping large volumes of products and commodities over increasingly longer distances has increased the consumption of fossil fuels as well as carbon dioxide emissions and other pollution hazards. Lastly, the growing worldwide poverty has pushed more people into unsustainable use of natural resources to earn a living. More forest land is being converted to agricultural use, and more chemical inputs are being used in farming.

Equity

What is the effect of globalization on equity? Does globalization make the poor poorer? Empirical evidence has given mixed results on the question. Citing examples such as China and South Vietnam that saw "the most impressive poverty reduction in human history" as their economies opened up, Dollar (2000) argues that "to be against integration is not a rational strategy if you really want to help the poor." For Sub-Saharan Africa, the results are mixed. A study by Tsikata (2001) concludes that the impact of globalization on poor people in Sub-Saharan African countries depends on how it occurs (sequencing, pace, and government capacity) and on a government's response to it with supply-side and compensatory policies. Success stories include Ghana, Uganda and Mauritius. What is clear from all the studies is the growing inequity between Africa and the industrialized world under globalization. In relative terms, the annual average per capita income level of African countries fell from 14 percent of the level of industrial countries in 1965 to 7 percent in 1995 (Reed and Sheng, 2002). Between 1966 and 1996, the income ratio of the shares of the richest 20 percent and poorest 20 percent of the world's population has doubled from 30:1 to 60:1 (UNDP, 1996). Thus, globalization has increased the rift between the rich and the poor by concentrating wealth.

Brain drain

Most Sub-Saharan African countries have experienced an exodus of skilled labor to industrialized countries. The large income differentials with other regions of the world, coupled with increasing labor mobility has resulted in a massive "brain drain" from the continent. Excluding students pursing further studies abroad, an estimated 70,000 highly qualified Africans leave their home countries annually (Odumasi-Ashanti, 2003). Given that education is highly subsidized in most Sub-Saharan African countries, the migration implies an investment transfer from poor to wealthy nations. The HIV/AIDS pandemic, which continues to kill and incapacitate the working population, has exacerbated the situation. Without skilled labor, Africa is likely to miss out on new opportunities presented by globalization.

Volatility in financial markets

Finally, financial globalization has caused increased volatility and risk in poor countries. The Asian financial crisis was a classic example of this previously overlooked effect. The increased international flow of capital that followed global financial deregulations led to vast amounts of foreign direct investment flowing into Asia for years resulting in unprecedented economic growth. But, high speculative investment obscured internal weaknesses and wrong decisions made by Asian economic players. In April 1997, the depreciating Thai baht triggered a domino effect on the currencies of Malaysia, Indonesia, Philippines, and then South Korea. A sudden reversal in international investors' sentiment turned the Asian miracle into a nightmare overnight. Inflation skyrocketed, real incomes fell, unemployment increased, poverty incidence increased, and income inequality widened (Knowles, Pernia and Racelis, 1999).

As noted by Prasad et al. (2003), "cross-country financial linkages amplify the effects of various shocks and transmit them more quickly across national borders." Perhaps reflecting its limited integration with global financial markets, Sub-Saharan Africa has not experienced much of this economic volatility. Table 1 compares SAPs with globalization from the perspective of LDCs. While the causes are different, many of the effects are similar.

Lessons from SAPs and Globalizations

We have shown some parallels between the biggest market-driven phenomena of our time, SAPs and globalization. Both have had a tremendous effect on developing countries. While SAPs have ended, or are in their final stages, in most countries globalization is only in its infancy. We note four key lessons from SAPs and globalization that can guide present and future policy in LDCs.

Markets have limits

Under certain conditions, market allocations maximize economic efficiency. Markets are better than a central command system at signaling supply and demand conditions and coordinating the activities of a multitude of economic players. However, markets are oblivious to equity considerations and often result in the concentration of wealth and economic power as seen under SAPs and globalization. The ability of markets to deliver socially desirable goals depends on market structure, participant conduct and the resultant economic performance. As most economies liberalize markets, governments should continue their active role in facilitating trade, providing public goods, designing and enforcing antitrust laws, and redistributing wealth.

Table 1 Comparison of between SAPs and Globalization for LDCs

Attribute	Structural Adjustment Programs (SAPs)	Globalization
Phenomenon	Reduction in government spending, higher interest rates privatization of parastatals, trade liberalization, debt repayment, currency devaluation.	Intensification of economic, political, social and cultural relations across borders.
Causes/Driving force	Promoted by IMF and World Bank. Facilitated by conditional and from USA.	Improvements in transport and communication technology. Trade liberalization supported by SAPs, GATT, NAFTA.
Coverage	Sub-Saharan Africa, South America, Asia, Eastern Europe.	Worldwide, expect poor and remote areas. Limited only by access to technology.
Opportunities	Improved economic efficiency in some industries. Increase in FDI and intellectual capital to LDCs. Improved product range and quality, lower prices.	Improved economic efficiency in some industries. Increase in FDI and intellectual capital to LDCs. Improved product range and quality, lower prices.
Threats	Increased unemployment. Increased inequity within countries. Reduced government expenditure on public health, education and social welfare programs. "Race to the bottom" — lower regulations and standards attract FDI.	Increased inequity between countries, Increased inequity within countries, Loss of control of domestic economies to global trends resulting in increased volatility. "Race to the bottom"-lower regulations and standards attract FDI.
Impact on environment	Increased pressure on environment due to increased poverty.	Increased consumption of fossil fuels due to increased shipping costs and industrialization.

Policies should be pro-poor

Every economic reform program has winners and losers. Poor people continue to bear the brunt of SAPs and globalization. When designing policies, governments should focus on the impact on the most vulnerable members of society. These often include women, children, minorities, and other economically disadvantaged groups. Aggregated statistics mask the effects of economic programs on these vulnerable groups. Ameliorative measures targeting the poor should ensure food security, and provide free or subsidized education.

Protect the environment

Once a village level phenomenon, the tragedy of the commons now applies at a global scale. Economic pressures, increasing human population, and consumerism have resulted in unsustainable over-exploitation of finite natural resources at both local and global levels. As countries compete for foreign direct investment from transnational cooperations, environmental regulations are being relaxed or ignored. Developing countries are more dependent on natural resources and are especially vulnerable to their exploitation. Minimum environmental regulations should be imposed globally to avoid a 'race to the bottom' in environmental standards.

No single pill for development

For the sake of analysis, it is useful to group countries that are at the similar levels of development or in close geographic proximity. However, it is important to keep in mind that each country has a unique set of physical resources and history that impact directly on its development path. Public decision-makers should be skeptical of blanket reform processes that disregard the unique circumstances facing each economy. As volatility increases with globalization, policy markets should put in place contingency measures that will minimize the adverse effect of situations beyond their immediate control. In fact, the success of any economic system depends to some extent on its ability to deal with both endogenous and exogenous shocks.

Conclusions: Informing Choice between Imperfect Options

Our closing remarks are directed toward applied economists in their role as suppliers of information to public decision-makers. Central to this discussion is the role of markets in achieving society's desired ends. The current view, that unfettered markets are superior in achieving efficiency, growth, and welfare gains has encouraged a larger role for the private sector. But the relative roles of market-oriented versus government-oriented solutions to problems are often not well appraised. As a result, the complementarity, and need for appropriate balance of, public and private roles are not well understood.

The choice between markets and government is influenced by social, political, and economic considerations. It is not an all-or-nothing proposition. Rather than being a pure choice between markets or governments, it is usually a choice between different combinations of the two, and different degrees of one or another mode of allocating resources. If the preferred choice favors the market, government then plays a role in providing pure "public goods," contract enforcement and, if necessary, redistributive services and programs that reflect distributive justice (Wolf). If the preferred choice favors allocative decision-making by government, a significant role for the market will remain largely due to the private good needs involved and to provide support in case of government failure. In any case, without distributive justice, a democratic society eventually will face serious social unrest and disorder.

Although the choice between market and government is essentially a matter of emphasis and degree, the differences between the two have great influence on economic performance: efficiency, equity, and accountability. To this end, we follow Wolf's suggestions on several guiding propositions:

(1) As a general allocative mechanism, markets do better than governments. Market systems tend to be more efficient in the use of resources at a given point in time, and are more innovative, dynamic, and expansive over time. If efficiency were the sole policy criterion (or the only thing that counted), then many public policy problems could be solved by turning all economic activity over to markets. However, efficiency is inadequate as the sole criterion for evaluating the performance of an economy (Lang, 1980; Shaffer, 1987; Bromley, 1991). Efficiency

is the product of a unique set of values, and a power distribution embedded in the initial resource endowment. Therefore, economists would do well to make use of a broader array of performance criteria and acknowledge trade-offs inherent to their analysis when displaying the distributional impacts of alternative policies. Well-trained economists have long accepted this guideline, but too many policy participants today are innocent of this knowledge or are driven by ideology.

(2) When equity is used as a performance criterion, both market and government systems have serious flaws. Markets are impersonal. They do not consider distributional impacts (although some economists would argue so) and do not address the distributional issues associated with initial resource endowments. Similarly, governments can be flawed when equity is used as a criterion. Consider the bureaucratic behavior of centrally planned systems and its potential for favoritism, arbitrariness, and delay when making allocative decisions.

(3) If broader social-political criteria are used (i.e., participation and accountability) government in a pluralistic democracy has specific advantages over markets. Citizens can exercise their voice option to bring political consequences to bear on government. Interest groups that are well organized and financed can apply a great deal of influence in shaping the size and direction of government policy and programs.

The views we have presented here call for economists to obtain a better understanding of policy analysis consistent with a socially complex and globally integrated economy. Many in our profession are involved in economic analysis that relies primarily on the application of tools of economic theory in problem- solving. In contrast, policy analysis requires the use of a group of disciplines, recognizes a characteristic of policy decision as involving values (good and bad), and focuses on achieving a prescriptive statement about what ought to or should be done (Bonnen, 1987).

"What can markets do and what can they not do?" has long been one of the central concerns of economics as it applies to questions of public policy. Public policy issues are increasingly a part of a larger interconnected world. It may not readily be apparent that urban and rural poverty, globalization of capital, and the survival of the nation-state are connected directly to the functioning of markets. Policy questions are becoming more interrelated. Because we simply cannot draw boundaries around our applied disciplines, a broader view of societal problems must be incorporated into our analyses. The challenge for applied economists is to design and evaluate alternative institutional arrangements within an economy and, consequently, provide guidance for public and private decision-makers. Economic fads and ideology aside, it will take the combined efforts of the private sector and an enlightened public sector to solve the entrenched and emerging economic problems of our times.

References

Adger, Neil W. (1999). Social Vulnerability to Climate Change and Extremes in Coastal Vietnam. *World Development*, 1, pp. 249–269.

Bhagwati, Jagdish N. (1994). Policy Perspectives and Future Directions: A View from Academia. In *United States Department of Labor: International labor standards and global economic integration: Proceedings of a symposium.* Washington, DC, July, pp. 57–62.

Bonnen, J. T. (1989). Relevancy of the Social Sciences in the Policy Arena: Implications for Agricultural Economics. *So. J. Agric. Econ.*, 21, pp. 41–50.

Bromley, Daniel W. (1991). *Environment and Economy: Property Rights and Public Policy.* Cambridge: Basil Blackwell.

Caves, R. E. (1992). *American Industry: Structure Conduct and Performance.* New York: Prentice Hall, 1992.

Christy, R. D. (1996). Markets or Government? Balancing Imperfect and Complementary Alternatives. *American Journal of Agricultural Economics*, 62, pp. 1145–1156.

Dollar, D., and J. Svensson (2000). What Explain the Success or Failure of Structural Adjustment Programs. In *The Economic Journal*, 110, pp. 894–917.

Easterly, W. (2001). The Effect of International Monetary Fund and World Bank Programs on Poverty. Working Papers — Poverty. Income distribution, safety nets, micro-credit. 2517, World Bank.

Holm, H. H., and G. Sorensen. (1995). *Whose World Order? Uneven Globalization and the End of the Cold War,* Boulder, CO: Westview Press.

Hayami, Y. (1998). Community, Market and State. In *International Agriculture Development*, edited by Eicher, C.K., and Staaz, J.M. Maryland: John Hopkins University Press.

IMF (International Monetary Fund). *World Economic Outlook October 1997,* Washington, D.C., IMF, 1997.

Knowles, C., E. Pernia, and M. Racelis. Social Consequences of the Financial Crisis in Asia: The Deeper Crisis. Paper read at the Asian Development Bank Manila Social Forum. Philippines, November 9–12, 1999.

Lang, Mahlon G. (1980). Economic Efficiency and Policy Comparisons. *Am. J. Agric. Econ.*, 62, 4, pp. 772–777.

Lundberg, M., and L. Squire. The Simultaneous Evolution of Growth and Inequality. World Bank, December 1999.

Mandle, J. R. (2003). *Globalization and the Poor*. Cambridge University Press.

Odumasi-Ashanti, D. P. N., Africa 'brain drain': 70,000 Scholars leave yearly, *Ghanaian Chronicle* (Accra), 13. March 2003, available online at http://www.warmafrica.com/index/geo/1/cat/5/a/a/artid/208.

Pamela Sparr (2001). Making the Connections between Debt, *Economic Justice News Online*, Vol. 4, No. 3, http://www.50years.org/ejn/v4n3/gender.html.

Prasad, E., K. Rogoff, S. Wei, and M.A. Kose. Effects of Financial Globalization on Developing Countries: Some Empirical Evidence. Staff Paper, International Monetary Fund (IMF), March 17, 2003.

Reed, D. (1996). *Structural Adjustment, the Environment, and Sustainable Development*. London: Earthscan Publications Ltd.

Robertson, R. (1992). *Globalization: Social Theory and Global Culture*, London: Sage.

Shaffer, James D. (1969). On Institutional Obsolescence and Innovation — Background for Professional Dialogue on Public Policy. *Amer. J. Agric. Econ.*, 51.

Steger, M. B. (2001). *Globalism: The New Market Ideology*. Oxford: Rowan and Littlefield Publishers.

Stiglitz, J. E. (1998). Markets, Market Failures and Development. In *International Agriculture Development*, edited by Eicher, C.K., and Staaz, J.M., Maryland: John Hopkins University Press.

Stiglitz, J. E. (1992). Another Century of Economic Science. In *The Future of Economics*. Cambridge, MA: Blackwell Publishers, pp. 134–141.

Stiglitz, J. E. (1995). Economic Organization, Information and Development. In *Handbook of Development Economics Volume 1*, edited by Srinivasan. Amsterdam: Elsevier.

Sparr, P. (2001). Making the Connections between Debt, Trade & Gender. available at http://www.50years.org/ejn/v4n3/gender.htm

Tsikata, Y. M. Globalization, Poverty and Inequality. In "Sub-Saharan Africa: A Political Economy Appraisal." Technical Paper, OECD Development Centre, France, No. 183.

UNDP (United Nations Development Program), *Human Development Report 2001*, New York, 2001.

Welch, C., and Oringer, J. (1998). Structural Adjustment Programs. *Foreign Policy in Focus*, 3.

Wolf, C., Jr. (1993). *Markets or Governments: Choosing between Imperfect Alternatives*. Cambridge, MA: MIT Press.

chapter six

$\mathcal{F}$inancial Market Integration and the Fate of Small and Micro Business Lending in Emerging Economies

Mark Wenner

Financial markets play an important role in the economic development of countries. Strong correlations exist between the depth and efficiency of financial markets and rates of economic growth (Levine, 1996). In recent times, financial markets have become increasingly interlinked and integrated. Increased financial integration is but one feature of globalization. In last three decades, a wave of financial liberalization has swept most countries. In the late 1970s and early 1980s, the early reformers abandoned repressive financial policies — interest rates ceilings, high reserve requirements, credit quotas, bans on foreign ownership of banks, multiple exchange rates, repatriation of capital, repatriation of profits, deposit accounts in foreign currency — for laissez-faire policies. Many early reformers were Southern Cone Latin American countries but macroeconomic disorders combined with weak supervision and regulatory frameworks led to bankruptcies, massive government interventions, and

Mark Wenner is a micro- and rural finance specialist at the Inter-American Development Bank. The views expressed herein are personal and do not necessarily reflect those of the institution.

financial crises in the early 1980s (Diaz-Alejandro, 1985). In the beginning
of the 1990s, a larger number of Latin American countries attempted
another liberalization effort. The main difference was that at this time,
regulatory and supervisory mechanisms were strengthened to avoid the
previous type of crises. One other region, Eastern and Central Europe, in
its transition from centrally planned economies to market-oriented
economies, had a marked and rapid financial liberalization. Other regions
such as sub-Saharan Africa, Asia, and Western Europe, followed a more
gradual course of reform. But the quality and depth of reforms varied widely
from country to country (see Figure 1).

In countries with auspicious investment climates, attractive market
size, a modicum of quality infrastructure, and some political stability, net
private capital flows soared (Table 1). Countries with larger, more open,
and deeper financial markets tended to attract more private capital flows.
In 1997, 15 emerging market economies mostly in Asia, Latin America,
and Eastern Europe, received 83 percent of foreign direct investment (FDI)
whereas sub-Saharan Africa received only 5 percent (World Bank
Development Indicators, 2001).

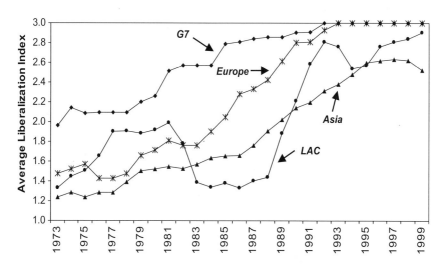

Figure 1: Financial Liberalization across Regions, 1973–1999
Source: Galindo et al., 2002a.

Table 1: Net Private Capital Flows of Selected Emerging Market Countries, 1990 and 1999 (US$ millions)

Countries	1990	1999
Argentina	−203	32,296
Brazil	563	22,793
Chile	2,098	11,851
Mexico	8,253	26,780
Czech Republic	876	4,837
Hungary	−308	4,961
Poland	71	10,452
Russian Federation	5,556	3,780
China	8,107	40632
Indonesia	3,235	−8,416
Malaysia	770	3,247
Thailand	4,399	2,471
Cote d'Ivoire	57	74
Egypt	682	1,558
Nigeria	467	860
South Africa	na	4,533

Source: World Bank Indicators 2002.

In the 1990s, FDI increased significantly for a handful of "emerging market countries." FForeign direct investment in these markets increased fourfold from 1990 to 1999, from US$200 billion to US$884 billion (World Development Indicators, 2001). However, financial crises during the decade in Mexico, the Russian Federation, Brazil, Indonesia, Thailand, and Malaysia, slowed private capital flows by decade end. After the crises, flows improved but annual growth rates did not match those of pre-crisis years for those countries nor did the distribution of private capital inflows between developing and developed countries. In 1997, a year of financial crisis in Asia, developing countries received 38 percent of world FDI. In 1999, the share fell to 21 percent. Table 2 provides a summary of leading financial indicators for selected emerging market economies.

In the wake of the global economic slowdown and the profound economic crisis in Argentina, a former paragon of neo-liberal reforms, there is a growing disillusionment with the neo-liberal paradigm of privatize, stabilize, liberalize, and democratize. Many claim that the pain of

Table 2: Core Financial Indicators of Selected Emerging Market Countries, 1990 and 1999

Emerging Country	PPP GDP Per Capita (US$)		Domestic Private Credit as Share of GDP		Interest Rate Spread (Lending Rate − Deposit Rate)	
	1999	1998–99 Per Capita Growth Rate	1990	1999	1990	1999
Argentina	11,940	−4.4%	32.4	35.6		3.0
Brazil	6,840	−.5%	89.8	51.8		
Chile	8,410	−2.4	73	72.5	8.6	4.1
Mexico	8,070	2.1	36.6	28.8		16.3
Czech Republic	12,840	−.1		62.7		4.2
Hungary	11,050	5.0	105.5	52.1	4.1	3.1
Poland	8,390	4.1	18.8	39.3	462.5	5.8
Russian Federation	6,990	3.6		32.7		26
China	3,550	6.1	90	130.6	.7	3.6
Indonesia	2,660	−1.3	45.5	60.5	3.3	1.9
Malaysia	7,640	3.3	75.7	151.6	1.3	3.2
Thailand	5,950	3.4	91.1	141.9	2.2	4.3
Cote d'Ivoire	1,540	.1	44.5	25.9	9.0	
Egypt	3,460	4.1	106.8	99.8	7.0	3.7
Nigeria	770	−1.5	23.7	19.5	5.5	7.5
South Africa	8,710	−.5	97.8	155	2.1	5.8

Source: World Development Indicators, 2001.

adjustment is very high, if not too high, there are many uncompensated losers, and that inequality is rising. Given this mood, what should be the role of the private sector in improving financial intermediation, especially intermediation benefiting the low-income, rural residents, and agriculture based firms? Should the paradigm be abandoned or should efforts be increased? This report seeks to address three questions. First, how integrated are financial markets in selected emerging economies? Second, what are the impacts of financial liberalization and observed levels of financial integration on investment efficiency and degree of credit access by small and micro- businesses, the broadest segment of firms in emerging countries? Third, what strategies and policy measures should be pursued to assure fuller participation of such businesses in the ongoing wave of financial integration?

Patterns and Trends in Financial Integration in Selected Emerging Economies

Financial integration is the process in which a country's financial market becomes more closely liked with those in other countries. It implies the elimination of barriers that prohibit the foreign ownership of banks and the ability to offer cross-border financial services such as the participation of foreign institutions in insurance markets and pension funds securities trading abroad, and direct borrowing of domestic firms in international markets. Financial integration can be achieved through formal means and de facto or informal means.

Formal membership in regional integration agreements (RIAs) such as the North America Free Trade Agreement (NAFTA) that allows U.S., Canadian, and Mexican financial institutions to operate freely in all three member states, is one example of a formal means of financial integration. CARICOM and the European Union are other examples. But this is not the most common or the most important means. The most important formal means of financial integration is a unilateral opening of financial markets, in particular, the allowance for entry of foreign owned banks and borrowings by domestic firms. The rationale for the "opening" is that foreign banks will bring more competition resulting in lower cost of funds, greater efficiency in the allocation of investments, more security for depositors because large international banks are less likely to fail than local ones, and innovations in products and services. Other ancillary benefits of foreign bank presence and general financial market liberalization is the development and adherence to better prudential norms, the creation and strengthening of rating agencies and credit bureaus, a movement to adhere to international standards of accounting and information disclosure, and transfer of management know-how and more modern information technologies.

One debatable point is whether foreign banks help stabilize or worsen host country credit and deposit crunches. Some authors claim that foreign banks, due to their access to foreign liquidity, are less dependent on erratic local deposits, and therefore can stabilize credit in the host country. In addition, foreign banks tend to enjoy a brand reputation that permits depositor-fly-to quality to occur within the domestic financial market thus helping to stabilize both deposits and credit. But others argue that foreign banks decrease their exposure to a country when domestic conditions deteriorate, increasing credit volatility. Also changes in a foreign bank's claims at home or in other countries can spill over to the host country. In many cases, the home countries of foreign owned banks have extensive trade relations with the host country. A drop in import demand in the foreign owned bank's home country can contract external demand as well as contribute to local credit reduction.

Degree of foreign bank ownership as a proxy for financial integration

One of the easiest indicators of financial integration is the extent of foreign bank presence in a country. Since only a handful of regional integration agreements are explicit about financial integration (NAFTA, CARICOM, and European Union), foreign bank penetration can serve as a proxy. In Table 3, 47 percent and 41 percent of bank sector assets in Latin America (excluding off-shore banking centers such as The Bahamas, Cayman Islands, and Panama) and Transition Economies are foreign owned (See last column in table). The region with the highest degree of intra-regional integration is Europe with 15.9 percent. Other regions of the world do not exhibit such a high degree of penetration.

In Latin America, most of the foreign bank entrants are Spanish (Banco Santander Central Hispano (BSCH) and Banco Bilboa Vizcaya Argentaria (BBVA), Canadian (Nova Scotia) and American (Citigroup and Fleet Boston Financial Corporation). The three countries with the highest degree of foreign bank entry in 2001 were Mexico, Argentina, and Peru, where foreign banks account for more than 50 percent of total bank assets in each country (IDB, 2002). Other countries that surpass the 50 percent mark are Czech Republic, Hungary, and Poland. These six countries can be said to have a very high degree of financial integration using our proxy of foreign bank ownership of assets (Table 4).

Table 3: Percent of Bank Sector Assets Owned by Foreigners in Given Host Region and by Asset t Source Region, 2001 (Percent)

Host Region \ Source Region	Africa & Middle East	Asia & Pacific	Latin America[2]	USA & Canada	Transition Economies[3]	Europe[4]	TOTAL
Africa & Middle East	7.68	0.14	0.00	1.89	0.03	3.66	13.39
Asia and Pacific	0.05	1.32	0.00	1.22	0.00	3.30	5.89
Latin America[2]	0.11	0.23	1.47	18.81	0.06	26.64	47.32
USA & Canada	0.08	0.68	0.03	0.95	0.00	8.61	10.34
Transition Economies[3]	0.01	0.26	0.02	4.45	1.39	34.69	40.82
Europe[4]	0.34	2.49	0.03	3.34	0.02	15.89	22.11
TOTAL	0.34	1.64	0.05	2.47	0.02	11.25	15.77

Source: Estimates based on data from Fitch IBCA's Bankscope database.
[1] Ownership data reflect changes up to July 2001 while balance sheet data are the most recent available.
[2] Excludes The Bahamas, Caymand Islands and Panama.
[3] Includes economies in transition from central and eastern Europe.
[4] Excludes Europe in transition.
[5] Excludes Czech Republic, Hungary, Korea, Mexico, Poland and Slovakia.
Source: Bankscope op. *cit.* Galindo, Micco, Serrá, 2002.

Table 4: Importance of Foreign Bank Ownership in Selected Emerging Markets and Developed Countries in 2001

Region	Total Assets (US$ Billions)	Number of Banks	Share of Total Bank Assets Foreign Owned (%)
European Emerging Market			
Czech Republic	50.3	21	92.99
Hungary	28.2	29	68.84
Poland	85.4	39	63.58
Turkey	156	45	6.68
Latin American Emerging Markets			
Mexico	156	38	76.53
Argentina	166	97	54.5
Peru	20.1	17	53.75
Chile	77.1	28	43.71
Brazil	397	138	30.61
Asian Emerging Markets			
Malaysia	180	51	16.76
Korea	496	27	8.73
Thailand	155	23	6.37
Indonesia	87.4	67	4.92
China	1,090	37	.21
Developed Countries			
United States	10,800	744	10.3
Japan	8,720	211	.02
Sweden	557	28	.42

Source: IDB estimates based on data from Fitch IBCAA's Bankscope database.

One of the reasons that the Spanish banks dominate the other foreign entrants in Latin America is similarity in legal code (both Spain and Latin American countries share the same Napoleonic or French civil code vs. Anglo-Saxon common law code for American based-banks)(Galindo et al. 2002b). Legal and institutional differences across countries increase entry costs and reduce the participation of banks in foreign countries. Galindo et al (2002) found that controlling for variables usually used in the analysis of determinants of bilateral trade and FDI flows significantly reduced foreign banking activity between countries that have different legal origins. Also, differences in banking regulation and institutional framework (corruption, law enforcement, the burden of regulations and the efficiency of the judiciary system) between the source and host country reduced cross border banking.

Impact of Financial Liberalization and Financial Integration

Financial liberalization and financial integration impacts several variables of concern: investment efficiency (i.e. whether firms with higher marginal returns to capital receive more investment or external financing); economic growth rates; and access to external financing by small and medium scale firms. This section reviews the literature for patterns.

Impact on investment efficiency

The micro-evidence on the effect of financial liberalization on resource allocation is limited. Jaramillo, Schiantarelli, and Weiss (1992) using panel data of Ecuadorian firms during the 1980s found an increase in the flow of credit accruing to more efficient firms after liberalization, controlling for other firm characteristics. Siregar (1992) obtained the same results for Indonesian establishments in the 1980s. Chari and Henry (2002), using firm level data for Jordan, Korea, Malaysia, and Thailand, show that the typical firm experienced an increase in investment after liberalization.

Galindo, Schiantarelli, and Weiss (2002c) using firm level data for 12 developing countries — Argentina, Brazil, Chile, India, Indonesia, Korea, Malaysia, Mexico, Pakistan, Philippines, Taiwan, and Thailand — find that financial liberalization in the majority of cases leads to an improvement in resource allocation. This conclusion holds for different measures of marginal returns and of financial liberalization. This relationship is robust when using a sales based index and when other potential determinants of investment efficiency, (i.e. trade liberalization and financial stability) are included in the econometric analysis.

Impact on economic growth

Rajan and Singales (1998), using industry level data, show that sectors with a greater need for external finance, grow faster in more liberalized and financially developed countries. Demirguc-Kunt and Maksimovic (1998) show that firms in countries with a more developed financial system grow at a faster rate relative to a benchmark growth rate that would hold in the absence of external finance. Levine has produced a number of papers that show that aggregate growth rates are positively correlated with degree of development of financial markets. Galindo, Micco, and Ordoñez (2002a), show results similar to Rajan and Singales but go further and determine which of the two components of financial liberalization, reform of domestic banking and stock markets or opening of capital accounts, are more important. They find that liberalization of domestic markets is the key component in explaining faster growth in external finance intensive sectors. In addition, they also find that countries with weak legal protections for creditors do not take full advantage of possible effects of liberalization.

Impact on small business lending

Financial liberalization and the entry of foreign banks in particular, can affect the small and medium enterprises (SME) sector through two channels, one direct and one indirect. The direct channel involves a lowering of the cost of funds in the domestic market as foreign banks through greater operational efficiency and access to external liquidity can offer lower rates of interest or firms can borrow directly from overseas banks. The more technically efficient firms (high marginal rate of return to capital) in the SME sector, theoretically should be able to access these funds, probably not internationally but from banks operating in the domestic market. In short, the entry of foreign banks expands the size of the financial market. In practice, however, SMEs are collateral constrained, have management weaknesses, and tend to operate in super competitive, low margin markets, and thus are not attractive clients for foreign owned banks. Many times, foreign owned banks enter a country to finance a multinational corporation from its same home country and is a long-time preexisting client in local currency to allow that client to avoid currency mismatches. Secondarily, the foreign owned bank may "cheery pick" the local market by attracting the better host country corporations who may need hard currency financing by offering better terms than domestic banks can. In some cases, such as Banco Santender and Banco Bilboa Vizcaya in Latin America, the corporate strategy is different. It is more retail oriented and consumer lending is aggressively pursued.

The indirect channel, is where domestic banks have been forced "down market" by foreign owned banks who have lured away their "better corporate clients" or eroded their market share in the "consumer finance segment." Theoretically, one can reason that the displaced domestic banks either have to become more operationally efficient to compete with the foreign banks or they have to look for underserved niches in the marketplace. Two huge underserved niches are small- and medium-sized businesses that demand US$5,000 to 1,000,000 loans and microenterprises that demand loans up to US$5,000. Most business surveys estimate that small (fewer than 50 employees) and micro- (fewer than 10 employees) businesses easily account for more that 50 percent of all employment and in some countries approach 80 percent. More important, SMEs and microenterprises are accustomed to paying high informal rates of interest and so the domestic bank does not have to compete on price as much as it would in the consumer and corporate market segments. In practice, however, domestic banks are reluctant to enter the SME and microenterprise markets because radically different lending technologies are needed, reliable information on SMEs and microenterprises is expensive to gather, provisioning requirements may be ill suited, guarantees are problematic, and legal enforcement mechanisms are weak. In short, the information, risk, and transaction costs obstacles of serving these two sectors are daunting if expansion into these segments occurs.

Empirically the record is mixed and no conclusive econometric results can be drawn on the impact of foreign bank entry and SMEs. A recent study by Berger et al. (2001) finds that small businesses in Argentina were less likely than larger ones to receive credit both from large banks and from foreign banks. However, also analyzing the case of Argentina, Escudé et al. (2001) find that while foreign banks dedicate a smaller share of the lending portfolio to SMEs, they lent almost half of the total credit to this sector in the year 2000. Clarke et al. (2002), studying a larger set of countries, find that foreign banks in Argentina, Chile, Colombia, and Peru generally lent a smaller fraction of their funds to SMEs than domestic banks in the late 1990s. Nonetheless, they find that differences between foreign and domestic banks were far less pronounced for large banks than for small banks in all four countries and that in some instances large foreign banks (Chile and Columbia) appear to have lent more to SMEs than large domestic banks. Mester (1997) argues that advances in credit scoring methodologies coupled with enhanced computer power and data availability will revolutionize small and microbusiness lending. This technology allows large banks to overcome the diseconomies associated with SME and microlending, as was the case in Chile and is suspected for Colombia. Even if foreign banks do not lend directly to SMEs, evidence suggests that the indirect channel works. Jenkins (2000) in a survey of 78 countries, finds that 44 percent of those banks that lent to small and microenterprises indicated that changed market conditions and increased competition in lending to large enterprises were the two most important reason for doing so. Bonin and Abel (2000) provide similar evidence consistent with this argument in the case of Hungary, one of the most financially integrated economies. In short, a U shaped curve may exist, wherein to the left, small banks dominate in small business lending because relationship lending technologies are commonly used and information is costly to generate and share. As banks get bigger, small business lending declines because of the high unit costs associated with traditional lending technologies. Then at the far right, large banks that use modern, cost reducing lending technologies such as credit scoring can profitably engage in small business lending.

Policy options and strategies for improving access for small and medium enterprises

In summary, the benefits of financial globalization are (1) increases in the supply of capital that can smooth consumption at the country level and provide access to lower cost of funds for domestic borrowers; and, (2) improvements in the financial infrastructure such as convergence to international accounting standards, improved corporate governance through closer monitoring by shareholders of managers, imposed market discipline and competition because investments can easily shift from one country to the other, deepening of financial markets through increase in the scope of financial products, instruments, and services, and transfer of new management practices and information technologies. Evidence exists that shows that increased financial integration contributes to faster economic growth at both the aggregate level and at the firm level. Further evidence exists that suggest the investment efficiency increases after financial liberalization.

On the other hand, the risks of increased financial globalization are increased frequency of financial crises in countries that have liberalized and possible contagion that lead to output losses. Evidence suggests financial crises today are more frequent compared to the Gold Standard Period (1880–1913) and the Bretton Wood Period (1945–1971) but equivalent to the Inter-War Period (1919–1939). Nonetheless, the average duration and output losses are less compared to previous historical periods (Bordo, Eichengreen, Klingebiel, and Peria, 2001). Domestic factors tend to be more important in financial crises, especially unsound macro- and financial fundamentals (fiscal deficits and inflation) and are often exacerbated by weak banking supervisory authorities and weak contract enforcement mechanisms. What seems to be of more concern is the risk of contagion because a country can be "virtuous" in the sense of having good macroeconomic fundamentals but still fall victim. Contagion, namely shocks that are transmitted across borders, is primarily caused by disturbances in trade and capital flows, but non-fundamental factors such as herding and speculative behavior on the part of investors can play a role. Financial linkages between countries can exacerbate the situation and obviously the stronger the linkages, the worse the contagion. For example, banks and mutual funds can spread crises across countries as the sellout of shares in companies that are based in the crisis country or decide to stop lending and/or to write-off losses in the crisis country by foreign banks resulting in depressed stock value in the parent holding company and income losses due to repayment problems in the crisis country. This then may trigger a liquidity or credit crunch in a neighboring contagion country where branches of the same foreign owned bank operate. The more dominant the foreign owned bank is in the country and the less dependent the foreign bank is on the mobilization of local deposits, the worse the problem is in the contagion country. The more open a country, the more channels of transmission for contagion.

In terms of impact on small business lending, rural lending, and incomplete data prevent conclusive statements, but in general financial globalization does not seem to have had a dramatic and direct positive impact across a large number of countries on SME. There is evidence to suggest that some positive benefits have been realized (Clarke et al., 2001). In the case of Chile, foreign bank entry lead to the introduction of credit scoring technologies that allowed SMEs to be attended. No explicit data are available on how many rural SMEs benefited. The question becomes what should we do to mitigate the risks of contagion and financial crises and what should we do to improve access for SMEs, especially rural ones that are more risky than urban-based SMEs.

Option 1: Restrict capital movements but continue to promote banking and integration

This view holds that cross-country capital flows should be restricted because inefficient international financial markets debilitate the argument for lassez-faire, unregulated financial intermediation, as has been the case. Anomalies such as asymmetric information, moral hazard, asset bubbles, speculative attacks, herding behavior, and contagion are present in international financial markets and have deleterious effects. Open economies suffer from these market imperfections and corrections or buffers are needed. Crises in the 1990s show that countries that are similar in size and trade dependence but with different fundamentals and institutional settings are similarly punished. As a response, Krugman (1998), Tobin (2000), and Stiglitiz (2000) argue that governments should intervene to restrict capital movements across countries, and that such restrictions can be socially beneficial. Capital controls as imposed by Chile and Malaysia are held up as examples of "intelligent" controls (i.e., minimum amount of time a capital inflows must remain in country before it can be repatriated as a means to avoid speculative attacks and the use of unremunerated reserves requirements to give the Central Bank an opportunity to undertake a more independent monetary policy). Governments can mitigate the cost of volatile capital flows, reducing excessive risk taking and making markets more resistant to external shocks while at the same time continuing to pursue banking integration, in order to capture the documented benefits.

The critique of this argument is that the literature is quite mixed on the efficacy of capital controls, and if the controls are efficacious it is only for a short period of time and only in the case of small external shocks (Soto, 1997; Gallego, Hernandez, Schmidt-Hebbel, 1999). As time passes investors find ways of circumventing the controls and the distortions induced exact high costs of the economy in terms of foregone growth.

Option 2: Strengthen the domestic financial sector and sequence liberalization

Another view concentrates on risk management and mitigating microeconomic imperfections. This view argues that opening a weak domestic financial sector to large capital movements is too risky. If the domestic financial sector does not manage risk properly, does not have sufficient reserves, or does not have the right incentives, large capital inflows and outflows can create severe problems in the domestic financial sector. Foreign bank competition can debilitate local financial intermediaries and obliterate "information capital" that local lenders have developed over time in the absence of large and well-functioning credit bureaus. Since financial crises can be very costly, this view proposes an adequate regulation and supervision of the domestic financial system without distinguishing between foreign and domestic capital. Active management of reserve requirements and implementation of contingent liquidity arrangements are additional proposals under this option.

In addition, to rethinking how and when financial liberalization occurs, this approach places heavy emphasis on mitigating microeconomic imperfections, namely asymmetric information, high levels of risk, and high levels of transaction costs that stifled domestic financial intermediation targeting the small and microbusiness sectors, the naturally most risky niches. Assuming that economic policies biases are not so grave as to eliminate profitability in many informal and rural productive activities, the specific reforms are listed below.

- Improved secured transactions frameworks that would lower the costs to create, perfect, and enforce security or creditor claims rights and allow a wider range of moveable property to be used as effective collateral (i.e., accounts receivable, equipment, livestock, commodities, inventory) and permit the introduction of new liquidity enhancing instruments such as securitization.

- Enhanced credit information systems that would capture indebtedness and repayment patterns for moderate- and low-income individuals so as to permit the use of credit scoring technologies as a substitute for traditional, high-cost loan evaluations on individual clients demanding small loans.
- Consolidate and modernize deed registries to lower the costs of searches and registration of property. At present in many countries, multiple registries exist and systems are manual, requiring physical visits to all registries to assure that no prior liens or mortgages exist on the collateral proffered. Also, the act of registering property can be overly complex and costly for moderate and low-income clients.
- Create mechanisms that would allow indigenous peoples to pledge collective lands by delegating the authority to the tribe to punish individual defaulters or to insure individual defaulters and thus avoid falling into the politically unpopular choice of having to foreclose on collective parcels or refusing to lend to indigenous peoples prima facie because they lack individual land titles.
- Create a roster or registry for the ceding usufruct rights on a particular parcel of land. Indigenous peoples in Latin American and Asia and much of sub-Saharan Africa would benefit greatly from a legal recognition and codification of user or lease rights.
- Strengthening price and production risk management systems so that intermediaries are not discouraged from lending for agriculture. Specific proposals include piloting of index based and area yield insurance products, futures, options, and inventory (warehouse receipts) as feasible means to diminish risk in rural economies.
- Reform civil commercial codes so that agricultural input suppliers, traders, and agroindustrial processors can assume a larger role as non-bank intermediaries. At present in many countries, agricultural input suppliers and food processors play an important role in on-lending funds from formal banks to small agricultural producers through interlinked contracts but are liquidity constrained due to inability to have pledged mortgages and liens transferred from themselves to banks in an expeditious manner.
- Reform the judiciary system to expedite the processing of creditor claims.

- Remove embargos on the pledging of homesteads.
- Continue to strengthen banking superintendencies and create non-bank superintendencies for microfinance institutions and credit unions so that sound and robust financial systems can be built.

Conclusions

Financial globalization is not a new phenomenon in the world; it is a process that started with the invention of trade finance. What is different is the depth and breadth of financial globalization today. The volume of FDI flows in the 1990s was unprecedented. The degree of financial integration in Europe is high and the amount of FDI investment flowing to the banking sectors of Eastern Europe and in Latin America is impressive. Six emerging market countries, Mexico, Argentina, Peru, Hungary, Poland, and the Czech Republic have over half of total banking assets in their respective systems owned by foreigners. They can be considered the most financial integrated developed countries.

Financial integration has clear and well-documented benefits but also implies risks, namely vulnerability to more financial crises and contagion. The record shows that the frequency of financial crises has increased in the 1980s and 1990s, but the severity in terms of duration and output losses is not as severe as in other historical periods. In terms of the impact of financial integration on SME access to credit, the main channel that financial integration seems to work is indirectly. Foreign banks force domestic banks to move "down market" and penetrate underserved niches. The empirical evidence is limited but suggests that SMEs have benefited from financial integration and the entry of foreign banks into local banking markets. In terms of rural SMEs, disaggregated data are not readily available but they are presumed to be more disadvantaged than urban SMEs in gaining access to formal bank credit since formal banks normally tend to have their branches concentrated in larger cities. Only when the country is predominately agrarian do you see more rural bank branching. The countries that have tended to be more financially integrated have tended to have a larger urban population.

The lessons seem to be the following. Much of the discomfort with financial integration stems from the liberalization of capital accounts and less so from the removal of restrictions on banking (Schmukler and Zoido-Lobat-n, 2001). Thus, one primordial objective is to reduce the negative impacts of volatility in movements of capital flows, yet to continue to promote financial integration in the banking and stock markets. In the case of rural SMEs, it is critical to expand the frontier of formal finance. Foreign bank entry can force domestic banks "down market" but formidable legal, economic, and institutional barriers exist that need to be attacked systematically.

The more promising of two policy options is to manage risk and to deepen domestic financial markets by carefully sequencing liberalization, strengthening prudential norms and bank supervision capacities, and removing legal and institutional imperfections that conspire to make SMEs and microenterprises — both urban and rural but more so rural ones — undesirable credit clients. The proposed reforms essentially strengthen creditor property rights, introduçe new risk management tools, and widen the class of collateral acceptable to intermediaries. In conclusion, financial globalization should not be rejected but it should be better managed.

References

Berger, A. and G. Udell (1995). Relationship Lending and Lines of Credit in Small Firm Finance. *Journal of Business*, 68.

Berger, A., L. Klapper, and G. Udell (2001). The Ability of Banks to Lend to Informationally Opaque Small Businesses. *Journal of Banking and Finance*, 25(12).

Bonin, John and István Abel, *Retail Banking in Hungary: A Foreign Affair?* Wesleyan University manuscript, 2000.

Bordo, M, Eichengreen, B., Klingebiel, D., and Martinez-Peria, M. S. (2001). Financial Crises: Lessons from the Last 120 Years. *Economic Policy*. April.

Chari, A. and P. B. Henry (2002), Capital Account Liberalization: Allocative Efficiency or Animal Spirits? NBER Working Paper No. 8908. April.

Claessens, Stijn, Asli Demirguc-Kunt, and Harry Huizinga (2001). How Does Foreign Entry Affect Domestic Banking Market? *Journal of Banking and Finance*, 25.

Clarke, George, Robert Cull, Maria Soledad Martinez Pería, and Susana Sánchez (2002). Bank Lending to Small Businesses in Latin America: Does Bank Origin Matter? World Bank Finance Working Paper No. 2760, Washington, D.C.

Clarke George, Robert Cull, and Maria Soledad Martinez Peria (2001). Does Foreign Bank Penetration Reduce Access to Credit in Developing Countries? Evidence from Asking Borrowers. Mimeo.

Demirguc-Kunt, A. and Maksimovic, V. (1998). Law, Finance, and Firm Growth. *Journal of Finance*, 53, pp. 2107-2137.

Diaz-Alejandro, Carlos (1985). Good-bye Financial Repression, Hello Financial Crash. *Journal of Development Economics*, 19.

Escudé, Guillermo, Tamara Burdisso, Marcelo Catena, Laura Dámato, George McCandless, and Tomas Murphy (2001). Las MIPyMes y el Mercado de Crédito en la Argentina. Documento de Trabajo Nro. 15, Banco Central de la República Argentina.

Galindo, A., Micco, A. and G. Ordoñez (2002a). Financial Liberalization: Does it Pay to Join the Party? *Economia*, forthcoming.

Galindo, A., Micco, A., César Serra (2002b). Better the Devil that You Know: Evidence on Entry Costs Faced by Foreign Banks. Research Department, Inter-American Development Bank, Washington, D.C.

Galindo, Arturo, Fabio Schiantarelli, Andrew Weiss (2002c). Does Financial Liberalization Improve the Allocation of Investment? Micro Evidence from Developing Countries. Research Department, Inter-American Development Bank, Washington, D.C.

Gallego, F., Hernandez, L., and Schmidt-Hebbel, K. (1999). Capital Controls in Chile: Effective? Efficient? Endurable? Mimeo Central Bank of Chile.

IMF (2000). The Role of Foreign Banks in Emerging Markets. In *International Capital Markets, Developments, Prospects and Key Policy Issues*.

Inter-American Development Bank (2002). Financial Integration. In *Economic and Social Progress Report*. Inter-American Development Bank, Washington D.C.

Jaramillo F., F. Schiantarelli, and A. Weiss (1992). The Effect of Financial Liberalization on the Allocation of Credit: Panel Data Evidence for Ecuador. Policy Research Working Papers, The World Bank, WPS 1092.

Jaramillo, F. F. Schiantarelli, and A. Weiss (1994). Capital Market Imperfections Before and After Financial Liberalization: An Euler Equation Approach to Panel data for Ecuadorian Firms. *Journal of Development Economics*, 51, pp. 367–386.

Jenkins, Hatice (2000). Commercial Bank Behavior in Micro and Small Enterprise Finance. Development Discussion Paper No. 741. Harvard Institute for International Development, Harvard University.

Kaminsky, G. and S. Schmukler (2001). On Booms and Crashes: Financial Liberalization and Stock.

Kaufmann, D., Kraay, A. and P. Zoido-Lobaton (2002). Governance Matters II: Updated Indicators for 2000/01, The World Bank.

King, R. and Levine, R. (1993a). Finance, Entrepreneurship and Growth: Theory and Evidence. *Journal of Monetary Economics*, 32, pp. 513–542.

King, R. and Levine, R. (1993b). Finance and Growth: Schumpeter May Be Right, *Quarterly Journal of Economics*, 108, pp. 717–737.

Krugman, P. (1998). Saving Asia: It's Time to Get Radical, *Fortune*, pp. 74–80.

La Porta, Rafael, Florencio Lopez-de-Silanes and Andrei Shleifer (1997). Legal Determinants of External Finance. *Journal of Finance*, 52, pp. 1131–1150.

La Porta, Rafael, Florencio Lopez-de-Silanes and Andrei Shleifer (1998). Law and Finance. *Journal of Political Economy*, 106, pp. 1113–1155.

Levine, Ross (1996). Foreign Banks, Financial Development and Economic Growth. In Barfield, C. (ed.), *International Financial Markets*, Washington, D.C.: AEI Press.

Mester, Loretta J. (1997). What's the Pont of Credit Scoring? *Federal Reserve Bank of Philadelphia Business Review*, pp. 3–16.

Rajan, R. and L. Zingales (1998). Financial Dependence and Growth. *American Economic Review*, 88(3), pp. 559–586.

Schmukler, S. and Pablo Zoido-Lobatón (2001). Financial Globalization: Opportunities and Challenges for Developing Countries. World Bank, Washington, D.C., Mimeo.

Siregar, M. (1992). Financial Liberalization, Investment, and Debt Allocation, unpublished Ph.D. Dissertation, Boston University.

Stiglitz, J. E., (2000). Capital Market Liberalization, Economic Growth, and Instability. *World Development*, 28, pp. 1075–1086.

Tobin, J. (2000). Financial Globalization. *World Development*, 28, pp. 1101–1104.

World Bank. *World Development Indicators 2001*. World Bank, Washington, D.C.

Market Cycles. World Bank Working Paper.

Part Three

Achieving Sustainable Communities

chapter seven

$\mathcal{E}$ssential Forms of Capital for Achieving Sustainable Community Development

Daniel V. Rainey
Kenneth L. Robinson
Ivye Allen
Ralph D. Christy

The 1990s saw rural communities in the United States lose many manufacturing jobs. Rural areas were losing manufacturing jobs well before the 2001 recession started in March of that year (Henderson). Overall employment growth in rural areas has lagged that of metropolitan areas since 1995. The majority of the growth that has occurred has been in the service and trade sectors. However, the trade sector had even begun to decline in the last quarter of 2001 (Henderson). Much of the losses in the trade sector were due to the economic slow down across the country. However, the decline in manufacturing activity is likely the result of other forces that rural leaders need to address before they can change the direction of their local economies.

Changes in production technologies and management strategies in the past 10 to 20 years have changed such that companies no longer produce

Daniel V. Rainey is Assistant Professor in the Department of Agricultural Economics at the University of Arkansas at Fayetteville. K. L. Robinson and R. D. Christy are research associate and professor, respectively, in the Department of Applied Economics and Management, Cornell University, Ithaca, NY. Ivye Allen is Chief Operating Officer at MDC, Inc., Chapel Hill, NC.

This chapter was published in the *American Journal of Agricultural Economics*, Vol. 85, No. 3, August 2003, pp. 708–715.

many of their intermediate goods internally. Instead production of intermediate components has been outsourced to companies with a comparative advantage in producing those components. The comparative advantage could arise due to specialized technologies owned or patented by the contracting company. Alternatively, the comparative advantage could be due to lower production costs that develop from lower wages or governmental regulations in different locations.

This new management philosophy has led to production of many of the intermediate goods being manufactured in components across diverse geographic regions, creating global networks of production processes (Weinberg). Harrison (1997) stated, "The business system is increasingly taking the form of lean and mean core firms, connected by contract and handshake to networks of other large and small organizations, including firms, governments and communities" [cited in Weinberg].

Though changes in communication and transportation technology have made it possible for most locations to take part in the global economy, some feel that rural communities are deficient in other categories that are necessary for local economies to survive. Porter, in his 1990 book The Competitive Advantage of Nations, proposes that clusters play a significant role in economic growth. Porter defines clusters as, "geographic concentrations of interconnected companies, specialized suppliers, service providers, firms in related industries, and associated institutions (e.g., universities, standards agencies, trade associations) in a particular field that compete but also cooperate." (Porter, 2000, p. 15).

Rural areas by definition do not have a concentration of anything in the Porter sense, with the exception of agricultural and natural resources, and would appear to be limited to a minor role in the growing global economy. However, Isserman points out that over the past 50 years many rural communities have grown into metropolitan areas. His research indicates that while many rural communities will continue to stagnate and decline, many more will grow and blossom into thriving metropolises. The following sections present the foundation needed by communities to develop sustainable economic growth. But first let us give a brief definition of sustainable community development.

Sustainable development encompasses a set of policies and activities that work together to create economic vitality, environmental stewardship and social equity. Economic vitality implies increasing and strong standards of living during current times as well as the ability to adjust to changes over time so that local operators and individuals remain globally competitive. Environmental stewardship implies that current and future activities do not degrade the resources such that the communities become less productive and/or attractive over time. Social equity entails encouraging development that will benefit all segments of local society. This implies educational training that prepares current and future laborers to not only meet current employee needs but to be capable of becoming entrepreneurs and rapid adapters of new technology.

Components of a Sustainable Community Development Strategy

For rural communities to succeed in the global economy they must be able to compete not only with other rural communities both at home and abroad, but also with urban areas. Technological advances in communication and transportation have enabled rural communities to overcome the problems of geographic and information isolation.

While globalization and new technologies opens opportunities for rural communities to develop, it does not ensure that development will occur. Weinberg states for rural development to succeed, in a global environment, three things are essential: "human capital, physical infrastructure, and adequate financing." We combine physical infrastructure and adequate financing together under financial capital (public and private) and add another element — social capital. Each of these elements is discussed more fully in the following sections.

Financial capital

Public capital

A building block in a community's sustainable economic development strategy is adequate infrastructure. Though new technologies exist to reduce the communication and transportation problems that have isolated rural locales, communities need infrastructure to implement those technologies. Increasingly this means access to high-speed data transmission, digital communication equipment, international airports, and overnight transportation services (Weinberg).

In regards to sustainable economic development policies, Harrison (1997) states, "I also define 'productive' local economic development policy (as contrasted with a tax-and wage-cutting race to the bottom, in which localities compete with one another by reducing their standard of living) as the building of stronger attractors for catching multilocational or networked capital. This is done by providing high-quality infrastructure — roads, bridges, waste disposal, telecommunications, transportation — and highly skilled labor." (p. 33)

Communities that want to participate in the global economy must be able to provide access to quality communication and transportation infrastructure. Communities that are deficient in those areas will find themselves at a considerable disadvantage for attracting and/or maintaining firms in a global environment.

Kantor (1995) states, "Professionals are recruited on a national and international basis; companies need to make sure that their home city has maximum amenities and minimum problems in order to compete for talent in a global labor market." In addition to adequate infrastructure, sustainable community development should also include clean, safe communities with plenty of recreational, entertainment, and cultural amenities.

However, advanced infrastructure and quality amenities cannot be developed without the resources to pay for the improvements. This poses a problem for many rural communities because of their limited tax base and the sensitivity of firms to high tax rates. However, research has shown that when taxes are raised to make improvements in infrastructure and/or labor quality, communities may become more attractive to locating firms (Aschauer; Eberts, 1986, 1991; Gerking and Morgan; Miller and Russek). This is not to imply that raising taxes alone has a positive impact on development. Holding everything else constant, higher taxes will tend to have a negative impact on capital investment. However, if higher taxes are used to make investments in public services that improve the productivity of private capital, the negative impact of the high taxes may be diminished or overcome by the positive productivity benefits (Rainey and McNamara, 2002).

Private (Equity) capital

Many rural communities have existing small firms that could compete competitively in the global economy. But many of these small businesses have not taken part in the global economy because they have been undercapitalized by existing financial institutions (Weinberg). Those small firms also have been overlooked by state agencies that tend to provide technical assistance to medium and large size firms (Weinberg; Rainey and McNamara, 1997).

An important facet of many of these small businesses is that they are "anchored to the community" through personal ties of the owner/operator (Rainey and McNamara, 1997; Weinberg). As such they are less likely to relocate their facilities to other locations, thus providing more security for jobholders and the local tax base. These firms also tend to have more economic connections to the local economy (Rainey and McNamara, 1997). In their research on strong home towns, Irwin, Tolbert and Lyson (1997) found that institutions like small manufacturing establishments, small retail gathering places, and similar businesses enhance "rootedness" by encouraging connections among diverse groups and making connections between individuals and their community. They conclude that places characterized by strong social institutions, including small businesses, may be more likely to retain a core of nonmigrating residents which could help maintain long-term population growth and economic health.

Historically, local banks serviced rural communities. These banks had personal connections to the community and its businesses. However, banking deregulation and improved technology have combined to decrease the number of local community banks in rural areas. The larger state and national banks that have moved in do not have the ties to the local community and are more likely to provide fewer business loans in rural areas. Another reason bigger banks lend less in rural communities is it is less costly to make one large loan as opposed to several smaller loans. Sustainable communities will need to develop small business leaders that are able to access equity markets in a competitive global environment.

Human capital

The association between human capital and economic well-being is derived from the early work of Schultz (1961). Schultz's research suggests that economic growth is largely the result of investments in human capital. Schultz argues that increases in the capital-income ratio are largely due to human capital development, not material capital (i.e., reproducible, nonhuman capital) which was originally thought to account for all increases in income and subsequent economic growth. The premise of his argument is that by giving too much weight to material capital, the large increases in real earnings of workers, which represent a return to the investment that human beings make in themselves, are overlooked. He suggests that investments in human knowledge and skill are the critical determinants of economic growth and are necessary if regions lacking human capabilities ever expect to attract and fully benefit from infusions of new capital.

Researchers studying economically disadvantaged regions like the South continue to cite human capital, or the lack thereof, as the reason for low earnings and high poverty rates among low income populations and individuals living in rural areas (Schultz, 1961; Moen, 1989; Jensen and McLaughlin, 1995; Stallmann, et al., 1995). Describing areas with low human capital, Harbison remarks:

Capital and natural resources are passive factors of production; human beings are the active agents who accumulate capital, exploit natural resources, build social, economic, and political organizations, and carry forward national development. Clearly, a country which is unable to develop skills and knowledge of its people and to utilize them effectively in the national economy will be unable to develop anything else (as quoted in Hansen 1979).

Today, global competition and technological advancement necessitate that machinery and labor continuously change to meet consumer demand and competitive pressures. To accomplish this global firms implement flexible organizational structures and high-performance work practices (Weinberg). These structures and practices include work teams, flexible job assignments, and information sharing between labor and management (Applebaum and Batt, 1994; Jones and Kato, 1995). High-performance work practices rely on skilled workers (Weinberg, Porter, 2000).

No matter how powerful the computer hardware and how user-friendly the software; most functions provided by computers (such as word processing, spreadsheets, database management, computer aided design, robotic manufacturing, global positioning systems) still require hands-on human contact to be productive (Gordon). It is the ability to effectively use the advances in technology that will determine which communities will flourish and which will be left behind. Communities that are able to train and/or attract a technologically competent labor force will be better able to attract and retain globally competitive firms.

Social capital

Prodded by persisting rates of poverty and growing levels of inequality, policy makers, program planners and social scientists alike are now looking beyond conventional market-driven policy solutions to alternative, more equitable and balanced forms of development. In recent years, social capital theory has begun to receive widespread attention as a possible alternative to neoclassical explanations for regional differences (Putnam, 1993; Flora, 1995; Fukuyama, 1995). Social capital theory is situated in a growing body of literature that seeks to challenge the idea that only the market-driven path of development can lead to improved social and economic conditions. Social capital theory explains development from a structural rather than an economic perspective. Its emphasis on the "embeddedness" within which economic relations take place is based on the notion that both individual and group decisions are embedded in a particular social context, which includes community traditions, norms, networks and the like (Granovetter, 1985). Literature in the structural tradition is divided into three primary strains, each focusing on some aspect of the organization of economic production and the individual and household opportunities it provides (Lobao, 1990). One of the strains, upon which this research is based, focuses on the effects of small firms, regional trade associations, industrial districts, and local entrepreneurs on community well-being. It examines the association between the organizational embeddedness of small-scale, locally-controlled, economic enterprises and community well-being. Research by Putnam (1993) and others suggests that the relationship between organizational embeddedness and sociocultural factors can help determine why some regions flourish while others remain underdeveloped.

Globalization and Its Impact on Sustainable Community Development

Globalization is the process by which national boundaries are becoming less significant in regards to the location or production of economic activity. Production is much less dependent on access to natural resources and materials but is ever more determined by the knowledge of individuals and entities to produce or assemble goods from whatever resources are available locally or purchased from abroad.

Michael Porter stated in his recent article on the location of economic activity, "It is widely recognized that changes in technology and competition have diminished many of the traditional roles of location. Resources, capital, technology, and other inputs can be efficiently sourced in global markets. Firms can access immobile inputs via corporate networks. It no longer is necessary to locate near large markets to serve them." (Porter, 2000, p. 15).

Global production is becoming increasingly more dependent on the creation, management, analysis, and dissemination of information. Communities that rely on natural resources are becoming less significant in global production unless they also are able to produce and effectively utilize new information and technology.

Globalization's impact on key components of sustainable development

The rapid changes taking place in the global economy have already had a significant impact on rural communities and will continue to affect how communities develop in the future. Hundreds of communities have lost textile and light industrial activity to lower-cost overseas sites. As the United States continues to enter into bilateral and multilateral trade agreements, competition will only intensify in these and other industries. The following sections discuss the implications of these developments on the importance of the three forms of capital (human, financial, and social) that are essential for sustainable community development.

Financial capital

Two forms of financial capital are public and equity. Public capital is the tax and fee revenue collected by governments to provide public services. Equity capital is the availability of equity financing available in the local market.

Recent research has indicated that communities with good quality and management of public services are more likely to be successful in sustaining stable and growing economic bases. Historically, when development agents discussed public capital it meant water and sewer capacity and transportation infrastructure. These areas are still necessary for future growth in the global economy, but a more important factor is the availability of information and communication infrastructure.

In today's market place, firms are constantly sharing and receiving information from vendors and customers. Access to up-to-date information is essential for most companies to operate efficiently and competitively in the current economy. Communities that cannot provide access to digital infrastructure will find their economy in a very vulnerable position.

Businesses also need access to equity capital for updating equipment and for normal operating expenses. However, several forces have taken place over the last decade to threaten access to equity capital for small business entities. Bank deregulation and the subsequent flurry of bank mergers have had a significant impact upon how capital markets operate in smaller economies. Towards the end of the 1990s several bank mergers occurred where larger national banks bought out or merged with many of the smaller local banks across the country. These mergers have resulted in a decline in the number of loans being determined at the local level. The close interaction and personal contacts that local residents have or had with their local bank are no longer taken into account when seeking capital for business upgrades. Those loan applicants must now compete with a bigger pool of applicants which requires small local businesses to become more professional in how they present their expansion plans to lending officers. For those that are successful, this development has likely made these companies more competitive as they become more adapt at managing financial resources. However, there are likely some small businesses that would have remained in business if the local contacts had remained in place, but are now going out of business. Sustainable communities will be able to find institutions to assist these small firms more effectively as they compete in the global market.

Human capital

Most rural communities have simply provided the bare basics in primary and secondary education and many have not done a good job of doing that. This has led to a work force that has not been able to adjust quickly to technology changes. These workers also are less able to think of creative ways to make the production process more efficient. In many of today's production techniques, line workers are required to make adjustments during the production process and to work in teams on ways to improve productivity and solve problems as they arise. However, many workers have not received the critical thinking skills to function in these environments. For communities to develop sustainable economies they must develop workers who can make creative adjustments to the production process and adapt new technology quickly.

Entrepreneurial activity is another area in which improved human capital will play an important role. Research over the past several decades has indicated the importance of small firms in economic growth (Birch, 1987). Though there is much debate over the relative importance of small firms' impact on economic growth (Harrison, 1997), there is little doubt that rural communities will have to rely more upon small scale and medium size firms due to their inability to attract larger production facilities.

Successful entrepreneurship requires individuals who are not only risk takers but visionaries and effective managers as well. Successful entrepreneurs are visionaries in that they are able to identify new markets for existing products/services and/or create a demand for new products/services. This requires skills in creative thinking and market and product analysis. Management skills are needed to run the day to day production and insure proper financial decisions.

Social capital

Small towns, particularly those in the U.S. South, have been plagued for decades with a lack of social capital. According to Wilkinson (1988:72), the problems of the South, for example, reflect, in part, a crisis of community, which cuts across the whole of local social and economic life, involves jobs and income as well as services and group life and affects the quality of social relations among people who live and work together. He warns that "The effects of this historical context of everyday life in the South continue, despite much change, to constrain the potential for cooperation among local population segments." In this respect, we refer to the open inclusion of everyone in the decision making process, a functioning local network where entrepreneurs and business leaders can share problem solving strategies, and governments that seek the best interest of the entire community as opposed to special interest of a connected elite.

Sustainable communities include everyone in the decision making process. Many local economies have stagnated or declined because leaders are too concerned about protecting the special interests of a small group of business leaders. Decisions must be made to benefit the entire community; and for this to happen, formerly excised segments of the community must be brought into the strategic planning process at the beginning not as mere cheerleaders after the decisions have been made. Lyson and Young (n.d.) elaborate on this theme in an analysis of the effects of structural pluralism on community well-being. In their study of economic well-being among U.S. counties, they find that structural pluralism — the degree to which a diversity of associations and population segments may participate in political debate — tends to be associated with higher income and lower rates of poverty and income inequality. They argue that these results are possible because structural pluralism influences the kinds of economic organizations that locate and stay in a community, the diversified employment structure that it encourages and the types of poverty-oriented agencies that the community adopts. They conclude that the link between structural pluralism and economic well-being suggests that economic outcomes cannot be reduced to aggregated individual behaviors. Unless business and local leaders work together rather than serving their own special interests, communities will continue to waste time and resources as different segments of the community struggle to obtain the upper hand concerning key decisions.

Sustainable communities have well functioning business and community networks. Cited as two of the most important ingredients needed to revitalize regional economic growth, network-building and collaboration among small and medium-sized enterprises is now seen as a prerequisite for communities attempting to achieve the economies of scale necessary for participating and competing in the global economy (Rosenfeld, Bergman and Rubin, 1989, p. 63). Admitting that the policy of branch plant recruitment and its dependence on nondurable manufacturing has become less effective in today's worldwide marketplace, Rosenfeld and his colleagues (1989) suggest that program planners and policymakers should do more to actively encourage the kind of collaborative networks that characterize industrial districts. Because regions home to industrial districts (e.g., the "Third Italy," Spain, Germany, and Denmark) generally fared well during the global economic crisis of the 1970s and early 1980s, researchers have begun to look at industrial districts for what they might reveal about perspectives and ingredients for development. For Harrison (1992:477), the logic behind industrial districts is that "proximity promotes the 'digestion' of experience which leads to trust which promotes recontracting (and the sharing of common support services) which ultimately enhances regional growth." He further points out that trust enables firms to "relate to one another by interpenetrating one another's formal organizational boundaries, rather than solely through the price-mediated exchange of commodities. The result is that firms plan together, bid on contracts together, and receive technical, financial and other services from the 'commons' together, rather than on a firm-by-firm basis." Moreover, economic actors and agents are willing to 'take a chance' on doing business with one another because of the belief that one party will not take undue advantage of the other by changing the rules of the game in mid-stream. By contrast, without viable networks, once a party has entered a business deal, it takes on a risk that an investment or hiring decision may become dead weight if the relationship does not proceed as planned. Businesses within a network, however, have support to solve internal and external business problems as well as links to resources.

Sustainable communities have effective governments. With the rapid changes that are taking place in the global economy, local leaders must become more proactive in identifying local resources and how those resources can be put to productive use in the new economic environment. The relationship between sustainable communities and effective government is introduced in Putnam's (1993) work on the institutional performance of regional governments in Italy. Using the term "civic community" to describe the link between institutional performance, patterns of civic involvement, and social solidarity, Putnam (1993) provides empirical evidence to show how norms and networks of civic engagement affect the performance of government institutions and prospects for regional development. Putnam's civic community thesis is based upon the social capital approach, which assumes that economic behavior is determined by the social context within which it occurs. Social capital theorists maintain that economic behavior is motivated by beliefs, values, and traditions that occur outside of the market. They take the position that the kinds of social structures that make, sanction, and enforce social norms benefit not only the person or persons whose efforts would be necessary to bring them about, but all those who are part of such a structure (Coleman 1988: S116).

Governments must also serve the entire community. For example, prior to the civil rights movement, the political, social, and economic structure in the southern U.S. was extremely stratified, across racial and demographic lines. Because certain population segments were typically excluded from mainstream social and economic institutions, many residents today are less productive than others. Research by Rosenfeld et al. (1989) suggest that counties with large black populations are less well off in terms of. economic growth than counties with smaller black populations. They find that counties with the fastest employment growth between 1977 and 1982 were those with low minority population. Likewise, their analysis of employment growth from 1977 to 1984 suggests that counties with a minority population of one-third or more are especially slow growth areas. In fact, counties with more than 50 percent minority population had an annual growth rate of only 1.1 percent compared with 2.1 percent for counties with less than 25 percent minority population. More than one-half of the counties with populations more than 50 percent black are classified as "persistent poverty" counties by the U.S. Department of Agriculture. Persistent poverty counties are defined as counties in which the poverty rate rate has exceeded 20 percent in each decennial census since 1960. As communities seek to create sustainable economies, they must insure that their populations are effective producers.

Global competition is also driving governments to be more efficient in providing services. High taxes and fees or poor public services can be a deterrent to attracting new economic activity. Local governments of sustainable communities need to provide good services with a small tax base. Many governments have already cut taxes significantly in recent years; now they must make sure that the quality of services does not diminish.

Examples of Sustainable Community Development

Following are examples of sustainable community development efforts. These communities looked within themselves and formed networks across business, public, and social strata to find ways to stop the economic decline in their area. In fact, the local networks and community cooperation have been so effective that the local economies have begun to expand.

Morrilton, Arkansas

Morrilton is a small rural community in central Arkansas with a population of about 7,000. In the spring of 1999 the city was rocked with the announcement that two of its major employers were shutting down: Levi Strauss operated an apparel plant that made jeans and had operated in the city for over four decades; and Arrow Automotive, which rebuilt engine starters and alternators in its plant for nearly three decades.

The overwhelming majority of the employees at the two plants had no more than a high school diploma and many had not obtained even that level of education. Most of the workers had only worked in their respective plant. The workers had specialized skills for their industry but were not transferable to other activities. In addition, the two industries represented by the plants — apparel and automotive parts manufacturing — are rapidly declining in the U.S. as production is being shifted to other countries with lower wages and fewer regulations. Many small communities have collapsed when facing similar situations and several analysts thought Morrilton would do the same.

However, four years earlier, city leaders began the process of creating a sustainable community in Morrilton. Mark KcKuen, the current economic development officer for the local chamber of commerce, attended a meeting where he learned the importance of community involvement and strong leadership. He read the writing on the wall for the city's labor force and was prepared to take the lead in aiding the newly unemployed.

When the plants announced their closings, the city immediately began finding new jobs and providing training and assistance to the displaced workers. Knowing that it would be impossible to find immediate employers to replace the closing facilities, the city organized a job fair that brought employers from surrounding towns to the city. Workers were fortunate that the closings occurred during a strong economic expansion nationally, and labor markets were tight across the region.

To address longer-term needs of finding new industries to locate in Morrilton, the city raised funds and purchased land to build a new industrial park. Leaders obtained a grant from state and federal sources to provide infrastructure to the new industrial park. Just a year after the park's completion a new firm announced its intentions to locate there. The city also obtained outside assistance to provide digital infrastructure to a closed grocery store, which allowed a national customer service center to locate in the city.

The city worked with the local community college to update the skills and knowledge base of the displaced workers. The college made adjustments to its class schedule so that many of the community's residents could take class at night or on weekends to upgrade their skills. The technology classes currently offered will enable the city to recruit higher paying jobs in the future.

Morrilton has participated in several leadership-training programs and conducts an annual local leadership development school that trains residents and leaders on the importance of effective governance. The leadership school also educates current and future leaders on the resources available from state and federal programs. Students spend a significant portion of the program focusing on the future of Morrilton and Conway County and developing a strategic plan toward that future.

Hot Springs, Arkansas

Hot Springs is a small city in southern Arkansas that was once a popular vacation area because of its natural hot springs and legalized gambling. However, the state outlawed gambling in the early 1960s and the city went into a slow decline. By the late 1980s most of the hotels and stores on Main Street had been boarded up, and many of the young families were departing for Little Rock or Dallas for better employment opportunities.

The primary cause of the decline in the city was the elimination of the gambling industry and local leaders neglecting to seek other avenues for economic opportunity. There was little change in leadership philosophy from the 1960 to the 1980s; the primary development strategy was to lobby state leaders for the reestablishment of legalized gambling. Little effort was put into developing infrastructure and human capital for other opportunities.

That all changed in the early 1990s when several younger, aspiring leaders forced a change in government and focused development on the city's strengths. The city had several natural amenities — the hot springs, lakes, mountains, and forest — as well as its size and low cost of living. The new leadership set out to develop a tourism and retirement industry and to develop the city into a regional health and retail trade center.

Though Hot Springs declined significantly from the 1960s, in the early 1990s it was still the largest economic area within a 45-mile radius. The city raised over $1 million for downtown revitalization and economic development initiatives. The city's natural amenities and low cost of living made it a popular destination for relocating retirees who helped stimulate the local health and retail sectors; and today Hot Springs is one of the most visited communities in the state and hosts several regional and national conventions.

The city does not focus on any particular industry for development but does look for firms that will complement the city's existing industrial base. Leaders work with local and regional educational institutions to help identify industries that will fit the community's resources. Working with the University of Arkansas Medical School enabled the city to land a biotech firm out of Houston. The city and university continue to work together to bring other biotech firms to the area.

Local leaders also convinced the technical college and community college in the area to merge to take advantage of synergies that existed. The merger also allowed the two institutions to stop fighting over revenue sources and focus more on providing educational needs in the community.

The leadership actively looks for opportunities that will enhance and diversify the local economy. While Hot Springs has an active industrial recruitment program, unlike most cities it does not offer industrial incentives. The natural amenities and productive workforce provide enough incentive for the size of firms the city recruits. This strategy allows the city to improve the quality of services being offered as the economy expands.

Setting the proper environment for sustainable community development

Creating a sustainable community development program requires participation from local residents as well as local and regional institutions and agencies. Individuals across all segments of the community must get involved in the decision-making and strategic planning process. Public agencies must be proactive and efficient. Similarly, local and regional private institutions must work together to form a cooperative environment for making a positive change in the community and abandon their turf wars.

One of the primary roles public institutions play is improving the human capital of current and future workers. Curriculums must emphasize critical thinking abilities. Rural educational systems can no longer focus on providing the bare basics to meet state educational requirements. If they are to take an active part in creating sustainable communities they must be proactive in insuring that students not only understand basic math and science, but also can think creatively and work within groups to solve problems.

Educational systems must also put emphasis on providing basic technology training. Almost every industrial sector involves some form of electronic technology to operate efficiently. Communities that provide a technically sophisticated workforce will position themselves well for economic advancement.

Educational institutions also need to help foster strong entrepreneurial skills in order to enhance local economic opportunities. Many rural communities are not able to attract outside investment and will have to develop from within or face continued decline or stagnation. Development from within requires strong entrepreneurial activity.

State and federal educational agencies can help foster the adoption of more advanced curriculum by setting guidelines and raising minimum curriculum standards. Communities have typically resisted to educational programs mandated by federal and state agencies, but many communities have not made adequate investments in human capital. Local institutions can reinforce the importance of improved education and act as a liaison between the governmental agencies and local residents resistant to requirements imposed from outside the community.

The lack of advanced technical infrastructure is becoming an increasing hindrance to many communities's ability to develop sustainable economies. Global businesses require instant access to information from around the world. Communities seeking to create sustainable economies must provide industrial clients the ability to connect to high speed transmission lines and other forms of digital infrastructure.

Many rural school systems need financial assistance to develop improved curricula, particularly as it relates to technology advancements. Technology grants and aid for salary support is needed from state and federal sources. Aid also is needed in providing infrastructure improvements in many rural locations.

The local chamber of commerce, Small Business Administration, lending institutions, local banks and branches of national banks, must work with smaller businesses to ensure that they know how to access equity markets. The continued operation of many of these institutions in small communities is dependent on the competitiveness and survivability of these small local businesses. This is particularly true as communities try to develop entrepreneurial talent.

Though almost everyone agrees that both human capital development and economic development are essential components of any local development program, the verdict is still out on social capital — or the need to promote "a sense of community." Perhaps this is because of the fragmentation or isolation among groups that often characterizes economically disadvantaged communities. Or, it could simply reflect the notion that "community" is a much more nebulous quality to understand than is human or physical capital. In any event, if government authorities want to help communities address local development needs they must design a set of policies that cultivates and enhances the capacity of civic community-oriented organizations.

Pulver's (1995:59) call for "economic development literacy" is a step in this direction. According to Pulver, any comprehensive strategy to address economic development issues must include an economic development literacy program. Such a program is designed to provide educational and technical assistance in understanding community economic development policy to local government officials, community organizations, and private business people. The intent of economic development literacy programs is to enable local communities to understand critical changes in global economic forces, analyze their specific economic problems and opportunities, and build comprehensive strategies to address them. They also help citizens transform their own neighborhoods by nurturing leadership from within those communities, often through what Harris (1996:26) refers to as the "organizing tradition." The organizing tradition involves local residents teaching and recruiting each other to organize and become actively involved in community problem-solving activities, rather than relying on charismatic leaders or well-meaning volunteers, who may have little firsthand knowledge of the community. In building greater local capacity among themselves, residents become better equipped to make informed decisions about the future health and welfare of their communities.

References

Applebaum, Eileen, and Rosemary Batt (1994). *The New American Workplace*. Ithaca, NY: ILR Press.

Aschauer, D. A. (1990). Highway Capacity and Economic Growth. *Economic Perspectives: A Review from the Federal Reserve Bank of Chicago*, 14, pp. 14–24.

Bates, Timothy (2002). Government as Venture Capital Catalyst: Pitfalls and Promising Approaches. *Economic Development Quarterly*, pp. 49–59.

Birch, David (1987). *Job Creation in America*. New York: Free Press.

Coleman, James S. (1988). Social Capital in the Creation of Human Capital. *American Journal of Sociology*, 94, pp. S95–S120.

Eberts, R. (1986). Estimating the Contribution of Urban Public Infrastructure to Regional Growth. Working paper 8610, Federal Reserve Bank of Cleveland.

Eberts, R. (1991). Some Empirical Evidence on the Linkage between Public Infrastructure and Local Economic Development. In *Industrial Location and Public Policy*, edited by H. Herzog and A. Schlottmann, pp. 83–96. Knoxville, TN: The University of Tennessee Press.

Gerking, S., and W. Morgan (1991). Measuring Effects of Industrial Location and State Economic Development Policy: A Survey. In *Industrial Location and Public Policy*, edited by H. Herzog and A. Schlottmann, pp. 31–56. Knoxville, TN: The University of Tennessee Press.

Gordon, Robert J. (2000). Does the "New Economy" Measure Up to the Great Inventions of the Past? *Journal of Economic Perspectives*, 14, pp. 49–74.

Hanushek, Eric A. and Dennis D. Kimko (2000). Schooling, Labor-Force Quality, and the Growth of Nations, *American Economic Review*, 90, pp. 1184–1208.

Harris, Fredrick C. (1996). Will the Circle Be Unbroken? The Erosion and Transformation of African American Civic Life. Institute for Philosophy and Public Policy, pp. 20–26.

Harrison, Bennett (1992). Industrial Districts: Old Wine in New Bottles? Regional Studies, 26, pp. 469–483.

Harrison, Bennett (1997). *Lean and Mean*, New York: Guilford Press.

Henderson, Jason R. (2002). Will the Rural Economy Rebound with the Rest of the Nation. *Economic Review — Federal Reserve Bank of Kansas City*, 87, pp. 65–83.

Jones, Derek and Takao Kato (1995). The Productivity Effects of Employee Stock-Ownership Plans and Bonuses: Evidence from Japanese Panel Data. *American Economic Review*, 85, pp. 391–414.

Irwin, Michael Tolbert, Charles, and Lyson, Thomas, (1997). How to Build Strong Home Towns, *American Demographic*.

Kantor, Rosabeth (1995). *World Class*. New York: Simon & Schuster.

Lyson, Thomas A., and Frank W. Young. *Structural Pluralism and Economic Well-Being*. Ithaca, New York: Cornell University Press.

Miller, S., and F. Russek. (1997). *Fiscal Structures and Economic Growth at the State and Local Level*. *Public Finance Review*, 25, pp. 213–37.

Porter, Michael. (1990). *The Comparative Advantage of Nations*, New York: Free Press.

Porter, Michael E. (2000). Location, Competition, and Economic Development: Local Clusters in a Global Economy. *Economic Development Quarterly*, pp. 15–34.

Pulver, Glen C. (1995). Economic Forces Shaping the Future of Rural America. In *Investing in People: The Human Capital Needs of Rural America*, edited by Lionel J. Beaulieu and David Mulkey. Boulder, CO: Westview Press, pp. 49–64.

Putnam, Robert D. (1993). *Making Democracy Work: Civic Traditions in Modern Italy*. Princeton, NJ: Princeton University Press.

Putnam, Robert D. (1993). The Prosperous Community: Social Capital and Public Life. *The American Prospect*, 13, pp. 35–42.

Rainey, Daniel V. and Kevin T. McNamara (1999). Taxes and Manufacturing Site Location Decisions. *Review of Agricultural Economics*, 21, pp. 86–98.

Rainey, Daniel V. and Kevin T. McNamara (2002). Tax Incentives: An Effective Development Strategy for Rural Communities? *Journal of Agricultural and Applied Economics*, 34, pp. 319–325.

Rosenfeld, Stuart A., Edward M. Bergman, and Sarah Rubin (1989). *Making Connections: After the Factories Revisited*. Research Triangle, NC: Southern Growth Policies Board.

Schultz, Theodore W. (1961). Investment in Human Capital. *The American Economic Review*, 51, pp. 1–17.

Weinberg, Adam S. (2000). Sustainable Economic Development in Rural America. *Annals of the American Academy of Political and Social Sciences*, 570, pp. 173–85.

Wilkinson, Kenneth P. (1988). The Community Crisis in the Rural South. In *Rural South in Crisis: Challenges for the Future*, edited by Lionel J. Beaulieu. Boulder, CO: Westview Press.

chapter eight

Innovative Community Strategies in Sustainable Agriculture and Natural Resource Management: Landcare in South Africa

Monique L. Salomon

"You cannot discover the ocean unless you have the courage to loose sight of the shore."

—Anonymous

The eyes of the world have been focused on South Africa since its first democratic elections, in 1994. How will this young democracy address the injustices of the past and create opportunities for all its citizens, and at the same time gain its rightful place in the global economy and become a strong competitor in the world market? Emerging economies such as South Africa are challenged to address the needs and demands of the poor and destitute, and at the same time provide products and services that compare and compete with the First World.

This report argues that governments and civil society can learn from trends in market research. People with different lifestyles require different levels of service and care. Practitioners are challenged to review the

Monique Salomon is director of the Farmer Support Group, a development organization in sustainable agriculture and natural resource management in South Africa based at the University of Natal.

premises behind projects to alleviate poverty and environmental management. Notions of community participation and ownership in natural resource management are unpacked. The work of the Farmer Support Group is introduced. The Okhombe Landcare project shows that complex problems cannot be solved with simplistic answers and confirms the many critical issues raised by practitioners and scientists.

South African Lifestyles in a Global Economy

Worldwide, emerging economies are growing at twice the pace of the industrialized West. Their populations are young and possess growing household spending power, often moving from peasantry to full-blown consumers in a short time. South Africa is both a transitional society and an emerging economy. The first democratic elections were held in 1994, and the new sociopolitical order has brought about incredible social changes. Globalization of trade, information and computing has stimulated pockets of strong economic growth and human development, in some cases up to the level of industrialized countries (Burgess).

Burgess uses the concept of social identity to explain a wide range of commercial, social and political attitudes and behaviours in South African society. He argues that the complex nature of social identity, rather than racial differences, explains the choices people make. He undertook a survey of 3,500 households. Researchers held in-home personal interviews probing into people's propensity to experience certain situations, identity characteristics, demographic characteristics, and values.

The study revealed four major lifestyle typologies and 16 more detailed subgroupings. The lifestyle types are Rural Survivalists, Emerging Consumers, Urban Middle Class, and Urban Elite. Rural Survivalists form some 26 percent of South Africans. They live far from the major cities in the rural areas. Their lifestyle is mainly agrarian, producing their own food and engaging in informal trade and barter. Most Rural Survivalists are Black South Africans. Traditional tribal life and customs are very important. Many live in abject poverty and could not survive without the financial support from family members living in the metropolitan areas. Four sub-groups of this typology are: Agrarian Lifestyles; Border Survivalists; Highveld Survivalists; and KwaZulu Natal Survivalists.

Emerging Consumers (39 percent) are poor, but have reached a basic standard of living that includes running water, electricity and a flush toilet. However, development is low, with only 20 percent having hot water. They are mainly Black and Coloured, among which five sub-groups are: Free State Emerging; Matchbox Suburban Youth; Gauteng Township Youth; Cape Coloured Emerging; and Prime Skills.

The Urban Middle Class (21 percent) has electricity, running water, a flush toilet, a geyser and a car. Many also have a television, hi-fi music system, refrigerator-freezer, telephone and microwave oven. Four sub-groupings of this typology are: East Coast Settlers, The Believers, Suburban Bliss, and Suburban Challenge.

The Urban Elite (8 percent) live a lifestyle that competes with their counterparts in Europe and North America. Their homes show a high state of development. Most have personal computers at home and half of those are linked to the Internet. The Urban Elite is divided into three sub-groups: Earth Mothers; Family Focus; and Achievers.

These lifestyle groupings can be used for market segmentation and service strategies. The Urban Elite is settled and happy. They aspire to standards of living, and levels of service and care, that compare with their peers in developed countries. The Urban Middle Class are on the edge of consumer society, and are coping in different ways. They can afford what many others consider luxuries. Emerging Consumers, the largest group in South Africa, have survival needs filled but struggle in difficult economic circumstances. Programmes to empower people through basic education and enhancement of skills can make them employable and uplift their standard of living. The Rural Survivalists have just the most basic of needs. Self-help, small enterprise and other educational programmes, especially directed at women, can make a difference to them.

Dimensions of poverty

According to Chambers and Topouzis, "The poorer people are hard to reach. They are typically unorganized, inarticulate, often sick, seasonally hungry, and quite frequently dependent on local patrons. They are less educated, less in contact with communications, less likely to use government services, and less likely to visit outside their home areas than their better-off rural neighbours. Further, they are relatively invisible, especially women and the children." Having household members in both urban and rural areas is an important risk-reduction strategy.

At least four schools of thought can be distinguished around the causes of poverty.

- Domestic policy management: Internal factors in a country are seen as main cause of poverty such as price discrimination against agriculture produce, inefficient bureaucracies, insufficient or inappropriate investment in rural infrastructure.
- Political culture and governance: Ineffective government, weak accountability particularly to rural constituencies, and active repression of autonomous development are causes of poverty.
- Lack of resources, debt and economic structural adjustment: Poverty is understood primarily in terms of economic forces, social relations, property rights, and power. War, destabilization, discriminating terms of trade, and post-colonial clauses are constrains to development and reform.
- Population growth, climate and resources: Food shortages and environmental degradation occur as a result from rising populations and poor resource management (Whiteside; Chambers).

Different interpretations lead to different development interventions. Those who see social causes of poverty may seek to change social and property relations. Those who see physical causes of poverty may seek programs in soil conservation, family planning, and resettlement.

Chambers proposes a pluralist approach, which is empirically based and recognizes multiple causation, multiple objectives, and multiple interventions. He describes the situation of poor rural people as a struggle against five interlocking disadvantages that trap them in deprivation:

- Poverty: Defined as lack of wealth or assets, and low, unreliable, seasonal, and inadequate flows of food and cash (food insecurity);
- Physical weakness: The high ratio of dependents to able-bodied adults;. the dependents may be young children, old people, the sick (with a rapid increase in people living with HIV/AIDS) or handicapped;
- Vulnerability: The lack of buffers against contingencies such as social conventions (e.g. dowry, weddings and funerals), disasters (man-made or

natural), physical incapacity (e.g. sickness, child bearing, and accidents), unproductive expenditure (e.g. alcohol, drugs, bad judgement).

- Isolation: Peripheral location, either in an area remote from town and communications, or removed from the village and the center of trading, discussion, and information. Often illiterate and without a radio, rural poor are not well informed about events beyond their neighbourhood.
- Powerlessness: Rural elites intercepting benefits intended for the poor, the ways in which the poor are robbed and cheated, and the inability of poor people to bargain, especially women, and those who are physically weak, disabled, or destitute.

He continues to argue that, for rural projects to be successful and effective in poverty reduction, a shift in focus is needed towards projects that are:

- Small;
- Administration intensive rather than capital intensive;
- Difficult to monitor and inspect. Those will be highly dispersed and focused on the formation of groups or the construction of small items of infrastructure;
- Slow to implement. Local participation implies going at peoples' pace. Poor people often take time to realize what they can achieve and to become organized;
- Not suitable for complex techniques for project appraisal.

Much of the aid and investment programs, however, still point in other directions. Decentralization, simple appraisal procedures, and direct exposure of officials to village life can help refocus on projects that benefit the poor people (Chambers).

Community-Based Natural Resources Management

In the year 2000, agriculture in South Africa constituted 4 percent of the national formal economy, employing 30 percent of the workers and contributing to the economy in terms of manufacturing, services in rural towns, and consumer spending. The informal economy, particularly in rural areas, is closely linked to the productivity of land. Land degradation is an important concern, and is costing the country dearly.

Desertification and land degradation in South Africa are the result of a combination of factors: inappropriate policies and legislation in the past; inappropriate management structures; land tenure systems that do not encourage responsible stewardship; bad management practices, particularly in agriculture; high population densities relative to the available resource base; poverty and the livelihood strategies adopted by the rural people to survive; lack of, or inappropriate government support; and ignorance.

Degradation of veld in terms of changes in plant species composition (including less palatable grassland, bush encroachment, and alien plant invasion) is more prevalent in commercial farming areas. Loss of biological and economic productivity of land (including deforestation, loss of plant cover, and soil erosion) is strongly associated with the former "homelands." Large numbers of people, with few resources, had to scrape a living from these lands. This coincided with the breakdown of traditional institutions that would normally regulate communal tenure.

Many individuals and households living in rural areas still rely on locally available natural resources such as fuel wood harvesting and subsistence agriculture. Cropping on marginal land, particularly on erosion sensitive soils, and heavy grazing in arid areas contributes to land degradation (Farmer Support Group).

In 1998, the South African Department of Agriculture launched the Landcare program as "an innovative approach for promoting sustainable land management." It distinguished between Landcare as government-supported program and Landcare as an approach. The Landcare approach is defined as aiming at:

- Community-based natural resource management;
- Building partnerships between the public community and private sectors;
- Local economic development through employment creation, and access to technical information and advice;
- Greater productivity, food security and poverty relief;
- Integrated and innovative approaches to natural resource management;
- Addressing the needs of formerly disadvantaged groups.

Main strategies employed in the national Landcare program are: major works in land and water degradation; capacity building; awareness; policy and legislation; and research and evaluation.

The concept of community-based natural resource management is debated among both scientists and practitioners. Bell describes community-based natural resource management as a wide range of activities from collection of wild caterpillars in communal woodland to commercial farming of genetically modified maize on private land. He makes a distinction between informal and formal resource use. The informal sector is based on rules, laws, and policies that are unwritten and flexible; resource tenure is often characterised by communal access. The formal sector is based on written laws and policies; resource tenure tends to emphasise individual (private) access. The term community-based natural resource management is commonly used by formal sector practitioners and refers to resource use systems that:

— Include a significant element of communal, as opposed to private, resource use;
— Are sustainable in terms of ecosystem and biodiversity conservation, economic viability, skills and capacity, and sociopolitical viability;
— Distribute benefits from resource use equitably through the community;
— Have some degree of democratic processes and a significant element of communal, as opposed to private, resource use.

Ostrom seems to focus more on formal resource use when she lists design principles for effective management of natural resources requiring:

• Clearly bounded and relatively homogeneous groups;
• Clear rules of operation;
• Collective decision making;
• Overt monitoring systems; and
• Clearly agreed and applied sanctions (Peters).

Peters challenges this distinction between formal and informal resource use as artificial. She describes resource users generally as highly heterogeneous, and resource system boundaries as flexible and difficult to define outside particular circumstances. She also states that one often finds competing interpretations of principles and rules governing claims and use, and patterns of use that are flexible and negotiable related to highly variable ecological conditions and embedded in complex social and political relations.

Thus, the term "community" in community-based natural resource management is contested and by many considered as misleading. Dore, et al., describe the notion of community as referring to individuals and groups who collectively make up the social groupings of a locality, region, or nation. The term implies that social cohesion or identity exist, which is generally not the case at all. In recent debate, the concept of "governance of natural resources" is used.

Governance of Natural Resources in South Africa

Until a century ago, the Southern African region was largely dominated by the informal sector and by informal resource use systems, which changed drastically through the colonial experience. Community-based natural resource management developed here out of two modes of thinking:

— The conservation strand, which developed in an attempt to recreate a set of economic and social incentives that would motivate rural communities living with wildlife to participate in preventing illegal off-take; and
— The social equity strand, which the primary motivation was to redress the problems of rural poverty and inequitable access to resources (Bell).

The South African Landcare program seems to lean more towards the equity strand in community-based natural resource management.

The Farmer Support Group is a civil society organization in South Africa that has been working in community-based natural resource management for over a decade. The national Department of Agriculture's Landcare program has provided it with a new label and government funding to support its work. The Farmer Support Group's Landcare program involves projects in land rehabilitation, wetland management, sustainable farming, enterprise development, and youth development in the communities of Okhombe, Mbongolwane, Mpumalanga township, Ngazana, and Amaswazi in the province of KwaZulu-Natal.

The Farmer Support Group has been working with the Okhombe community since 1999 to address land degradation. The Department of Agriculture has funded the Okhombe project through the Landcare program. Activities focused on the promotion of sustainable farming practices, grazing management, and soil conservation measures, and on building capacity within the community to continue the work. Over 400 people have been employed for periods of four to six months to control soil erosion, rehabilitate dongas and revegetate degraded areas. Three community facilitators were appointed and trained to initiate capacity building and income generating activities. Training focused on Landcare principles, permaculture, nursery management, grazing management, and institutional development. A job creation facilitator was appointed to monitor work teams and Landcare facilitators and liaise with groups and committees. In 2001, a group of 25 volunteers formed the Okhombe Inthathakusa Monitoring Group. Their mission is to continue to promote sustainable management of natural resources among community members. They are currently monitoring the structures built by the project and developing plans for new land rehabilitation and conservation works.

Framework for intervention in landcare

"The development paradigm which we are articulating here has little to do with the transfer of resources ... development is about facilitating resourcefulness ..." (Kaplan)

Based on experiences in Landcare and years of work in integrated catchment management, the Farmer Support Group has developed a framework to guide interventions in Landcare. Four main areas of intervention have been identified in Landcare, each covering a range of activities: sustainable land use; entrepreneurship; Landcare ethos; and structures for collective action. Figure 1 illustrates these interventions undertaken within the Okhombe Landcare project. The diagram also indicated that work in Landcare is highly diverse and complex and that facilitation of such processes requires a wide range of skills or competencies.

Sustainable Land Use

Project activities are aimed at analyzing existing land use practices of individuals (e.g., homestead gardens, cropping fields) and communal practices (e.g., community gardens, grazing management, landscape). Appropriate technologies are needed for ecologically sound cropping and

Figure 1 Areas of intervention in med Okhombe Landcare project

livestock management, other sustainable land use practices such as rainwater harvesting, and technologies for land rehabilitation. Resource poor farmers and their households obviously need technologies that work in their context, are affordable and effective, and can be maintained by people themselves after project interventions end.

Peters states that natural resources are not mere "assets to be managed," but ways of life. Poverty does not necessarily lead to unsustainable use, nor does control over resources lead to unsustainable use. This is illustrated by a community member who is very active in the Okhombe Landcare project:

"I have been fighting fire burning in this community and trying to let people understand what happens to the grass when it is burnt all the time. The Landcare facilitators are assisting me in playing that role in the community. There are a lot of things in the community that I have to do. Since the selection of these youngsters, my burden has become less."

Entrepreneurship

The majority of people in rural areas rely on multiple sources of income such as sales from products (e.g., farming, craft) and services, pension, grants, and money from relatives. Yet for many, income is unstable, seasonal, and greatly fluctuates. A week in which cash flows in is often preceded by weeks with little or no money and scarce food. Many people in South Africa live below the poverty line and have limited or no access to basic services.

The Okhombe Landcare project has experienced that long-term investments must have short-term returns to keep people involved. After two years of job creation, community members were expected to continue with land rehabilitation on a voluntary basis. The Okhombe Inthatakusa monitoring group has volunteered with a larger community group to explore the establishment of small enterprises such as seedling production, craft development, and tourism. However, many people in Okhombe are in dire need for income to sustain their livelihoods. Some group members have left the area to find jobs in Durban and Johannesburg. and the project has not yet succeeded in establishing viable enterprises, which puts the continuity of the project in jeopardy.

Landcare ethos

People do not necessarily identify themselves with the land on which they live or work. Their identity is more likely to be centred around their residential area, working environment, or social group. Taking care of the land is often low on peoples' agendas as their primary objectives may be providing food for their households, passing math in school, or increasing household incomes.

However, people also have goals other than economic and materials that define their relationship to a place (Peters). Environmental education is an important instrument to raise awareness about social, ecological, and economic issues in an area and to mobilize collective action to address land degradation. At the beginning of the Landcare project, a competition was held in Okhombe for a Landcare slogan in Zulu. "Thandizwe," or love for the land, was chosen by community members. Other activities to promote Landcare within the community are the celebration of events such as Arbour Day, Water Week, and the formation of environmental action clubs at schools and among unemployed youth.

Structures for collective action

Local structures are necessary to sustain project activities in all other areas of intervention. These structures are the glue that holds it all together, the energy that makes the vehicle drive. Governance of natural resources requires that individuals, groups and the community as a whole are able to pursue their own development and negotiate (improved) access to training, advice, and technical support services.

Communities and institutions are sites of social interaction, negotiation, and contestation of heterogeneous actors with diverse goals (Peters). For example, while Rural Survivalists can be divided into four sub-categories, it cannot be assumed that a village in a remote rural area would consist solely of, say, the sub group KwaZulu Natal Survivalists. In fact, different major lifestyle groupings can be distinguished together in one village as well. This may shed light on why some villagers become leaders — formal or informal — in a community, and others not, and provides clues on how to develop leadership in development situations.

Power differences among community members strongly affect the degree and type of their participation. Empowerment requires structural changes within a community and between the community and the rest of society. In the context of South Africa this means addressing injustices from the past and reducing conflict, and also enabling each person to know and exercise their rights and to articulate their issues and needs, regardless of race, sex, gender, age, etc. To do this requires capacity building at local level. Capacity building is a process that improves peoples capacity to determine their own values and priorities, and to act on these priorities. Groups are formed around specific interests such as farming, environment, and water use, and collaboration among those groups is promoted. Local leadership must be accountable to ensure that benefits are spread widely throughout a community. Without adequate social organization and effective leadership of community members (outside formal leadership), resource degradation is very likely to continue and aggravate. Thus, group dynamics, resource use negotiation, and conflict management should be part of a Landcare facilitator's standard tool kit (Bhana; Campbell; Oxfam; Peters).

Furthermore, service providers are called to be responsive to the needs of farmers and other land users, to be sensitive to their context, and become partners in development. Partnerships — such as a Landcare forum — should become venues where stakeholders discuss differences and identify commonalities; where they develop a vision and negotiate how resources can best be managed. Effective linkages between community members and service providers are essential in making the structure work. Community facilitators play an important role as movers and shakers in Landcare. They can keep communities focused and accountable, and motivate them to action.

Conclusion

Emerging economies like South Africa are faced with the challenge to offer a wide range of products and services that can compete with those from First World markets, as well as to respond to the needs of the poor and destitute. Governments and civil society can learn from trends in market research to identify and cater to peoples' different lifestyles. Countries where a large proportion of the population depends on agriculture are challenged to find ways to manage their natural resources in a sustainable manner. Community participation and ownership are considered key in this process.

Although popular, the term community-based natural resources management is contested by scientists and practitioners. Governance of natural resources is preferred since it emphasizes processes of negotiation and contestation among resource users and within a community as good, or bad, governance. In the past, many development programs have failed to alleviate poverty. The Okhombe Landcare project shows that complex problems cannot be solved with simplistic answers. Alleviating poverty and sustaining the environment are indeed slow and complex processes that require interventions and competencies in different fields and at different levels. The case study confirms the many critical issues raised by practitioners and scientists. Natural resources are not mere assets to be managed, but integral to ways of life. People do have goals other than economic and materials that define their relationship to a place. Thus, poverty does not necessarily lead to unsustainable use, nor does control over resources lead to sustainable use. But long-term investments must have short-term returns to keep people involved. Power differences within communities heavily impact on degree and type of participation possible. Accountability of local leadership and community facilitators as movers and shakers are key to ensure that benefits are spread widely within communities. Empowerment will lead to structural changes within a community and between the community and the rest of society. Governance of natural resources requires 'facilitating resourcefulness' and technologies and structures that work for all people involved.

References

Anonymous (2002). In *Oprah Magazine, May*.

Ashley, C. and Hussein, K. (2000). Developing Methodologies for Livelihood Impact Assessment: Experience of the African Wildlife Foundation in East Africa. Working paper 129. Overseas Development Institute, London. February 2000.

Bell, R. (1999). CBRM and Other Acronyms: An Overview and Challenges in the Southern African Region. Paper presented at the CASS/PLAAS Inaugural Meeting in Harare, 21–23 September.

Bhana, A (1999). Participatory Action Research: A Practical Guide for Realistic Radicals. In *Research in Practice: Applied Methods for the Social Sciences*, edited by M. Terreblanche and K. Durrheim. Capetown: University of Capetown Press.

Burgess, S. (2002). SA Tribes. Who we are, how we live what we want from life. Groundbreaking research into the new South African society. Epping: ABC Press.

Campbell, A. (1998). Fomenting Synergy in Australia. In *Facilitating Sustainable Agriculture. Participatory Learning and Adaptive Management in Times of Environmental Uncertainty*, edited by N. G. Roling and M. A. E. Wagemakers. Cambridge: Cambridge University Press.

Chambers, R. (1983). *Rural Development. Putting the Last First*, Essex: Longman Group Ltd.

Department of Agriculture, undated. Landcare — Looking after our land so that our land can look after us. Brochure.

DFID (1999). *Sustainable Livelihoods Guidance Sheets*. London: DFID.

Dore, J., C. Keating, C. Woodhill and K. Ellis (2000). Sustainable Region Development. SRD Kit — A resource for improving the community, economy and environment in your region. Greening Australia.

Farmer Support Group in preparation. Framework for Community Participation in Integrated Catchment Management. Water Research Commission, Pretoria.

Farmer Support Group unpublished. Strategy document.

Kaplan A. Annual Report 2000. Capetown: CDRA.

Oxfam. *Monitoring and Evaluation*. Oxford: Oxfam.

Peters, P. (2002). Grounding Governance: Power and Meaning in Natural Resource Management. In *Contested Resources. Challenges to the Governance of Natural Resources in Southern Africa*, edited by T. A. Benjamin, B. Cousings, and L. Thompson. Capetown: PLAAS.

Stefano L. Empowering Rural People: Can Development Initiatives Really Make a Difference? Paper for mini seminar research methods. University of Natal, Pietermaritzburg, unpublished.

Topouzis, D. and Guerny de J. (1999). Sustainable Agricultural/Rural Development and Vulnerability to the AIDS Epidemic. FAO and UNAIDS joint publication. UNAIDS Best Practice Collection, Geneva.

Whiteside, M. (1998). Living farmers — Encouraging sustainable smallholders. In *Southern Africa*. London: Earthscan Publications Limited.

chapter nine

"𝒮how Me the Money": Asymmetric Globalization and Relative Deprivation in Sub-Saharan Africa

Parfait Eloundou-Enyegue
Amani McHugh
Jalamang Orcutt

In the 1990s, "show me the money" became a mantra for skeptics wary of dubious promises. First popularized in a movie pitting a promising athlete against shady recruiters, the mantra eventually came to symbolize a hard-nosed insistence on proof and quid-pro-quo. While popular metaphors are hardly the ware of academic argument, this one does capture two relevant facets of the impact of globalization on African societies. The first is about absolute deprivation, i.e., whether globalization has *shown the money* in the sense of delivering on its promise to stimulate growth in Africa. The second facet of this metaphor, which the paper emphasizes, is about relative deprivation. We argue that globalization has largely been about *"showing"* the money, in the alluring sense of exposing Africa to Western consumer culture and raising its consumer aspirations without commensurate improvements in the means to achieve these new aspirations. The

---

Parfait Eloundou-Enyegue is an Assistant Professor of Development Sociology at Cornell University. At the time this chapter was completed, Amani McHugh was a student in Natural Resource Management, and Jalamang Orcutt was a student in Development Sociology with an interest in political sociology.

globalization of urban Africa, we argue, is so far an asymmetric process of cultural Westernization without economic or demographic integration.

How do African households respond to this asymmetric process? A full assessment is beyond the scope of this article. Instead, we simply propose an analytical framework then use it to examine a small subset of responses. The framework describes globalization as an asymmetric process, both in direction and coordination (Appadurai, 2001). Globalization involves a series of uncoordinated processes and can be understood as an uncoordinated flow across national borders of (a) values and aspirations, (b) capital and technology, (c) labor, and (d) global and non-governmental institutions. Much of the impact of globalization, we argue, depends on the coordination of these flows. We further posit that household responses to globalization can be captured in a matrix covering four behavioral domains and types, including migration, consumerism, individualism, and opportunism.

We discuss evidence on some of these responses by drawing from personal observations and from existing national statistics. By combining the bird's eye perspective of macro-level analysis with insights from a ground-level observation of daily life in Africa, we achieve some measure of triangulation and are able to suggest possible reasons for the disagreements often noted between macro-level analysts and grass-roots observers about the impact of globalization in poor countries (Stiglitz, 2003).

This chapter is organized as follows. The first section restates our general argument in order to reduce misunderstandings. We then discuss sources of disagreement about the impact of globalization. The third section documents the extent of globalization in Africa, outlining its partial and selective nature. Finally, we examine the impacts on selected domains of African life.

The General Argument

The core argument in this article is that the process of globalization currently strains the fabric of African societies. It does so because the process is selective, reaching the urban middle class more than the rural poor and spreading Western consumer culture more than economic opportunity. This selective process disconnects individual aspirations from the material conditions within African countries.

Families subjected to this strain cope in several ways that can include emigration, consumerism, individualism, and opportunism. All these expected responses constitute attempts to reduce the inconsistencies generated by an asymmetric globalization. Emigration, for instance, seeks to reduce the inconsistency between the geographic location of aspirations and the location of opportunity. Consumerism seeks to reduce the inconsistency in status between occupational prestige and real incomes of workers, particularly mid-level civil servants. The tendency towards individualism (through both delayed fertility and family nucleation) is an attempt to reduce the inconsistency between norms of family size and extension and current resources. Finally, opportunism — in the form of increased involvement in high-risk or illicit activities — is a rational response to the cultural inconsistency between the ideals of the local culture and the means offered to achieve these ideals.

It is unclear whether African families respond as expected. It is also unclear whether these responses ultimately hurt Africa's development prospects. Several of these responses clearly challenge the sustainability of African communities by promoting inequality, corruption, or divestment from classic forms of human capital. Others such as the reduced fertility are generally expected to be beneficial. However, many adjustments (e.g., migration and family nucleation) can have both positive and adverse consequences. Reaping the benefits of globalization ultimately depends on African societies' capacity to avoid the traps of consumerism and individualism while taking advantage of the interstitial opportunities offered by globalization.

Sources of Disagreements

As one of the most powerful forces of our lifetime, globalization is the subject of lively debate. Some development practitioners regard globalization with great optimism, as the inevitable and permanent future of world commerce, or as a medium to spread modern technology to the masses, along with the means to live longer, healthier, and more secure lives. Critics on the other hand view globalization as developmentally uneven, controlled by, and driven by the interests of Northern countries. While a handful of states can integrate successfully, this is not guaranteed for all. African States in particular are casualties — not partners — of capital globalization. Globalization creates inordinate constraints on African governments and erodes their sovereignty. At best, globalization is a peep window for Africans to spectate Western luxuriance while the doors of opportunity remain closed. At worst, globalization is simply colonization by another name.

Much of this polarization in the debate between the proponents and the "discontents" of globalization can be traced to basic differences in definition and perspectives. While most can agree on a generic definition of globalization, scholars from different disciplines will emphasize either global governance, trade and markets, cultural change, or labor migration as the key element. Defining globalization therefore resembles a Rorschach test where individual readings reflect disciplinary background. Beyond definition, each discipline brings different assumptions to the debate regarding the proper role of national governments, the regulatory efficiency of markets, the need for competition, the inevitability of inequality, or the appropriate level of analysis. This combination of definitional and paradigmatic biases has contributed to crystallize each discipline around its parochial view of globalization. One participant at the Conference that generated this volume thus offered in jest that a self-respecting economist would be expected to be pro-globalization while a sociologist would be anti-globalization. Indeed, in the internal quarrels between academic disciplines, one's perspective on globalization has almost become a litmus test of disciplinary loyalty.

Beyond bias in perspective, studies seeking to evaluate the impact of globalization must also overcome real methodological difficulties. The concurrence of globalization with other social and demographic changes in Africa makes it difficult to isolate its net effects. Ambiguities about proper control groups and time frames introduce further difficulties. By definition, the process is supposed to embrace all countries, leaving few countries to serve as control groups. The starting point of the process is itself elusive, making pre- and post-comparisons difficult. Nor can one really determine what would have happened if the process of globalization had not occurred.

Given these biases, can one draw any reliable conclusion about the impact of globalization? One strategy is to confront differing experiences.

The authors of this chapter came to this project from different disciplinary perspectives and backgrounds. Between all three, they had visited or resided in more than a dozen countries including the Gambia, Senegal, Ghana, Mali, Nigeria, Cameroon, Kenya, Tanzania, Rwanda, Madagascar, and South Africa. While spending each at least one third of their lives (and receiving some of their education) in Africa, they also spent a substantial portion of their lives outside the continent and they have different citizenship connections to Africa. Coming into this project, they initially held different views about the prospects for globalization in Africa, from mildly optimistic to agnostic to critical. The confrontation of their diverse experiences served as one check against obvious bias. A second check was to examine the aggregate evidence, i.e., whether African countries whose globalization process had been most asymmetric turned out to be worse off than other countries.

Globalization in Africa

Is Africa really present in the world globalization scene? International trade statistics and Africa's representation within international trade and financial organizations clearly relegate Africa to the role of a marginal player. Within international mass media, the portrayal of contemporary life in Africa still alternates between images of desolation as seen on CNN, or isolation as portrayed by National Geographic. The first conjures up images of wars, famines, and pestilence, while the latter propagates bucolic images of a land where wildlife roams free and where local Bushmen have been spared further brush with modernity ever since that empty Coke bottle fell from the heavens. Both images misrepresent reality and the dramatic changes in this region over the last two decades. To begin, Africans have a long experience with trade since the days of the ancient empires. Exchange occurred between the various empires as well as with traders from North Africa, Arabia, and Southern Europe, most notably the Roman and Greek Empires. These exchanges only intensified during the last century or two with improvements in transportation and, more recently, with the development of global communication systems such as the telephone, fax, Internet, radio, and television. The growing transportation infrastructure facilitated the exchange of natural resources and manufactured goods. Communication infrastructure allowed the flow of cultural ideas and practices as well as current market information.

The pace of change in media use has quickened over the past two decades. During this period, the growth in television ownership, and the increasing use of phones and Internet have brought Africans even closer to Western events and consumer culture. Most communities — even rural areas — have access to radio and an increasingly wide audience has gained access to television. Figure 1 depicts the trends in access to televisions, phone main lines, mobile phones, and the Internet in Africa between 1976 and 1998.

The general pattern is one of rapid growth in recent years. In 1975, fewer than 3 out of 1,000 Africans owned a television set. Two decades later, this number had multiplied by nearly 20, reaching 52 per 1000 in 1998. Phone lines, mobile phones and Internet access have increased rapidly since the mid 1990s. The range of communication services offered has continued to grow since 1998. The phone and Internet industry in urban Africa is experiencing remarkable expansion, with a rise in mobile phone usage, phone and Internet cafes, and "call boxes." In Kenya today, the number of mobile phone users is an estimated 1 million, or about 1 in every 32 residents (allafrica.com, 2003). The provision of services has

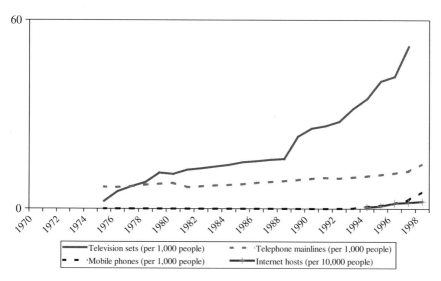

Figure 1: Trends in access to television, telephone, and internet, sub-Saharan Africa 1970–98

created much-needed employment and the resulting competition appears to have been beneficial: The density of coverage has improved in large cities and access has grown surprisingly fast among marginal groups such as sex workers and street children (Wiehler, 2000). Prices have also fallen. A three-minute call from Cameroon to the U.S. cost about 12 dollars in 1996 (World Bank, 2000) but less than 1 dollar today. While Africa is often described as a lagging region, the pace of its telecommunication expansion matches that of other developing regions. Figure 2 shows the trends in television ownership within four developing regions, including sub-Saharan Africa (SSA), South Asia, the Middle East and North Africa, and Latin America and the Caribbean. While SSA and South Asia have fewer television sets per capita than the other two regions, the expansion rate is similar across all four regions.

There are of course important variations within Africa. For instance in 1998, the Democratic Congo boasted an ownership rate of nearly 135 television sets per 1,000 persons while neighboring Congo had 12 per 1,000 and Rwanda had fewer than 1 per 1,000. Other countries with low rates of TV ownership included Chad (1 per 1,000 persons), Ethiopia (5 per 1,000), and Mali (12 per 1,000). Because of its reach and content, television is arguably the most potent force of cultural globalization in

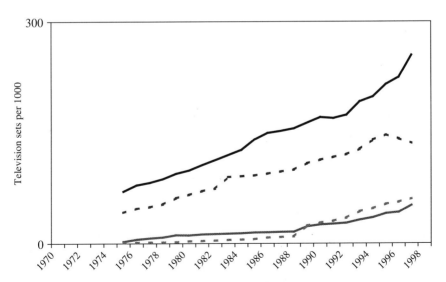

Figure 2: Trends in television ownership in developing regions, 1970–98

Africa. Much programming in Africa relies on foreign material — U.S. sitcoms, U.S. and Brazilian soap operas, Warner Brothers cartoons, Hollywood films, European soccer, and U.S. basketball. Local programs often are limited to political news, documentaries, and occasional African feature movies. While foreign material has captured the lion's share in national programs, the advent of cable television further disconnects viewers from local events and programs. Cabled viewers, a growing group, are more likely to tune in to Canal Horizon, CNN, or BBC for their international news. At times, African viewers in fact get better international news coverage than viewers in Western nations who rely exclusively on their domestic sources. Africans' connection to multiple Western media makes it possible to bypass censorship by any single Western country. For instance, unlike most U.S. viewers, African viewers were able to watch the execution of Timothy McVeigh, the Oklahoma City bomber.

Yet, the drift to foreign networks raises several concerns. First, local regulation agencies lose control over the material received by national audiences. Since African regulators have little control to match programming with local norms of decency or family schedules, offending material is easily aired during peak hours.

Second, the programming of major foreign events increasingly structures local activities. Young Africans have so embraced Western programming that they have incorporated European and the U.S. cultural events in to their daily lives. Local fans have developed surprising loyalty to European soccer teams and regularly bet on European sports events and horse races. African followers of US sport events must often disrupt work and family schedules in order to accommodate their sport interests.

Third, Western programming exports its racial stereotypes. International commentary on Africa seldom deviates from canned stories of gloom. More importantly, athletes and entertainers are the quasi-exclusive role models projected to black youth. Not surprisingly, African youth are embracing sports (most notably soccer) as one of the most viable routes to status attainment. Sports academies are growing as a result and many families are willing to sacrifice for the highly unlikely goal of attaining athletic stardom in Europe. While few aspiring stars actually succeed, there is a clear rise in the number of African youth contemplating a career in sports.

Fourth and most importantly for the purposes of this report, foreign programming exposes African households to Western consumer standards or perhaps more accurately, to a media-distorted and glamorized version of these standards. While viewers do not adopt these standards indiscriminately, mimetic behavior is evident among the younger generation, especially in fashion and entertainment. Replicas of Western brand names pirated in China or Nigeria now dominate popular fashion, while traditional African garb is increasingly reserved for special occasions. It is not uncommon to see urban African youth dressed in Wrangler jeans, Calvin Klein shirts, Fubu jackets, and Nike shoes, eating pizza, speaking American slang, while watching an NBA game on Canal Horizon (cable and satellite). Western popular music from hip hop to R&B to rock can be heard blaring from stereo systems throughout the marketplaces along with African popular music (itself a blend of traditional African music and Western instrumentation). Purely traditional African music is usually reserved for special ceremonies and is played mostly in rural areas.

The Asymmetry of Africa's Globalization

Africa's globalization is asymmetric inasmuch as (1) it selectively touches the urban (but not the rural) populations and (2) its sub-processes evolve at different rates. Table 1 compares rural and urban areas, and shows the urban/rural ratio in access to radio, television, and telephone. The data reveal a comparatively modest rural/urban gap with respect to radio, the most common medium. Within 40 percent of African countries, at least half of rural households own a radio and the urban/rural ratio in radio ownership rarely exceeds 2:1. In contrast, rural communities lag far behind urban centers in their access to television, telephones and thereby the Internet. Even though the recent influx of cellular phones is extending communication to rural areas, phone lines remain limited to urban areas. Fewer than 0.2 percent of rural households in most African countries have access to a phone, whereas rates in most urban areas exceeded 5 percent even before the recent influx of cell phones. Compared with rural-urban inequality in radio ownership, the gaps are larger with respect to phone services. South Africa and Côte

Table 1: The rural urban gap in telecommunication infrastructure in sub-Saharan Africa

	Radio (per 100)			Televisions (per 100)			Telephone (per 100)		
	Urban	Rural	U/R ratio	Urban	Rural	U/R ratio	Urban	Rural	U/R ratio
Benin 2001	80.7	66.3	1.2	33.3	5	6.7	8.7	0.7	12.4
Burkina Faso 1998/99	82.1	53.1	1.5	34	0.7	48.6	9.5	0.1	95.0
Cameroon 1998	71.3	43.4	1.6	35.8	7	5.1	5.1	0.1	51.0
CAR 1994/95	60.6	35.6	1.7	6.9	0.2	34.5	2.6	0	na
Chad 1996/97	60.7	19.8	3.1	6.8	0.1	68.0	1.4	0	na
Comoros 1996	67.4	43.6	1.5	22.3	4.9	4.6	9	0.9	10.0
Cote d'Ivoire 1998/99	76	59.2	1.3	51.4	13.3	3.9	10.2	1.6	6.4
Ethiopia 2000	61.3	12.8	4.8	11.7	0	na	7.9	0	na
Gabon 2000	79.4	54.1	1.5	64	11.4	5.6	17.2	1.1	15.6
Ghana 1998	64	42.7	1.5	40.6	9.7	4.2	5.3	0.2	26.5
Guinea 1999	72.9	48.6	1.5	29.5	0.9	32.8	5.6	0.1	56.0
Kenya 1998	78.2	58.4	1.3	33.4	6.7	5.0	9.1	0.7	13.0
Madagascar 1997	58.2	31.7	1.8	21.6	1.3	16.6	2	0.1	20.0
Malawi 2000	79.5	50.8	1.6	13.7	0.5	27.4	—	—	
Mali 2001	83.3	64.2	1.3	42.4	4.9	8.7	9.3	0.1	93.0
Mauritania 2000/01	61	42.7	1.4	45.1	2	22.6	6.8	0.2	34.0
Mozambique 1997	58.7	24	2.4	14.5	0.4	36.3	5.4	0	na

Namibia 1992	78.4	58.7	1.3	46.5	2.7	17.2	—	—	—
Niger 1998	55.8	28.4	2.0	25.5	0.4	63.8	3.3	0	na
Nigeria 1999	77.6	55.3	1.4	52.7	13.9	3.8	5.3	0.2	26.5
Rwanda 1992	62	30.5	2.0	—	—	—	—	—	—
Senegal 1997	76.4	59.8	1.3	42.6	5.4	7.9	—	—	—
South Africa 1998	84.5	73.5	1.1	73.2	35	2.1	43.3	6.1	7.1
Tanzania 1999	66.9	34.7	1.9	8.5	0.2	42.5	—	—	—
Togo 1998	69.3	41.8	1.7	32.2	3.1	10.4	—	—	—
Uganda 2000/01	77.5	47	1.6	26.6	1.9	14.0	14.5	0.6	24.2
Zambia 1996	64.9	31	2.1	43.4	2.1	20.7	—	—	—
Zimbabwe 1999	73.4	38.5	1.9	52.1	7.6	6.9	16.6	1.3	12.8

Source: ORC Macro. 2003. MEASURE DHS+ STATcompiler. http://www.measuredhs.com, 24 May 2003.

d'Ivoire were the only countries where the urban/rural ratio was lower than 10. Still, the most crucial differences concern access to television. Whereas television ownership has expanded in urban areas, the urban to rural ratio still exceeds 5:1 in all but a handful of countries such as Benin, Nigeria, Ghana, and South Africa. Vast fringes of rural populations in Africa thus remain relatively isolated from television's portrayal of international news and culture. While urban Africa seems poised to enter a globalized society, rural communities still lack the technological and communication infrastructure that is necessary for the process.

Different aspects of Africa's globalization (economic, political, cultural, and demographic) are proceeding at different rates, in part because they are regulated by different institutions (Stiglitz, 2003). The process of economic globalization largely falls under the purview of the International Monetary Fund and World Bank, along with regional banks and private banks and financial institutions. The United Nations plays a key role in political globalization, while individual countries control immigration. Unlike the other three components, cultural globalization is more diffuse and less subject to tight regulation because of media plurality. Still most media outlets depend on commercial sponsorship that explicitly or subliminally promotes consumerism. Cultural globalization thus works to raise consumer aspirations among African customers.

A rise in material aspirations is not problematic in itself and Africans are hardly the only targets of international businesses seeking new consumers. The problem in Africa arises from its low level of material opportunity. While cultural globalization proceeds briskly, the economic and demographic integration with other regions is slow to come. This asynchronous evolution places many African families in a situation where they desire goods and services that they cannot realistically obtain under their present environments. The gap between rising aspirations and stagnant resources fosters a frustrating sense of relative deprivation. Figure 3 illustrates this growing gap by showing the trends in economic conditions relative to growth in television exposure for sub-Saharan Africa. Until 1988 exposure to Western consumer culture via television was fairly limited though steadily increasing. Accordingly, the gap between material aspirations and local conditions was minimal. Since 1980, exposure to

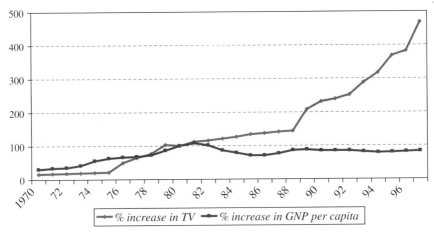

Figure 3: Growth in access to television and GNP per capita, sub-Saharan Africa, 1970–98

television has increased by 4.7 times. During the same period, the GNP per capita has declined, and by 1998, GNP was only at 83% of its 1980 level. As the growing gap between the two curves in Figure 3 suggests, the ratio of Western exposure to local means (an indicator of globalization asymmetry) has increased since 1980.

Again, substantial differences exist within Africa. Table 2 lists African countries and their index of globalization asymmetry, as measured by the ratio of the percent growth in television exposure to the percent growth in per capita GNP during the period 1970–1997. Within about 25 countries, this index was smaller than 10, indicating a fairly even globalization pattern where cultural globalization does not far outpace economic growth. Those countries include Rwanda (0.1), South Africa (1.4) Chad (1.5), Uganda (2.5), Malawi (2.5), and Côte d'Ivoire (3). Low indices are achieved either because countries experienced little growth in television access (e.g., Chad) or because countries experienced some economic growth (e.g., Uganda). For many other countries, the globalization experience was quite asymmetric. They include the Democratic Republic of Congo (760), Mauritania (121), Niger (58), Swaziland (43), Cameroon (34), and Senegal (29). Some of these countries registered their growth in television exposure at a time when they also experienced substantial economic declines.

Table 2: Growth in access to television and GNP per capita, and index of globalization asymmetry within African countries, 1970–98

Country	Growth in TV ownership (1)	Growth in GNP per capita (2)	Index of Globalization asymmetry (1/2)	Country	Growth in TV ownership (1)	Growth in GNP per capita (2)	Index Globalization asymmetry (1/2)
Angola	327.7	43.2	7.6	Madagascar	446.8	57.8	7.7
Benin	725.7	92.7	7.8	Malawi	271.9	110.5	2.5
Botswana	2042.2	249.6	8.2	Mali	1175.4	92.6	12.7
Burkina Faso	313.7	92.3	3.4	Mauritania	9120.2	75.9	120.1
Burundi	403.9	63.6	6.3	Mauritius	237.4	300.8	0.8
Cameroon	3228.8	93.8	34.4	Mayotte			
Cape Verde				Mozambique	492.8	75.0	6.6
C.A.R.	526.9	88.2	6.0	Namibia	766.3		
Chad	145.1	95.8	1.5	Niger	2656.6	45.5	58.4
Comoros	398.8	100.0	4.0	Nigeria	1048.6	42.3	24.8
Congo, Dem.	13485.0	17.7	760.1	Rwanda	10.2	92.0	0.1
Congo, Rep.	573.3	77.3	7.4	Sao Tome & P.			
Cote d'Ivoire	184.9	61.4	3.0	Senegal	2852.1	98.1	29.1
Equat. Guinea	3524.3	358.1	9.8	Seychelles	14935.0	304.3	49.1
Eritrea				Sierra Leone	212.5	36.8	5.8
Ethiopia	532.0			Somalia	1321.3		
Gabon	485.0	87.8	5.5	South Africa	183.0	130.3	1.4

Country			
Gambia, The	342.5	89.5	3.8
Ghana	1867.4	90.7	20.6
Guinea	3046.6	120.5	25.3
Guinea-Bissau		106.7	
Kenya	431.6	77.8	5.5
Lesotho	2547.2	129.5	19.7
Liberia	217.1		
Sudan	202.2	60.4	3.3
Swaziland	6222.2	144.3	43.1
Tanzania	2063.1	115.8	17.8
Togo	475.8	75.0	6.3
Uganda	493.8	206.7	2.4
Zambia	1306.9	52.4	24.9
Zimbabwe	293.9	65.3	4.5

* Source: Computed from World Bank data. Growth in TV ownership is measured by the ratio of 1998 (or 1997) TV ownership rates relative to 1970 rates. Growth in GNP was measured by the ratio of 1998 (or 1997) GNP to the 1970 GNP.

Responses to Globalization

How do African consumers respond to the strain of being shown the goods of a globalizing world and yet not having access to them? The most discerning can ignore the unrealistic standards set by mass media, but few consumers remain immune to the barrage of direct and indirect advertising in television programs. Those who increasingly desire, but cannot access, higher consumption may cope in various domains of behavior. Coping can take a variety of forms: migration; consumerism; individualism; and opportunism. Each of these responses can be understood as a mechanism for reducing the inconsistencies associated with an asymmetric globalization.

Table 3: Matrix of possible household responses to globalization in Africa

Domain Type	Demographic	Economic	Social	Political
Physical mobility	Cyber-dating; bride drain	Labor migration Brain drain, brawn drain	"Prestige" Tourism	Refugee migration
Redistribution of consumption over time	Delay in marriage & fertility	Savings and debt		
Redistributing of consumption priorities	Reduced fertility	Limited private investment	Assistance to relatives Status consumption	Rural-urban relations
Deviance from previous status-attainment strategies	Choice of marital partners	High-risk, high reward routes to status attainment (sports, arts, lottery) Reduction investment in classic forms of human capital (e.g., education)	Involvement in illicit activities (corruption, crime)	Political corruption

Migration: The brain, brawn, and bride drains

Poor populations bombarded with consumer advertising can cope by moving physically toward places of global opportunity. In addition to fuelling a desire to emigrate, globalization also facilitates migration by reducing barriers to mobility including the costs of moving, the costs of information about destinations, and the costs of maintaining contact with the community of origin (DeJong and Gardner, 1981).

The literature on African emigration is concerned with a so-called "brain drain" or the loss of educated Africans (Gordon and Gordon, 1996). Perhaps there should be equal concern with a "brawn" drain as young African men increasingly look to European professional sports as a ticket to status. Nor have researchers seriously explored the possibility of a "bride" drain, as young African women bank on the Internet to seek love and economic security abroad. Discussions about any of these drains must however recognize a shortage of hard evidence about the volume of emigration flows from individual African countries, let alone their economic impact. Despite the shortage of national statistics on emigration rates, observations at the ground-level leave little doubt about the fascination of African youth with Western emigration. The long lines for visa applications around European embassies in many African capitals are but one sign. Another, less visible sign is the cottage industry blooming around services to facilitate legal and illegal immigration. Researchers increasingly recognize the growth in legal and illegal immigration from Africa to Europe (e.g. Hatton and Williamson, 2001), but their analyses remain based on limited data and they lag far behind the recognition that these issues have received in the African popular press. By the 1990s, Western migration had become a rite of passage guaranteeing migrants a measure of status regardless of its economic payoff. Although this grass-roots evidence might be compelling to ordinary observers of African life, one still needs a rigorous assessment of emigration rates and how these have changed in response to globalization. Further, it is important to differentiate migration intentions from the ultimate migration outcomes. Because the legal and economic restrictions on immigration often thwart migration intentions, actual emigration rates are often much smaller than the yearnings of youth would suggest.

As the term "drain" connotes, the emigration of Africans is presumed to deplete the region of vital human capital. Yet, the evidence is weak. Evaluations of the macroeconomic loss to African economies often include items such as fees paid to international or foreign experts. Doing so attributes Africa's recourse to foreign experts to lack of local expertise, rather than to contractual obligations within the rules of foreign aid. Furthermore, the very process of globalization permits family remittances, an important source of revenue for many families. Wiring services make it possible for emigrants to remit and maintain a modicum of economic presence in their origin countries, even while they reside away. Again, although sound arguments warrant concern for African emigration as a net loss, the debate about emigration drains must acknowledge possible benefits in the context of increased mobility and communication between North and South.

Consumerism: Basic needs versus status consumption

Consumerism would not be expected to be a problem among poor populations in Africa. Yet the success of consumer advertising comes precisely from blurring the boundaries between foreign and local standards and from turning luxuries into apparent necessities. Further, consumers left to their own devices are easily mistaken or misled about the level of local opportunities. Youth are often optimistic about their future incomes and each generation expects to at least match the standards of living enjoyed by the parental generation. However, matching this standard is not guaranteed for the next generation of workers in African countries where economies have faltered and costs of living risen.

When workers ultimately acknowledge their incapacity to meet the standards of the global consumption culture, reason should compel the most disciplined to simply withdraw from the consumption race and focus on basic needs. Yet, the reality of household consumption is that middle-income families in Africa can forego what appear to be necessities in order to keep up with the distant Joneses of the global culture. One striking example is found in the subculture of *sapeurs*, or young adults who spend an inordinate amount of their income on designer clothing. Another example comes from a recent — perhaps hyperbolic — journalistic report describing how the relatively affluent in a particular West African country were turning away from purchasing Mercedes brand cars, because these were supposedly becoming "distressingly commonplace" (Afrik.com, 2000). This was especially remarkable in a country where annual GNP was less than $500 per person and at a time when gas prices were four times higher than in the U.S.! The paradox of luxury consumption among the poor reflects the success of the advertising industry to link individual sense of worth with consumption. While the drive to over-consume as a marker of status is universal (Packard, 1959; DeGraaf, Wann and Naylor, 2001), it assumes a tragic dimension in Africa where many poor families still lack the basic necessities. Middle-income groups in these countries often succumb to the pressures of status competition and lose sight of more urgent needs to save, invest, or assist kin in need.

Africa's asymmetric globalization should have visible consequences on consumption patterns and savings rates. Figure 4 (frames A and B) shows the correlation between the extent of globalization asymmetry and national savings and interest rates for African countries. While interest rates vary considerably within the region (from about 5% to 20%), they turn out to be unrelated to a country's globalization pattern. Even more remarkably, asymmetry is associated with higher — rather than the expected lower — rate of savings. Each unit increase in the index of globalization asymmetry is associated with a 2.4 unit increase in savings rates. Such findings raises doubt about the notion that asymmetric globalization would depress savings rates, these findings also question the relevance of common macroeconomic indicators to the daily lives of many Africans. Many African households work outside formal banking systems and rely on informal savings groups that are less stringent in their collateral requirements, but also charge higher interest rates. Observers familiar with the usury facing low-income families would indeed be surprised by national statistics on savings and credit rates. The world of formal banking scrutinized by macroeconomists has only indirect relevance to the credit markets faced by many, and perhaps most, African families. In that context, it should not be surprising that macro-level analysts of formal banking systems and ground-level observers of the daily realities of African families would disagree about the impact of globalization.

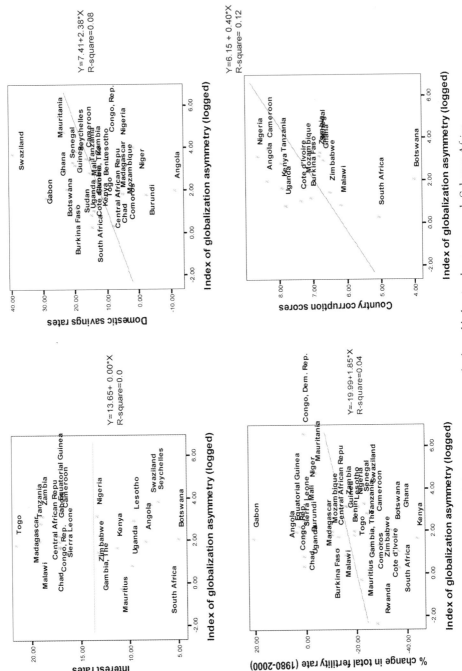

Figure 4: Correlation analysis of globalization asymmetry and selected behavioral outcomes, sub-Saharan Africa

Individualism

African workers bear a high dependency burden. This burden arises in part from the prevailing high fertility but also from the demands of an extended family system. Couples with smaller progenies are often solicited to support more prolific or poorer relatives through fosterage or through remittances (Isuogo-Abanihe, 1985; Mahieu, 1989). Because a high dependency burden competes with consumerism, a globalization process that promotes consumerism will work to reduce fertility and family extension.

However, the aggregate evidence contradicts our intuition, showing smaller declines in fertility within countries where globalization was more asymmetric. Again, while such evidence casts doubts on the presumed impact of globalization on fertility, it also illustrates a limitation of macro-level analysis. Detailed micro-level studies have confirmed the effects of economic downturns and rising aspirations in Africa on delaying marriage and births (NAS, 1993; Watkins, 2000). Studies also underscore the need to account for unwanted fertility, i.e., the inability of some couples who wish to curtail fertility to effectively do so (Westoff and Bankole, 1996). If unwanted fertility is more common among economically stagnant countries, the aggregate analysis will underestimate the impact of an asymmetric globalization. Again, the point is to draw attention to the limitations of macro-level analysis in revealing changes in behavior intentions at the household level.

Workers can also reduce their dependency burden by curtailing assistance to distant relatives. While most African families remain extended, middle-income couples are increasingly reluctant or unable to accommodate their relatives. Still, this desire to nucleate will face opposition from needy relatives. Given the important role of the African extended family system in buffering inequality, a trend toward nucleation will have serious consequences for the levels of economic inequality in the region.

Opportunism and deviance from previous modes of status attainment

The flip-side of consumption-reduction strategies is to supplement incomes. Public sector workers can respond by taking on additional jobs or getting involved in illicit activities. Families can encourage female partners to join the labor force. Because African countries under structural adjustment have frozen public sector hiring and because the private sector is still weak, the informal sector has become an important employment outlet. As workers increasingly flock to this sector, the prestige of informal-sector work is being reevaluated by workers and society alike. Civil sector jobs — once at the top of the local stratification structure — are increasingly compared with jobs previously considered less desirable such as street vending, taxicab driving, hair dressing. However, the informal economy cannot absorb all prospective workers and competition has become intense in this sector as well. In some cases competition has lowered prices and improved services. Unfortunately, it also has less desirable consequences. Winning in the informal sector competition now depends on businesses' ability to secure the support of regulatory agencies, often through bribery. In a context where civil servants feel under-compensated and relatively deprived, vulnerability to bribery is not surprising (Treisman, 2000; Eloundou, Arguilas, and Zalik, 2000). The general acceptance of bribery can be seen as an attempt by public sector workers to reduce their status inconsistency by bringing up their income to match their occupational prestige. Public sector workers are unfortunately not alone in breaking the rules. Other citizens follow the behavior which leads to generalized corruption and a proliferation of theft, drug trade, and sex work. If this argument is correct, the incidence of corruption and crime should be higher in countries where globalization has been most asymmetric. Data confirm the positive association expected between the asymmetry in globalization and the rate of corruption found within individual countries.

African citizens also exhibit deviance in ways that are legally-benign but still important for development prospects. One coping tendency is to engage in high-risk/high-reward investments. The rise of gambling and lottery participation among the urban poor is a visible phenomenon in many capital cities. In South Africa, it is estimated that at least one quarter of unemployed individuals regularly play the lottery (Allafrica.com, 2003). Players certainly are aware that the odds of winning a lottery are slim, but in the absence of realistic possibilities of steady accumulation, a large windfall appears to be the only way out of chronic insolvency or to meet expanding consumer needs. The same risk orientation increasingly pervades investments in human capital. While education achievement is still a good indicator of future economic status attainment, its appeal pales in comparison with the fields of sports, politics, business, or criminality where success is rare but perceived to be more dramatic.

Conclusions

Globalization is unfolding in Africa as an asymmetric process of cultural integration without its corresponding economic and demographic integration. In the process, African consumers are exposed to, but not getting access to, higher standards of living. This asymmetry can spur changes in behaviors that ultimately affect the region's development prospects. In theory, individuals can cope in multiple ways including migration, consumerism, individualism, and opportunism. The motivation behind these behavioral changes is to reduce inconsistencies associated with asymmetric globalization. Migration, for instance, reduces the inconsistency in geographic location between the locus of consumer aspirations and the locus of income opportunity. Consumerism would reduce the status inconsistency between the occupational prestige and real incomes of middle-income workers. Workers become individualistic both by reducing fertility and seeking nuclear family arrangements, because they seek to reduce the inconsistency between norms of family formation/ structure and the resources available to workers. Finally, workers' increased opportunism and proclivity toward high-risk/high-reward or illicit activities represents an attempt to redress the cultural inconsistency between new cultural ideals and the norms that regulate status attainment practices.

In practice, the actual behavioral responses to globalization are difficult to assess. One limitation emphasized in this report is the exclusive reliance on macro-level analysis of formal institutions. The bird's eye perspective of macro-level analysis is unlikely to capture the complexity of actual responses on the ground. Macro-level analysis is limited either because of lack of adequate data (in the case of emigration), a focus on formal rather the more popular informal systems (in the case of credit and savings), or failure to consider behavioral intentions (in the case of emigration, fertility, or family nucleation). For most of the behavioral responses we examined, a macro-level of comparison of African countries fails to support theoretical predictions about the impact of asymmetric globalization. We find little macro-level evidence showing higher emigration rates, lower savings rates, and more rapid declines in fertility in countries where globalization has proceeded most asymmetrically. The only supportive evidence pertains to corruption.

While our findings question the validity of grim predictions about the adverse effects of globalization, they also highlight the limitations of macroeconomic analyses that have typically supported the most optimistic assessments of globalization. Micro-level studies and observations on the ground can reveal insights that fall below the radar of macro-level analysis. The rising interest rates within informal saving and credit institutions, youth fascination with Western migration, the increasing pervasiveness of petty corruption, the growing preference for high-risk high-reward routes to status attainment are all important developments on the ground. A full account of globalization's impact requires both the panoramic view of macro-level analysis and the detailed observation of the daily lives of African households facing the challenge of globalization.

Even if families adjusted as theoretically expected, it is difficult to foretell the ultimate effects of these adjustments on Africa's development prospects. Some of these behavior changes represent a clear challenge to the cohesion of African communities. Others, such as the decline in fertility, are a potential bonus (Bloom, Canning and Sevilla, 2002). Most, however, contain both elements of risk and opportunity. The new values of individualism, risk taking, consumerism, deviance, and adventurism can become assets or liabilities, depending on how African communities recognize and modulate these pressures to change. The problem with globalization in Africa is not that it occurs at all. African economies and societies could well benefit from this process if African governments and civil society can organize a coherent response by drawing on the strengths of local institutions to avoid the trap of consumerism while banking on the adventitious opportunities of a globalizing world.

References

Appadurai, A. (2001). *Globalization*. Durham: Duke University Press.
Bloom, D. E., D. Canning and J. Sevilla (2002). *The Demographic Dividend: Consequences of Population Change*, MR-1274-WFHF, Santa Monica: RAND.

De Jong, G. F. and R. W. Gardner (eds.). (1981). *Migration Decision-Making. Multi-Disciplinary Approaches to Micro-level Studies in Developed and Developing Countries*, New York: Pergamon Press.

Eloundou-Enyegue P., F. O. Arguilas, Jr. and A. Zalik. (2000). *The Roots of Corruption: Historical and Present Roots*, Cornell University PDP Working Papers series.

Treisman, Daniel (2000). The Causes of Corruption. *Journal of Public Economics* 76, pp. 399–457.

De Graaf, J., D. Wann and T. H. Naylor. (2001). *Affluenza: The All-consuming Epidemic*. San Francisco: Berrett Koehler.

Hatton, T. J. and J. G. Williamson (2001). Demographic and Economic Pressure on Emigration Out of Africa, Working Paper No. w8124: National Bureau of Economic Research.

Gordon, April A. and Donald L. Gordon (eds.) (1996). *Understanding Contemporary Africa, 2nd Edition*. Boulder, CO: Lynne Rienner Publishers.

Isiugo-Abanihe, U. C. (1985). Child fosterage in West Africa. *Population and Development Review*, 11, pp. 53–73.

Mahieu, F. R. (1989). Transfers et Communauté Africaine. *Stateco*, June, 107–136.

National Research Council (1993). *Demographic Effects of Economic Reversals in Sub-Saharan Africa*. Washington, D.C.: National Academy Press.

Stiglitz, J. (2003). *Globalization and Its Discontents*. New York: W.W. Norton and Cie.

Watkins, S. Cotts (2000). Local and Foreign Models of Reproduction in Nyanza Province, Kenya. *Population and Development Review*, 26, pp. 725–759.

Westoff C.F. and A. Bankole (1996). The Potential Demographic Significance of Unmet Need. *International Family Planning Perspectives*, 22, pp. 16–20.

Wiehler, S. (2000). An Examination of Pull Factors Affecting Kampala's Street Children. Presented at conference on Street Children in East Africa.

World Bank (1994). *Adjustment in Africa, Reforms, Results and the Road Ahead*. Washington, D.C.: The World Bank.

World Bank (2000). *World Development Indicators*, CD ROM.

Online sources:

Afrik.com	http://www.afrik.com/journal/dossier/dossier-9002-7.htm
Allafrica.com	http://allafrica.com/stories/200304170305.html
Allafrica.com	http://allafrica.com/stories/200305300440.html

chapter ten

Globalization, Agricultural Development and Rural Community Livelihoods

Philip McMichael

In the words of José Bové, the logic of globalization is to flood the market with "food from nowhere" (Bové and Dufour, 2001:55). This phrase refers to the increasing separation of agriculture from its ties to ecological places and cultural cuisines. Across the world, farmers are resisting this separation with a range of activities — from organizing movements to protect property rights of products by denomination of origin, to those that seek to protect access to land and basic livelihood rights. While only 5 to 10 percent of food produced is traded internationally, the politics of globalization encourage and enable artificially low prices for agricultural commodities, squeezing farmers across the world.

This paper reviews those dynamics, relating them to historic political-economic and geo-political trends in the late twentieth century. It argues that the first step towards restoring sustainable rural livelihoods is to recognize the role of the "globalization project" in superimposing an increasingly socially and ecologically abstract pattern of agricultural

Philip McMichael is a Professor of Rural Sociology at Cornell University.

commodity chains on a world in which a specialized corporate food system has devastating consequences for rural cultures.

Global Restructuring of Agricultures

Global restructuring of agricultures is a legacy of the historic "empires of food," whereby food production and consumption was reorganized on a global scale within colonial relationships. The relocation of crops (e.g., sugarcane to the Caribbean, and maize and potatoes to Europe) and the incorporation of foreign foods in local cuisines (e.g., the tomato in Italian foods, sugar and bananas in to Western cuisine) express the impact of colonial and post-colonial relationships.

Beef has dramatically transformed ecologies and diets on a world scale (Rifkin, 1992). The introduction of the European cattle culture to the Western Hemisphere presaged an agribusiness complex that now links specialized soy producers, maize farmers, and lot-fed cattle across the world (see Friedmann, 2000). The global cattle complex embodies a series of commodity chains binding the world into an animal protein dependency that imposes feed grain and livestock monocultures on local ecologies. This dependency competes with the *direct* consumption of cereals like wheat, rice, and beans. By the mid-twentieth century, mass consumption of beef subdivided the industry into lot-fed high-value beef cuts, and cheaper, grass-fed, lean beef for the fast-food industry. This so-called "world steer," is an artifact of globalization as pharmaceuticals, chemical fertilizers, herbicides, grass strains, and sperm are all foreign inputs to the beef production. The industry caters to global consumers at one end of the chain, and at the other, it undermines diverse local agro-ecologies (Sanderson, 1986).

As some Southern societies have developed sizeable middle classes with Westernized diets, specialized domestic livestock industries have mushroomed alongside traditional farming systems. Between the early 1970s and the mid-1990s, meat consumption in the South grew by 70 million metric tons annually, compared with a growth rate of 26 million metric tons in the North. "In 1983 developing countries consumed 36 percent of all meat and 34 percent of all milk consumed worldwide. By 1993 those percentages had risen to 48 percent and 41 percent, respectively" (Delgado et al., 1999).

The International Food Policy Research Institute (IFPRI) reports that the world is in the early phase of a demand-led "livestock revolution," as distinct from the supply-led Green Revolution, which catered to national food security concerns. The livestock revolution caters to a global market anchored in a relatively affluent consumer segment of the world's population. These shifts have serious implications for the transformation of food security conditions. While noting the importance of roots and tubers as a principal source of food for small farmers around the world, IFPRI reports that a "rapid expansion in the demand for roots and tubers for livestock feed has been under way for some time, particularly in Asia, and is likely to continue as demand for meat products grows rapidly in coming years" (Pinstrup-Andersen et al., 1999). Meanwhile, IFPRI predicts that demand for maize in the South "will overtake demand for rice and wheat" and about "64 percent of the maize demand will go toward feeding livestock compared with 8 percent of wheat and 3 percent of rice in 2020" (Pinstrup-Andersen et al., 1999). During the 1990s, while food cereals production remained the same in Brazil and China, feed cereals production almost doubled in both countries (FAO Statistical Tables, 2000).

The link between this global reconstruction of diets and geo-political relations is central to the concept of the 'food regime.' The food regime defines an historically specific geo-political-economic organization of agricultural and food relationships. The food regimes corresponding to British and U.S. hegemonic eras were embedded in dominant state-building models organizing a particular structure of food production and consumption relations on a world scale (Friedmann and McMichael, 1989).

The first food regime, from 1870 to 1914, pivoted on the tension between the colonial and the national division of labor. The latter, anchored in a domestic farm sector, complemented and progressively displaced the colonial division of labor and involved a global exchange of tropical crops for manufactured goods. The national model found full expression in the settler states, where farm sectors replicated and rivaled European temperate crops, and partnered with domestic industrial sectors. The exemplar was the United States' commercial farm belt. After the inter-war period, when national food security was a priority, the U.S. model of inner-directed national development displaced the outer-directed British model, redefining the organization of agro-food systems in the mid-twentieth century era of universal state-building as colonialism collapsed.

During this era, development became identified with the ideal of consolidating a growing national economy fueled by an internal exchange between agricultural and industrial sectors. Just as the first food regime was defined as the progressive replacement of one model by another, so the second food regime, 1945 to 1970, pivoted on the contradiction between global integration and the coherence of national farm sectors. Also during this time, the U.S. deployed food aid to secure its geo-political perimeter in the Third World, underwriting industrialization in states such as India and South Korea as development showcases (Grosfoguel, 1996) where Third World regimes depended on Western foods to provide reconstructed urban diets (Friedmann, 1982). By extension, the Green Revolution consolidated the global movement under the guise of addressing the question of national food security. Green Revolution technologies further internationalized agro-food relations, supporting newly-introduced genetically modified crops with chemical and mechanical inputs, and elaborating agribusiness dependencies. With the global expansion of livestocking, Green Revolution technologies extended into feed cropping, promoting livestock commodity chains that link specialized agricultural sub-sectors across national boundaries (DeWalt, 1985). The tight nexus between agribusiness and dominant states fostered the global integration of agricultures, and underlay the movement to institutionalize this process in the 1990s (McMichael, 2000a).

The WTO regime

The 1994 Agreement on Agriculture was a key part of the Uruguay Round of General Agreement on Tariffs and Trade negotiations (GATT) and its focus on the liberalization of agriculture and agricultural trade. The original GATT agreement of 1947, which included anti-dumping protocols and provisions to avoid exporting of food surpluses, was soon subverted by U.S. and European practices, exempting their agricultural policy from GATT rules. In 1955, the U.S. moved to establish a price floor in order to protect its farm supply policies of price supports and production controls.

By the early 1960s, the European Common Agricultural Policy (CAP) negotiated border protection of its domestic food system with the U.S., in return for free entry of feedstuffs. The latter stimulated large food surpluses of animal protein supplied by cheap imported feed, which in turn closed local outlets for domestic feed grains. Both sets of policies, in generating food surpluses, led to an intensifying competition for world market outlets via export dumping. This market and price instability undermined the second food regime (Friedmann, 1993). World agricultural prices fell from a mean of 100 in 1975 to 61 by 1989 — a 39 percent decline. In 1986, U.S. Agriculture Secretary, John Block, observed: "the idea that developing countries should feed themselves is an anachronism from a bygone era. They could better ensure their food security by relying on U.S. agricultural products, which are available in most cases at lower cost" (quoted in Ritchie, 1993).

The Uruguay Round sought to reapply the GATT disciplines to U.S. and European Community agricultural policies (Dawkins, 1999). The context for this was twofold: first, the destabilizing impact of export competition between the U.S. and the European Union; and second, the escalating cost of farm subsidies, which became a political liability in the neo-liberal 1980s. Under pressure from the Cairns Group of 17 agricultural exporting countries, the Round was committed to liberalizing agriculture and services, paying lip service to market access for Southern exports, but essentially shaped by American and European needs to regulate Northern trade competition and lower the farm bill. The U.S. negotiation was fashioned and conducted by representatives of a transnational corporate alliance with a former senior vice president of Cargill, Inc. drafting the U.S. proposal and heading the U.S. delegation. Anticipating the outcome of the Round (arguably a U.S. weapon against the CAP's export apparatus), the E.U. switched from its original CAP farm price support policies to U.S.-style government subsidies (Dawkins, 1999) with the 'McSharry reform' in 1992. This switch towards market prices synchronized E.U. policy with that of the U.S. in favoring traders over producers.

The preference given to market prices reflected an ongoing restructuring of Northern agriculture and, in turn, was enabled by the GATT reforms. In the U.S., farm credit delivery shifted from a state-supplied credit system (Farmer's Home Administration loans) in the 1970s to President Reagan's policy of state-guaranteed private loans. The policy switch empowered private banks as rural creditors, shifting farming further towards a system of private accumulation, with the state socializing costs such as risk and rural welfare in the form of subsidies. An intensification of agricultural concentration followed: by the mid-1990s, 80 percent of farm subsidies in the OECD countries supported the largest 20 percent of (corporate) farms, rendering small farmers increasingly vulnerable to the vicissitudes of a deregulated (and increasingly privately managed) global market for agricultural products. For example, in 1994, 50 percent of U.S. farm products came from 2 percent of the farms, and only 9 percent from 73 percent of the farms (Lehman and Krebs, 1996). Since 1998, U.K. farm income has fallen by 75 percent, eliminating 20,000 farmers; U.S. farm income declined 50 percent between 1996-1999; and in 1999, 200,000 European farmers and 600,000 beef producers left the business (Gorelick, 2000:28–30).

The 1994 reforms included reductions in trade protection, farm subsidies, and government intervention. Free trade was the ostensible demand, but the underlying Northern agenda was an informal mercantilism of constructing a comparative advantage through de-regulating a highly unequal world market. The Agreement on Agriculture was designed to open agricultural markets by adopting minimum import requirements and reductions in tariffs and producer subsidies. Southern states signed on in the hopes of improving their foreign currency income from expanded agro-exports (under the imperative of servicing foreign debt). The effect was to open markets for Northern products and strengthen the position of the OECD countries in the international division of labor in agriculture. From 1970 to 1996, the OECD share in the volume of world cereal exports rose from 73 percent to 82 percent; the U.S. remained the world's major exporter of commercial crops such as maize, soybean, and wheat; and the share of Africa, Latin America, and Asia in world cereal imports increased to nearly 60 percent (Pistorius and van Wijk, 1999).

The privileging of Northern exports derived from the 1992 deal made between the U.S. and the E.U. is termed the "Blair House Agreement." This bilateral negotiation, essentially a 'protection racket' for U.S. and E.U. exports, became the norm for the whole GATT membership as the WTO formed in 1995. The agreement tied reductions in both domestic support and export subsidies to baseline levels of 1986, when stocks and subsidies were at their peak, thus giving both the E.U. and the U.S. ample flexibility in meeting their obligations, and established a peace clause regarding action against farm support programs and export subsidies (Dawkins, 1999). The legitimizing of export subsidies (for 25 of 132 WTO members) has, perversely, allowed the U.S. and the E.U. to intensify export dumping such that "just three (members) are responsible for 93 percent of all subsidized wheat exports and just two of them are responsible for subsidizing 94 percent of butter and 80 percent of beef exports" (Dawkins, 1999).

The Agreement on Agriculture institutionalized an historic shift in the meaning of food security, presaged by U.S. Agriculture Secretary Block at the opening of the Uruguay Round. Under this regime, states no longer have the right to full self-sufficiency as a national strategy. Rather, because of the minimum market access rule, the Agreement on Agriculture institutionalizes the 'right to export:' and this "applies to developed and developing countries alike, and even when the lower prices is made possible through export subsidies" (Einarsson, 2001). Related to this is a rule forbidding state restrictions on agro-food imports to protect population or livestock health, without scientific proof from experts recognized by the WTO. The complementary thrust of liberalization is to undercut public support of domestic production since "almost all remaining WTO-legal support options require direct payments through the government budget" (idem), and of course this discriminates particularly against Southern states whose public capacity has been severely eroded by debt and structural adjustment (McMichael, 2000a).

Since Northern commodities are cheaper on the world market because of export subsidies and economies of mechanized scale, the overall net effect of increasing minimum market access requirements and continuing general tariff reductions under the new Agreement on Agriculture would likely be to facilitate increased developed country exports to developing countries, not the opposite according to Einarsson (2001). Meanwhile, Northern states continue farm support with effective subsidies of 49 and 30 percent for U.S. and European farmers, respectively (Malhotra, 1996). Under such conditions of unfair trade, Oxfam asks: "How can a farmer earning US$230 a year (average per capita income in less developed countries) compete with a farmer who enjoys a subsidy of US$20,000 a year (average subsidy in OECD countries)?" (quoted in Bailey, 2000).

Accordingly, for a large minority of Southern states, food security has come to mean an increasing dependence on food imports. By the mid-1990s, half of the foreign exchange of the FAO's 88 low-income food deficit countries went to food imports (LeQuesne, 1997). FAO analysis has shown that the food bills of food dependent states grew, on average, 20 percent between 1994 and 1999, in spite of record low prices in the late 1990s (Murphy, 1999). This conception of food security conforms to the ideal of comparative advantage, which Murphy (1999) stated as: "The Agreement on Agriculture prescribes a model for agriculture that has basically only one dimension: increasing agricultural production for exports, importing what cannot be produced without tariff protection or subsidies to producers." Indian policy analyst Devindar Sharma writes that, "whereas for small farmers the subsidies have been withdrawn, there is a lot of support now for agribusiness industry ... The result is that the good area under staple foods is now shifting to export crops, so we'll have to import staple food" (quoted in Madeley, 2000). For example, in Chile, between 1989 and 1993 the food crop area fell 30 percent as beans, wheat, and other staples were replaced by fruit, flowers, and other export crops. While 90 percent of agricultural research expenditures in Latin America were devoted to food crop research in the 1980s, now 80 percent focuses on export crops (Madeley, 2000). Local food security is compromised by: the appropriation of land for export crops for affluent markets; the use of cheap food imports; and IMF Structural Adjustment Program-derived concessions. The globalizers' version of food security is realized: dependence on food from global grainbasket regions — or "food from nowhere."

The favoring of export crops over domestic food crops across the world is, of course, quite uneven. In particular, the Agreement on Agriculture agro-export model "is imperfectly articulated and includes various exceptions that have proved of more use to developed than developing countries" (Murphy, 1999:2). The imperfect articulation corresponds to Einarsson's subdivision of states in relation to world food trade patterns: The 'natural exporters' (the settler states of USA, Canada, Argentina, Uruguay, Brazil, Australia, and New Zealand) with favorable climates and soils, sparse population and late colonization; the 'artificial exporter,' namely Europe, created by agricultural policy, chemical-intensive farming, and huge feedstuff imports; net-importing developing countries (Japan, Korea, Switzerland, Norway and Eastern Europe); a large minority of net-importer Southern states; and a middle group of

Southern states more or less self-sufficient in food (Einarsson, 2001:4). The point of such a distinction is to emphasize the historic asymmetry in the state system, which is amplified by liberalization. It is precisely this asymmetry that stalemates WTO's attempts to impose a level playing field of trade rules.

Arguably, this contradiction between vision and reality is resolved by the process itself — of converting the world into a series of agro-export platforms as an alternative model to a world of states with farm sectors anchoring national food security (McMichael, 2000b). The alternative meaning of food security involves the wholesale subjection of agriculture to corporate relations, leading to far-reaching dispossession of farmers. This may take several forms depending on context and crop — the expulsion of rural populations through land concentration, the conversion of farmers into hired, plantation, or migrant labor, or their conversion to contract farming. The unifying feature of these diverse outcomes is the undermining of family or peasant farming (Araghi, 2000). A 1997 FAO study identified the impact of liberalization with:

> ... a general trend towards the concentration of farms, in a wide cross-section of countries. While this led to increased productivity and competitiveness with positive results, in the virtual absence of safety nets the process also marginalized small producers and added to unemployment and poverty (quoted in Madeley, 2000).

In West Africa, cheap tomato concentrate imported from Europe undermines local tomato production and processing. Subsidized E.U. dairy products undercut milk producers and co-ops in Jamaica and the Mercosur region (Uruguay, Brazil, Argentina and Paraguay), where dairy farms and co-ops are concentrating and transnational firms such as Nestlê (Swiss) and Parmalat (Italian) are reorganizing milk processing (Bailey, 2000; Madeley, 2000:75, 87). A Honduran farmer, interviewed in Seattle, noted:

> WTO regulations have extremely destructive effects on small farms in Honduras. Import barriers have come down, permitting the import of cheap food produce from Europe, Canada and the United States. Today, we cannot sell our own farm products on the markets because of these imports. Free trade is for multinationals, it is not for the small peasant farmers (quoted in Madeley, 2000).

While the FAO study did not provide data on expulsion, conservative estimates are that between 20 and 30 million people have recently lost their land — and relatively secure livelihoods — as a result of trade liberalization (Madeley, 2000).

Meanwhile, farm prices for the major commodities in world trade have fallen 30 percent or more since the WTO agreement was signed in December 1994 (Ritchie 1999). In April 1999, *The Economist* claimed that commodity prices were at an all-time low for the last century and a half. Many countries cannot meet their commitments to the Agreement on Agriculture because of this price collapse, which, according to the Chilean government, threatens to destroy much of their agricultural economies (Bailey, 2000). The U.S. has abandoned commitments by increasing farm subsidies and intensifying export dumping, using supply management to restore crop prices and to capture overseas markets (Ritchie, 1999). The recent U.S. Farm Bill promises considerably more of the same.

Agro-export platforms and 'food from nowhere'

A recent report from Public Citizen's Global Trade Watch on the North American Free Trade Agreement (NAFTA) documents the elimination of small farmers across the whole North American region as the legacy of NAFTA. While millions of Mexican *campesinos* have lost their maize farms, U.S. farmers fall prey to competitive imports from Mexico and Canada, replacing crops grown in the U.S. From 1994 to 2000, 33,000 U.S. farms with annual sales under $100,000 disappeared (six times the decline for 1988-93). Meanwhile, during the 1990s, a massive demographic shift occurred in Mexico where overall population growth was 20 percent, but urban population grew 44 percent and rural only 6 percent (Public Citizen, 2001).

As a world region, the NAFTA is a telling case study of the conversion of farm sectors to agro-export platforms. This shows up in two ways. First, is a general decline in U.S. agricultural trade surpluses as agriculture has shifted offshore (a noticeable trend since 1985). Second, since the mid 1990s when the WTO and NAFTA went into effect, the U.S. world trade surplus has declined almost 30 percent, while the U.S. trade surplus within North America has declined more than twice that, by 71 percent. This particular decline fuels a global substitution effect, whereby competitive imports (fruit, vegetables, and other labor-intensive foodstuffs) accounted for 80 percent of all U.S. agricultural imports during the decade of the 1990s (Public Citizen, 2001). This phenomenon has been termed 'the great food swap' in a recent study of Europe's food supply, detailing considerable replication of food exports and imports (Lucas, 2001).

Under NAFTA, the Mexican government followed the U.S./E.U. policy of privileging market prices by eliminating the floor price for, and obligation to purchase (under CONASUPO), staple crops such as maize and beans, replacing those guarantees with direct-assistance to farmers under PROCAMPO. Removal of price supports exposed *campesinos* to commodity markets controlled by the transnational grain traders, reducing real market maize prices to *campesinos* by 46 percent between 1993-1999 as U.S. corn shipments to Mexico grew 15-fold (Public Citizen, 2001).

While these shifts represented policy changes, they express and enhance the power of agribusiness. The WTO regime claim is that the generalization of an export model would render agricultural protections unnecessary because of expanding global food flows. As Public Citizen observes with respect to U.S. policy:

> Proponents of the legislation contended it would make farming more efficient and responsive to market forces; in reality it essentially handed the production of food to agribusinesss ... Ironically, to counteract the predictable failure of NAFTA and the similar farm deregulation policies embodied in the Freedom to Farm Act, Congress has had to appropriate emergency farm supports — in massive farm bailout bills — every year since the legislation went into effect.

As in Europe, 56 percent of emergency taxpayer assistance went to the largest 10 percent of farms. As states that could afford farm support ran up huge relief bills, agribusinesses took the opportunity to restructure, with input industries and output industries consolidating "within and across their narrow sectors and (creating) alliances with other food industries to encircle farmers and consumers in a web ... from selling seeds and bioengineering animal varieties to producing the pesticides, fertilizers, veterinary pharmaceuticals and feed to grow them to transporting, slaughtering, processing and packaging the final 'product'." (Public Citizen, 2001)

Such "food chain clustering" (Heffernan et al., 1999) exemplifies general global restructuring trends, where, for example, 60 percent of foreign direct investment in 1998 involved cross-border mergers and acquisitions. (Public Citizen, 2001) The Canadian National Farmers' Union testified in 2000 that "almost every link in the chain, nearly every sector, is dominated by between 2 and 10 multibillion-dollar multinational corporations." (quoted in Public Citizen 2001) And in Mexico, once NAFTA opened the door to 100 percent foreign investor rights in Mexican agriculture, Pillsbury's Green Giant subsidiary relocated its frozen food processing from California to Mexico to take advantage of cheap wages, minimal food safety standards, and zero tariffs on re-export to the US; Cargill purchased a beef and chicken plant in Saltillo, and Cargill de Mexico invested nearly $200 million in facilities such as vegetable oil refining and soybean processing in Tula. Meanwhile, anticipating the Free Trade Area of the Americas (FTAA) initiative, Tyson Foods has cross-border operations in Mexico, Brazil, Argentina, and Venezuela; ConAgra processes oilseed in Argentina; and Archer Daniel Midlands crushes and refines oilseed, mills corn and flour, and bioengineers feeds in Mexico, Central and South America; and Wal-Mart operates in Argentina and Brazil. (Public Citizen, 2001).

Through the device of cross-border operations, global firms exploit food market asymmetries between North and South, undercutting Northern entitlement structures and their institutional supports by optimizing the strategy of global sourcing. But global sourcing depends on the political restructuring of the market via the WTO. In relation to the neo-liberal regime institutionalized via NAFTA, Public Citizen observes:

> Multinational agribusinesses were positioned uniquely to take advantage of trade rules that force countries to accept agricultural imports regardless of their domestic supplies. The companies utilized their foreign holdings as export platforms to sell imported agriculture goods in the U.S., and by this increasing supply, put negative pressures on U.S. agriculture prices. (2001)

As Bové claims:

> less than 5 percent of agricultural production goes on to the world market. Yet those responsible for that 5 percent of international trade dominate the other 95 percent of the production that is

destined for national consumption (or neighboring countries), and force this sector to submit to their logic. (Bové and Dufour 2001)

The neo-liberal rhetoric of a level playing field imparts a very specific meaning to the image of leveling. By externalizing subsidies, U.S. and E.U. exports compete in world markets with artificially low prices. In comparison, Southern agriculture appears relatively inefficient. In privileging market prices as the criterion of survival, free trade rhetoric justifies the use of institutional means to extend markets for agribusiness at the expense of small farmers across the world. The idea of comparative advantage is revealed as a social construct, rather than an independent law, legitimizing a short-sighted and unsustainable social catastrophe that is destabilizing the remaining 3 billion of the world's population who live from the land. The 10s of millions of uprooted and migrant laborers circulating today foreshadow a future of redundant populations.

La Via Campesina's website declares:

> The specialization of production in regions that can export at lowest costs, importation of agricultural products at prices below the cost of production in the importing country, the agreement by the WTO of public support that allows the rich countries to export at prices below their cost of production, is destroying food sovereignty in all regions. Prices called global, are artificial and result in dumping. They are disconnected from the reality of production. Many countries are forced to export because of their debt and the structural adjustment programs imposed by the IMF and the World Bank. (http://ns.rds.org.hn/via/)

Implications of a corporate global agriculture

The undermining of food sovereignty in the South is matched by a farm crisis in the North. In the neo-liberal version, this is the result of a redistribution of efficiencies, where the disappearing family farmer is a rational outcome of a globalization market that incorporates lower-cost producers. In arguing that the market is in fact a political institution, I take issue with this naturalized scenario.

First, the "lower-cost producers" are often constituted by the very policies stemming from the consolidation of corporate power in the agro-food system. The effect of dumping farm goods on the world market routinely undercuts Southern producers, driving them into contract relations with agribusinesses, or to work as casual and migrant labor on *agro-maquilas* springing up across the global South (see, e.g., Barndt 2002). The expansion of agro-exporting is neither a natural process *in* the global South, nor a simple shedding of a superfluous economic sector. Rather, neo-liberal policies and related agribusiness practices generate low-cost producers as an unintended consequence of, and a competitive condition for, corporate strategies of global market success.

Second, the question of costs is far more complex. Farm prices for American farmers are artificially low because they face oligopolistic corporate processors on the one hand, and, on the other, they compete with farmers under contract with corporate processors overseas. The real costs of Northern government subsidies to corporate farmers, in the form of deficiency payments, in natural resource depletion, in oil and transport infrastructure, far outweigh the minimal supports to Southern producers.

Third, neo-classical economic theory views the (world) market as natural. Here life imitates art in very real sense since global economic policies are premised on the assumption of the superiority of markets in making efficient and profitable allocation of resources. As noted above, the market is essentially a political construct, expressing a balance of forces favoring corporate actors. But to recognize this is to posit and legitimize alternatives.

The debates over the American farm bill reveal the contradictory interests of different stakeholders in the farm system, in particular those of family farmers versus corporate farmers and processors. There is a mounting opposition to the neo-liberal policy of privileging corporate agriculture. In March 2000, over 3,000 farmers rallied in Washington, D.C., for Rural America, drawing their strength from a coalition of family farm, church, labor, consumer, and environmental groups. They called for a new farm bill that would restore a competitive market, support farmers with cost of production loans, enact conservation measures to reduce overproduction, create a farmer-owned grain reserve to ensure food security in times of scarcity and price stability in times of plenty, negotiate fair trade agreements with assurances that countries retain the right to develop farm programs responsive to the needs of their producers and consumers first, eliminate export dumping, and so forth, (Lilliston and Ritchie 2000). In Spring, 2001, a group of Catholic Bishops called for the reversal of corporate farming,

> which creates concern about market control and leaves little room for independent producers. These forces threaten to change the face of food production in our nation. They are already taking an enormous toll on those involved in family farming … Low prices and rising uncertainty about the future place a toll on personal relationships, marriages and the fabric of family life. Meanwhile the precarious situation of family farming threatens the welfare of businesses, schools, churches and community service. (Bishops' Statement 2001)

Fourth, the social consequences of U.S. farm policy are sufficiently severe, leading to U.S. Congress' emergency support of farmers, which clearly violates the principles of free trade as promoted through the WTO. The issue of subsidies was a central obstacle in the failed WTO Seattle Ministerial Round in 1999. Southern states view the Agreement on Agriculture as protecting the farm systems of the global North and in fact the U.S. has made it clear in negotiations for the Free Trade of the Americas (FTAA) that it will not negotiate the issue of farm subsidies.

The growing recognition of the contradictory policy of supporting a corporate food system via mechanisms in violation of WTO commitments, is a condition for generating real alternatives. Real reforms and alternative forms of agriculture will surely emerge to fill the gaps left by corporate agriculture. There is already a healthy movement for Community Supported Agricultures (CSAs) across the U.S., implementing the desire for localization (based potentially in new spaces like bio-regions rather than nations *per se*) and sustaining communities and farming simultaneously. Niche farming, for example with organics and local cuisines, is evolving in the wake of failed conventional farming. As U.S. farmers pull back from genetically modified crops, and face the displeasure of the processors, they also find their way towards alternative agricultures. Meanwhile, global economic policy controversies spotlight the subsidy system and its subversion of WTO protocols, and transnational movements like *Via Campesina* highlight the growing movement for food sovereignty based in democratic politics rather than food security based in euphemistic policies of free trade.

Arguably, global policies are stalled precisely because while all nations are presumed equal, some are more equal than others. The different stances, and groupings, of nations in the WTO negotiations regarding agricultural trade policies appear to be insurmountable. At the same time, governments experience growing pressure from destabilized farming populations, which provides an opening for a new envisioning of agricultural organization and food systems.

Conclusion

I have argued that the global food market is politically created and managed. Whether corporate power is embodied in subsidized Northern exports dumped on the world market, or in the proliferation of agro-export platforms, it depends on WTO rules and IMF structural adjustment conditions, respectively. The imposition of the price form, via such institutional regulation of market relations, politicizes the global economy. The market for food surpluses generated by subsidies or debt repayment strategies depends on political relations privileging Northern states and affluent consumers at the expense of a majority of the world's population. These relations, embedded in the WTO regime, are termed globalization, and they are justified in the name of broadening consumer choice via development efficiencies on a world scale. Much of the choice reduces to a questionable access to "food from nowhere," whose artificially low price depends on a disregard for the sustainability of local cultures and ecologies. However, because this contemporary empire of food rests on political foundations, it is fast generating counter-movements concerned with reinstating food sovereignties, or foods from somewhere.

Acknowledgments

The author thanks Rajeev Patel for helpful comments on a previous draft.

References

Araghi, Farshad (2000). The Great Global Enclosure of Our Times. *In Hungry for Profit. The Agribusiness Threat to Farmers, Food and the Environment*, edited by John Bellamy Foster, Harry Magdoff and Frederick H. Buttel. New York: Monthly Review.

Bailey, John (2000). Agricultural Trade and the Livelihoods of Small Farmers., Oxfam GB Discussion Paper — 3/2000. www.oxfam.org.uk/policy/papers/agric.htm.

Barndt, Deborah (2002). *Tangled Routes. Women, Work and Globalization on the Tomato Trail.* Lanham: Rowman & Littlefield.

Bishops' Statement. A Catholic Perspective on Rural Life in Illinois. Catholic Conference of Illinois, Spring, 2001. NCRLC2@aol.com.

Bové, Jose, and Francois Dufour (2001). *The World Is Not for Sale. Farmers against Junk Food.* London: Verso.

Dawkins, Karen. Agricultural Prices and Trade Policy: Evaluating and Correcting the Uruguay Round Agreement on Agriculture. Submitted to UNCTAD/NGLS Consultation with NGOs, Geneva, 12–14 December, 1999.

Delgado, C., M. Rosegrant, H. Steinfeld, S. Elui and C. Courbois (1999). Livestock to 2020. The Next Food Revolution. Washington, DC: IFPRI.

DeWalt, Billie (1985). Mexico's Second Green Revolution: Food for Feed. *Mexican Studies/Estudios Mexicanos*, 1, pp. 29–60.

Einarsson, Peter (2001). The Disagreement on Agriculture. *Seedling*, March 2001. www.grain.org/publications.mar012-en.cfm.

Friedmann, Harriet (1982). The Political Economy of Food: The Rise and Fall of the Postwar International Food Order. *American Journal of Sociology*, 88S, pp. 248–286.

Friedmann, Harriet (1993). The Political Economy of Food: A Global Crisis. *New Left Review*, 197, pp. 27–59.

Friedmann, Harriet (2000). What on Earth is the Modern World-System? Foodgetting and Territory in the Modern Era and Beyond. *Journal of World-Systems Research* 1, pp. 480–517.

Friedmann, Harriet, and Philip McMichael (1989). Agriculture and the State System: The Rise and Fall of National Agricultures, 1870 to the Present. *Sociologia Ruralis*, 29, pp. 93–117.

Gorelick, Sherri (2000). Facing the Farm Crisis. *Ecologist*, 30, pp. 28–32.

Grosfoguel, Ramon (1996). From Cepalismo to Neoliberalism: A World-Systems Approach to Conceptual Shifts in Latin America, *Review*, 19, pp. 131–154.

Heffernan, William, with Mary Hendrickson and Robert Gronski (1999). Consolidation in the Food and Agricultural System. Report to the National Farmer's Union. www.nfu.org/whstudy.html.

Lehman, Karen, and Al Krebs (1996). Control of the World's Food Supply. In *The Case Against the Global Economy*, edited by Jerry Mander and Edward Goldsmith. San Francisco, CA: Sierra Books.

LeQuesne, Caroline. The World Trade Organisation and Food Security. Talk to UK Food Group, July 15, 1997.

Lilliston, Ben and Neil Ritchie (1997). Freedom to Fail. How US Farming Policies Have Helped Agribusiness and Pushed Family Farmers toward Extinction. *Multinational Monitor*, 21, 7&8.

Lucas, Carol (2001). Stopping the Great Food Swap. Relocalising Europe's Food Supply. The Greens/Europe Free Alliance, European Parliament. www.europarl.euint/greens

Madeley, John (2000). *Hungry for Trade*. London & New York: Zed Books.

Malhotra, K (1996). The Uruguay Round of GATT, the World Trade Organization and Small Farmers. Focus on the Global South, Bangkok. www.focusweb.org/focus/library/Alternatives_to_Trade_and_Finance/ uruguay _round_of_gatt.htm.

McMichael, Philip (2000a). Development and Social Change. In *A Global Perspective*. Thousand Oaks, CA: Pine Forge Press.

McMichael, Philip (2000b). Global Food Politics. In *Hungry for Profit. The Agribusiness Threat to Farmers, Food and the Environment*, edited by John Bellamy Foster, Harry Magdoff and Frederick H. Buttel. New York: Monthly Review.

Murphy, Sophia (1999). WTO, Agricultural Deregulation and Food Security. *Globalization Challenge Initiative*, 4. www.foreignpolicy-infocus.org/briefs/ vol4n34wto_body.html.

Pinstrup-Andersen, Per, R. Pandya-Lorch and M.W. Rosegrant (1999). World Food Prospects: Critical Issues for the Early Twenty-First Century. Washington, DC: IFPRI.

Pistorius, Robin, and J van Wijk (1999). The Exploitation of Plant Genetic Information. Political Strategies in Crop Development. Wallington, Oxon: CABI Publishing.

Public Citizen. Down on the Farm: NAFTA's Seven-Year War on Farmers and Ranchers in the US, Canada and Mexico. *Public Citizen's Global Trade Watch*, June 26, 2001. www.citizen.org.

Rifkin, Jeremy (1992). *Beyond Beef: The Rise and Fall of the Cattle Culture*. New York: Penguin.

Ritchie, Mark (1993). Breaking the Deadlock. The United States and Agricultural Policy in the Uruguay Round. Minneapolis: Institute for Agriculture and Trade Policy.

Ritchie, Mark. The World Trade Organization and the Human Right to Food Security. Presentation to the International Cooperative Agriculture Organization General Assembly, Quebec City, August 29, 1999. www.wtowatch.org.

Sharma, Devinder (2001). WTO and Indian Agriculture: Trading in Food Security. *The Hindu Business Line*, October 1.

Sanderson, Steven (1986). The Emergence of the 'World Steer': Internationalization and Foreign Domination in Latin American Cattle Production. In *Food, the State and International Political Economy*, edited by F. L. Tullis and W. L. Hollist. Lincoln: University of Nebraska Press.

Watkins, Kevin (1991). Agriculture and Food Security in the GATT Uruguay Round. *Review of African Political Economy*, 50, pp. 38–50.